GUSTAV STICKLEY

DAVID CATHERS

TABLE OF CONTENTS

INTRODUCTION

This book is a narrative of the life and a critical study of the work of Gustav Stickley (1858–1942). Its emphasis falls on a brief period, 1900 through 1916, when Stickley presided over the Craftsman Workshops and achieved his greatest fame. Although it considers many facets of his Arts and Crafts endeavor, this is largely a book about furniture making—as an art, as a vocation grounded in idealistic impulses, and as the basis of a profit-making business enterprise. Stickley's Arts and Crafts furniture is central here because, at its best, it is a clear expression of integrity and exactitude, and the medium through which he most convincingly found his voice.

In the 1880s and 1890s Stickley had been an unheralded New York State furniture manufacturer, first in Binghamton and then in the town of Auburn, and he grew prosperous making reproduction period chairs. But at the end of the nineteenth century his conventional thinking about design and production was unsettled by his new awareness of the Arts and Crafts movement that had coalesced in England during the 1880s. This movement—although that word suggests a degree of unanimity and organization that the "movement" never really had—arose in part as a reaction against the meretricious household goods made possible by the spread of machine technology in the Victorian era.

There was a profound moral component to the Arts and Crafts movement. The shiny surfaces and overly elaborate ornamentation of factory-made household goods often concealed careless construction; the very existence of these shoddy products was thus an object lesson in superficiality and deceit that, in the Arts and Crafts view of things, inevitably tainted their possessors. Hence the movement's insistence on "honest" design and construction. Factory-made goods were also seen as pernicious because of the harmful effects they had on those who did the making. Workers were, at best, reduced to mere machine tenders, and whatever skills they may have had were devalued and ultimately rendered obsolete by the harsh imperatives of mass production; they were denied the satisfaction that comes from work well done. Arts and Crafts advocates spoke of restoring "joy" and "dignity" to labor by returning to the craft-based production methods of an earlier, idealized, preindustrial age. The revival of traditional handicrafts was also envisaged by its adherents as an essentially rural phenomenon, an antidote to the ills of crowded urban living and the pollution-spewing factories that fouled the air and water. By 1900 this earnest and humane movement had attracted many American followers, Stickley among them. Its admirable values, tempered in Stickley's case by the practical necessity of earning a living, were to affect his entire professional future.

Once started, Stickley's Arts and Crafts venture rapidly grew. It began modestly at the Grand Rapids Furniture Exposition in the summer of 1900, where he exhibited an assortment of chairs, benches, and a few small case pieces. By 1901 and 1902, the craftsmanship of the furniture made by his firm had reached a very high level. The adept handling of form, color, and proportion evident in his work of this period was convincing proof that he and his designers—following, at times, the lead of British counterparts—were mastering their new discipline. During these early years of its Arts and Crafts furniture production, Stickley's firm vigorously branched out. In addition to launching *The Craftsman* magazine, Stickley opened a metalworking shop and a textile department, and made his first forays into the field of domestic architecture. During this same period, he leased a substantial building in the city where he now worked and lived, Syracuse, New York. He remodeled the interior of this structure, adding office space, furniture display rooms, a design studio, and a lecture hall, and renamed it the Craftsman Building. By 1904, as his firm expanded, he began standardizing his furniture designs. At the end of 1905 he left the Syracuse Craftsman Building and moved his offices to New York City.

The firm became a sizable, thriving business making large quantities of handsome and robust Craftsman furniture. In 1910, Stickley and his family moved to a new home, Craftsman Farms, in a rural part of New Jersey, and he now worked in his New York City office full time. He opened a new Craftsman Building in 1913. In this twelve-story Manhattan tower he established all of his firm's offices and opened a vast Craftsman emporium. At the time he took over this building he was a nationally known maker of Arts and Crafts furniture, metalwork, and textiles. He was a successful retailer. He had become a prominent advocate for the sensible, affordable Craftsman house. And he was the publisher of the influential monthly journal that had established itself at the heart of the American Arts and Crafts movement, his *The Craftsman* magazine. The arc of his enterprise had attained its greatest height.

Stickley's life, at first glance, seems well documented. He left behind the fifteen-year run of *The Craftsman* and more than three dozen Craftsman catalogs and booklets. Many of his business papers survive, and they offer penetrating if intermittent glimpses into the day-to-day workings of the firm. The log house he built for his family at Craftsman Farms is now a museum and a National Historic Landmark. Yet Stickley's private life remains obscure; whatever personal papers he may have left behind have vanished, and almost none of his correspondence can be found today.

It is true that articles and essays with his by-line appeared frequently in Craftsman publications. They were at times suffused with fond, even sentimental, recollections of his youth. These writings, however, must be critically read: their purpose was primarily promotional and they were less concerned with offering a literal recounting of Stickley's life than with selling Craftsman goods. It must also be said that every essay signed by Stickley was ghostwritten or, perhaps, dictated by him and then given shape by an editor. He had the demanding job of managing his firm, and he did not have time for regular writing. Nor did he have the skills: despite the long hours he devoted to reading, Stickley's few remaining personal letters show that he never acquired

much mastery of spelling or sentence structure. When this book uses such phrases as "Stickley said" or "Stickley wrote," they have to be understood, in nearly every instance, to signify his ideas cast in prose by his firm's anonymous writers.[1]

Although the work of others, Stickley's writings were frequently expressed in the first person singular. For instance, this from a 1905 catalog: "I reached the conclusion...that the time was right for a simple, honest kind of furniture. I applied myself to this task.... I soon found that I was building better than I had planned."[2] Such statements probably *felt* true to Stickley. As president and principal owner of his enterprise, he was certainly conscious of the inevitable distance between himself and his employees. But most important, his Craftsman persona—the "I" who spoke to *Craftsman* readers—was a means of fostering a view of Stickley as the inspired artist/artisan inventing alone in his workshop, the source of everything emanating from his firm. This image-making enhanced his furniture's Arts and Crafts aura, and it was so successful, so captivating, that Stickley is still thought of principally as a furniture designer. That perception needs to be grasped in the broadest sense: he knew everything there was to know about furniture making and he had an uncannily acute eye. But he is unlikely to have spent much if any time designing at a drawing board. Nor did he work in a vacuum.

The creative process at the Craftsman Workshops was not the individual undertaking that Stickley depicted; it was collaborative. The core of his creativity lay in his astute selection of gifted designers and his ability to inspire them to produce superb work. He guided their efforts, critiqued every line they committed to paper, required revisions, and decided which designs would be put into production. In addition to designers, he attracted artists, architects, draftsmen, and artisans in wood, metal, textiles, and other media, as well as the writers, editors, and illustrators needed for his publications. Although largely unacknowledged by Stickley, these creative collaborators were essential to his firm, and one of the central aims of this book is to identify them and give them the recognition they are due.

The general outlines of Stickley's life and work are now well known; yet it can be difficult to penetrate the facade of his Craftsman persona. Nevertheless, Gustav Stickley is less of an enigma than his fragmentary biography might suggest. Evidence of his professional life reveals that he was inventive, demanding, personally magnetic, possessed of prodigious energy and ambition, and charged with a great talent for self-promotion. Although thoroughly grounded in the conventions of the late nineteenth-century American furniture manufacturing industry, he transcended those conventions and created an enduring body of work. Craftsman furniture was an exemplar of good design and sound workmanship, and it was also commercially viable. Stickley, to a great degree, was able to master the chronic Arts and Crafts conundrum about the retail pricing of goods. In its principled insistence on hand labor and its near-categorical rejection of that great bugbear "the machine" the Arts and Crafts movement, almost by definition, confined itself to making luxury goods for wealthy buyers. Many Arts and Crafts practitioners in England and America confronted this paradox, but few were able to resolve it as successfully as Stickley. Only a person with a keen aesthetic sense matched by a pragmatic blending of machine power and sound hand craftsmanship could have accomplished so much.

The sparser evidence of Stickley's personal life is that he was a loving but imperfect husband and father, intently pursuing his Craftsman vision and at times inattentive to his wife and children. He could also be astonishingly impractical and given to wishful thinking. He twice conceived of idyllic handicraft communities, the first in the California desert in 1904 and the second at Craftsman Farms, but neither plan became reality. As one of his daughters recalled more than thirty years after his death, "Father was a dreamer."[3]

It is no longer necessary to argue that Stickley was central to the American Arts and Crafts. Virtually any present-day book about the American movement must include Stickley within its purview. Another sign of his preeminence is the fact that few Arts and Crafts artifacts are now more avidly sought than the objects made by Stickley. Additionally, his successor firm, the Stickley Furniture Company, is producing "reissues" of his Arts and Crafts furniture designs with great success, and many contemporary craft workers make furniture modeled on or inspired by Stickley originals first made a hundred years ago. Despite this recognition and a general familiarity with Stickley's life and work, he remains a difficult subject to capture on paper.

Some writers in the past three decades have made Stickley the object of uncritical adulation, not seeing his flaws and failings. Others have damned him as a "popularizer," ignoring the reality that seeking publicity and making sales were essential pursuits for nearly all participants in the movement. Such one-sided views are inadequate, and this book attempts to steer a middle course between those extremes, admiring Stickley for his praiseworthy accomplishments and criticizing him when criticism seems deserved. It hopes to tell a much fuller and more detailed story of Stickley than has been told before, and to look past the surface of the Craftsman Workshops to see how things really worked there. It is therefore less concerned with placing Stickley in the social, cultural, and political contexts of his era than it is in recreating the more immediate professional contexts—his offices, design studio, retail shops, and factory—in which he spent his working days. The Stickley who will emerge in this book is in many ways a complicated and contradictory figure, a profit-seeking entrepreneur who was also idealistic, an ardent convert to his adopted cause, and the most significant protagonist of the American Arts and Crafts movement.

1 The cover of the first issue of *The Craftsman,* October 1901, dedicated to William Morris.

11

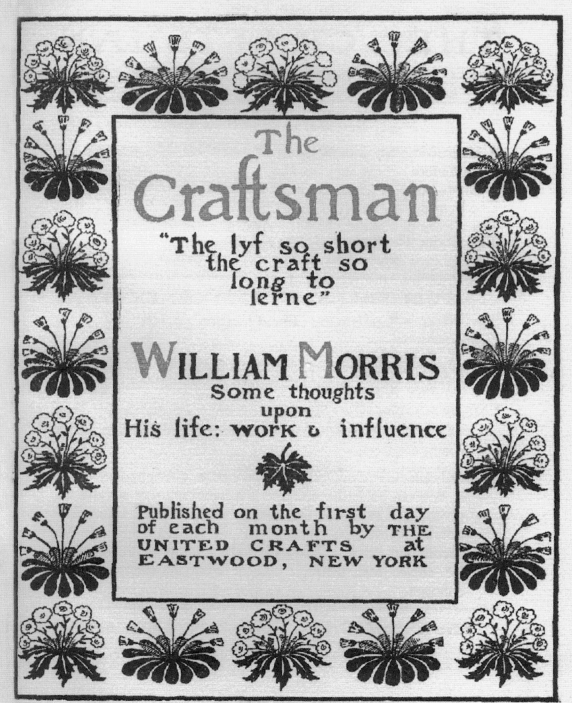

VOL. I   October, MDCCCCI   NO. 1

The Craftsman

"The lyf so short
the craft so
long to
lerne"

WILLIAM MORRIS

Some thoughts
upon
His life: work & influence

Published on the first day
of each month by THE
UNITED CRAFTS   at
EASTWOOD, NEW YORK

Price 20 cents the copy

Gustavus Stoeckel was born on 9 March 1858, the first son of German émigré parents, Barbara and Leopold Stoeckel.[1] Stoeckel, in German, means "little stick." The Stoeckels—the name later Americanized to Stickley—were a struggling farm family in Osceola, Wisconsin, then a rough-hewn frontier settlement on the banks of the St. Croix River. The story of Gustave Stickley's early life remains sketchy, although the decorative arts historian Marilyn Fish has tracked down many of the biographical facts that underlie this brief account.[2] The Stickley farm comprised forty acres, with about four acres under cultivation. Barbara Stickley gave birth to eleven children, of whom nine survived to adulthood. There were four girls, Louisa, Mary, Emma, and Christina, and five boys, Gustave (changed to Gustav in 1903[3]), Charles, Albert, Leopold (later called Lee or Leon), and George (later called John George).[4] Leopold senior earned a tenuous living as a farmer and stone mason, and the Stickleys were among the town's poorer families. As the eldest boy, Gustave began at an early age to contribute to the family's finances, helping his father at stone masonry, but deciding quickly that he hated this heavy work. He left school when he was about twelve. His formal education may seem sharply abbreviated, but it was not unusual for a child of mid-nineteenth-century America to have only five or six years of schooling.[5]

About the time Gustave left school his parents separated. Leopold, however, returned, and the family moved down river to Stillwater, Minnesota, where he could more readily find work. But by about 1875 he had abandoned his family once again, and Barbara swooped up her brood and carried them to Pennsylvania, where her prosperous brother, Jacob Schlager, could help keep her family secure. With his partner Henry William Brandt, Schlager operated two tanneries and a chair factory in the northeastern Pennsylvania town of Brandt.

By the time he was eighteen Gustave Stickley had entered the chair factory and was learning the rudiments of the furniture trade. Working with wood seemed like freedom to him, and according to his later accounts of this part of his life, he took to it naturally.[6] He became foreman of the plant within four years. Although Schlager and Brandt might have noticed the boy's abilities sooner rather than later because he was Schlager's nephew, this promotion cannot be chalked up merely to nepotism; the factory had the capacity to produce 96,000 chairs a year, and the pragmatic partners are not likely to have entrusted its operation to him solely out of family favoritism. Young Gustave possessed an aptitude for making furniture and, judging by his later life, the ability to manage workers. It was also during these years—again, according to reminiscences published decades later—that he began the life-long habit of reading books in pursuit of self-education.[7] In Pennsylvania he led a more stable and secure life than he had before, and his changed circumstances seem to have awakened him to books, music, and, apparently, to personal ambition. Surrounded by prosperous Brandts and Schlagers, he certainly observed how nice it would be to have money.

1 Detail of the Stickley-designed fall-front desk #521, oak, ca. 1901.

422   WILLIAMS BINGHAMTON CITY DIRECTORY.

BINGHAMTON

ELECTRIC RAILROAD,

RUNS FROM THE

Binghamton State Asylum,

TO

ROSS PARK,

Every 20 Minutes, Connecting with the

CABLE ROAD,

Making a Delightful Ride.

Strangers to the City,

Should Not Fail to Avail Themselves of it.

DISTANCE FIVE MILES,

For Ten Cents.

GUSTAVE STICKLEY,

PRESIDENT.

3

STICKLEY BROTHERS,

FURNITURE,

142 and 144 State St. and Commercial Ave.,

HEADQUARTERS FOR FURNITURE AT POPULAR PRICES.

Sold at Wholesale and Retail.

We buy for Cash, our expenses are Light and our profits Small, so we can sell Good Goods very Cheap.

Give us a trial and see.

4

In 1883, at the age of twenty-five, Gustave Stickley married Eda Simmons, a seamstress two years his junior. The same year, Gustave, together with his brothers Charles and Albert, established Stickley Brothers & Company in Susquehanna, Pennsylvania, where the newly formed firm began manufacturing furniture. Within a year the three brothers had opened a retail and wholesale furniture store in Binghamton, New York, a small but growing city about twenty miles northwest of Brandt. With a sound local economy rooted in manufacturing, retailing, and farming, it offered, potentially, a very good market for their wares. The brothers sold furniture made in their own factory and they also bought from larger firms whose plants were in the big manufacturing centers of Gardner, Massachusetts, Grand Rapids, Michigan, and New York City, thus establishing friendly and beneficial links with their industry colleagues. In 1885, the brothers expanded their business, opening a new shop on an adjacent block, and converting their first store into a wholesale outlet and a small factory that made serviceable Windsor and Shaker-like chairs. The Stickley Brothers firm was growing and, the evidence suggests, became modestly prosperous. But Gustave had greater aspirations.

By 1888, Gustave and Eda had been married five years and their first child, Barbara, named for his mother, was a year old. Their second child, Mildred, was born in August 1888. At this point Stickley was a thirty-year-old furniture man, by outward appearance perhaps conventional and unremarkable, and yet intelligent, fully versed in manufacturing, wholesaling, and retailing—and he was ambitious. It was about this time, for instance, that he made plans to open a large department store in Binghamton. Nothing came of this grand and probably impractical notion, and more than two decades would go by before Stickley, in New York City, would realize that particular dream. In 1888, Gustave bought an interest in a Binghamton streetcar line.[8] The following year he formed a partnership with G. Tracy Rogers to operate other street railroads that carried shoppers into the center of the city. Formerly a banker, G. Tracy Rogers (1854–ca. 1930) was a financier and budding railroad and utilities baron who was then buying up railway lines in New York State and Vermont.[9] He will appear only infrequently in this narrative, but Rogers was to remain involved with various Stickley enterprises for thirty years, playing a crucial role in Stickley's professional life.

Stickley's most significant step in 1888, however, had nothing to do with department stores or streetcar lines. It was his decision to leave Charles and Albert to begin a furniture-manufacturing venture with a new partner—Elgin Simonds. The same year, in England, Thomas Cobden-Sanderson invented the phrase "Arts and Crafts." Also in 1888, C. R. Ashbee (1863–1942) started the Guild and School of Handicraft and, in London, the Arts and Crafts Exhibition Society held its first exhibition. It was a watershed year in the history of the Arts and Crafts movement, but there is no reason to suppose that Stickley knew anything of these events in 1888.

2 The Stickley Brothers furniture store in Binghamton, New York, 1890.

3 Advertisement for the Binghamton electric railroad, Gustave Stickley, president, from the 1888 Binghamton city directory.

4 Advertisement for the Stickley Brothers furniture store, from the 1884 Binghamton City Directory.

5

6

In the summer of 1888, the trade journal *American Cabinet Maker and Upholsterer* reported: "It is rumored that Stickley Brothers of Binghamton will dissolve partnership and that Elgin A. Simonds and one of the brothers will form a co-partnership to manufacture rocking chairs."[10] Elgin Simonds (1854–1903) was a successful and well-liked furniture salesman widely known to the trade, and Stickley, at the time they joined forces, was only "one of the brothers." Yet his energy and manufacturing savvy made him a likely partner to the sociable, easygoing Simonds. The Stickley & Simonds Company was formed in December 1888, and Stickley took the title of treasurer, remaining in Binghamton to oversee the factory. Simonds, although his name came second in the firm's title, was the president, and worked from a sales office in New York City.[11] The board of directors had five members: Gustave and Eda Stickley, Elgin Simonds and his wife Jennie, and, by 1891, Gustave's younger brother Leopold.[12]

In January 1890, Stickley & Simonds decided to move its manufacturing operations northward from Binghamton to the state prison in Auburn, New York.[13] Assisted at first by Leopold, Gustave took over the prison's furniture workshop. The use of low-paid prison labor was then a generally unpopular practice within the furniture industry. It was one way to cut manufacturing costs and so, to the firms paying their workers a regular wage, it seemed an unfair competitive advantage and was eventually curtailed. Although both partners had agreed to shift manufacturing to the prison, the decision revealed two traits that would later resurface in Stickley's career. The first was his readiness, when it suited him, to flout industry norms. The second was his attraction to the role of mentor, in this instance training inmates to make chairs.[14] This urge to instruct eventually led him to publish his monthly magazine, *The Craftsman*, and later still, he would try to found a school for boys. Stickley managed furniture production in the prison workshop from fall 1891 until it was shut down in 1897.[15]

By early 1893, Stickley & Simonds was also manufacturing furniture in a large new factory it had built in the Syracuse suburb of Eastwood, New York.[16] Stickley began dividing his time between the house in Auburn that he rented for his family and a room he kept at the Yates Hotel in Syracuse; the demands of his business often kept him apart from his wife and children.

5 Elgin A. Simonds, undated photograph.

6 Gustave Stickley, ca. 1898.

7 Advertisement for the Stickley & Simonds "Rockingham" chair, from *Furniture World,* 19 November 1896.

8 The Yates Hotel, Syracuse, ca. 1900.

7

8

The firm closed its New York office by 1895—the partners must have felt that they no longer needed a presence in Manhattan—and Elgin and Jennie Simonds left their home in Brooklyn, New York, and moved to Syracuse. Both partners were now living close to their two manufacturing sites in upstate New York.

Stickley & Simonds followed standard industry practice by hiring professional furniture designers who worked without public acknowledgment. The name of only one is known today: Walter P. Plumb, a journeyman designer who joined the staff in November 1896.[17] After 1900, when his Arts and Crafts enterprise got under way, Stickley would continue to employ anonymous designers and grant public design credit only to himself and his firm.

Stickley & Simonds also followed industry norms in its manufacturing and marketing. The firm turned out eclectic renditions of seventeenth-, eighteenth-, and nineteenth-century chairs, making whatever seemed likely to catch the fancy of the market. These chairs were ornamented with elaborate machine-carved, machine-embossed, and in some instances, machine-inlaid, decoration. The partners employed traveling salesmen to call on retailers, issued illustrated catalogs, advertised in trade journals, and submitted self-promotional news items to the journals' reporters. Visiting merchants were taken through the warerooms at the Eastwood factory, and entertained over posh dinners at Syracuse's Century Club.[18] Stickley & Simonds was an unexceptional furniture manufacturer with an unremarkable line of revival style chairs. But it was growing.

The firm was doing well enough by 1895 that a visit to Europe now seemed a professional necessity. This was probably Stickley's first trip abroad.[19] He went again in 1896, spending his time looking at the furniture manufactured in England and France. The designs he admired were traditional ones, and *Furniture World*, reporting that fall on new additions to Stickley & Simonds's line, approvingly noted that "European sources have furnished inspiration for some of the best things."[20] The green and gold Vernis Martin "reception suite," decorated with sentimental vignettes of country life hand-painted in an antique manner, was a late Victorian rendition of French rococo. The "Rockingham" dining chair, despite a name that suggested English sources, reflected the interest in American colonial history that had been awakened with the Philadelphia Centennial Exposition twenty years before.[21] During these same months, American furniture trade journals were eulogizing William Morris, who had died on 3 October. Stickley, of course, read the trade papers and could not have missed these extensive obituaries. Yet the firm's output in the mid-1890s suggested little awareness of Morris and the Arts and Crafts movement.[22] There is no evidence that Stickley met anyone allied with the Arts and Crafts on either of these European trips, nor is there any reason to suppose, at this point in his career, that he had any interest in pursuing such acquaintances.

The Stickley & Simonds Company provided Stickley's main source of income during this decade, but he also looked for other moneymak-

9 Previous: Gustav and Eda Stickley canoeing, ca. early 1900s.

10 Eda Stickley in a rustic seat, probably on vacation in the Adirondacks, ca. late 1890s.

11 Gustave Stickley with his daughters, Mildred and Hazel, probably in Syracuse, ca. late 1890s.

ing opportunities. One came from the Yates Hotel. Financed by the heirs of a wealthy Syracuse wholesale clothier, Alonzo C. Yates, this opulent hotel opened in 1892.[23] In March of the following year, Stickley and G. Tracy Rogers helped the hotel's managers, Charles Avery and G. Fred Gregory, to secure a $30,000 loan. In return for endorsing the loan, Stickley and Rogers were promised a $5,000 fee. They had another financial agreement with Averill and Gregory that entitled them—for reasons now unknown—to ten percent of the hotel's annual profits. In 1896, Stickley and Rogers each earned the substantial sum of $2,468.44 from the profits of the Yates Hotel.[24] In 1895, Stickley invented an improved wood bending machine. He also invented a new kind of belt sander the same year.[25] Stickley had the furniture-making know-how—coupled with his all-American tinkerer's instinct and a desire to make money—to conceive of such machines, and he patented his inventions in the United States and Canada.[26]

Beside Stickley's trips to Europe, there were other signs of his increasing prosperity. By 1896 he could afford to settle his growing family in a substantial house at 1001 Walnut Avenue in Syracuse, and to furnish it with some luxurious objects, for instance, a costly Colonial Revival sterling silver tea service from a leading New York City manufacturer, Black, Starr and Frost. The family had grown throughout the decade. Gustave and Eda's third child, Hazel, was born in 1890, followed by Marion in 1893 and Gustav, Jr. in 1894. Ruth, the youngest, was born in Syracuse in 1897. About the time of Ruth's birth the family began taking summer trips to the Adirondack Mountains in northeastern New York State; these holidays were annual events until the Stickleys moved away from Syracuse in 1910. While Eda was generally content to spend her vacation time quietly knitting or doing needlework, Gustave was much more active. He led the children on vigorous overnight hikes, taught them to fish, and cooked the fish they caught over an open fire. As they grew older, his daughters began to wonder if these outdoor activities were suitably "ladylike." Stickley, however, thrived on strenuous activity and self-reliance in the woodlands, and when he later envisaged a boys' school these were the hardy virtues he planned to teach. During the summertime jaunts with his children Stickley certainly noticed the vast Adirondack camps and their mansion-sized log cabins and outbuildings. Those artfully rustic vacation palaces remained alive in his memory when he later came to build the woodsy compound for his family at Craftsman Farms in New Jersey.

In January 1897, Stickley & Simonds bought new machinery that could cut and shape cabinet wood into imitation bamboo. The firm's new "bamboo" furniture was its belated attempt to capitalize on the Japan craze that had taken hold in America after the great popular success of the Japanese exhibits at the 1876 Centennial Exposition.[27] By the late 1890s such furniture was passé, but in some ways it hinted at Stickley's Craftsman future. Many Americans, in the years following the Centennial, had embraced the appealing notion that for the Japanese artisan even the humblest domestic article could be a work of art. This was equally a central Arts and Crafts tenet, and while Stickley & Simonds' imitation bamboo furniture lamely embodied that view, it did suggest an awareness of it. The firm stained this furniture green, and green and green-brown were later to be Stickley's favored colors for Craftsman cabinet wood. Perhaps most significant, Stickley & Simonds did

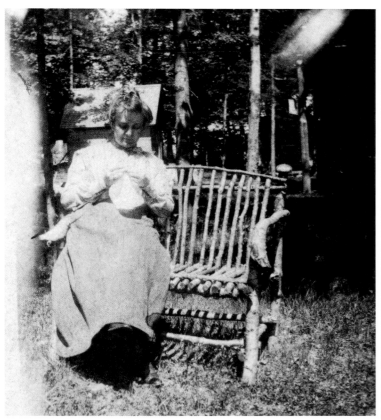

10

11

12

A ROOM IN FOREST-GREEN FURNITURE.

14

15

not introduce its bamboo line by mailing pictures of individual pieces of furniture to trade journals, although that was the usual method. Instead, the firm created what must be called an Aesthetic movement interior—stiffly drawn and marred by such visually jarring elements as a Renaissance revival fireplace—with a complete suite of matching furniture. This "Room of Forest-Green Furniture" was a coordinated ensemble of harmonizing shapes, colors, and textures, an ideal often sought by Arts and Crafts architects in the 1890s. The presentation of Stickley & Simonds's bamboo furniture suggests that Stickley, too, was beginning to think along these lines in 1897, and later polemics in *The Craftsman* would repeatedly stress this theme.

12 The Stickley family's sterling silver tea service from Black, Starr and Frost. Each piece is engraved "Stickley 1896."

13 The Stickley & Simonds "Room of Forest-Green Furniture," from *The Upholsterer*, March 1897.

14 Two Stickley & Simonds period reproduction chairs, from *The Upholsterer*, February 1898.

15 Two Stickley & Simonds chairs, one labeled "early American cottage furniture" and the other "Flemish oak," from *The Upholsterer*, February 1898.

Stickley & Simonds courted institutional customers as well as individual buyers, and in late 1897 won a commission to produce several hundred fancifully decorated chairs for the Waldorf-Astoria Hotel in New York City. The *Upholsterer* lavished these chairs with its utmost praise, calling them the "most important and most showy pieces of furniture" in the hotel. The firm supplied elaborate Empire chairs for the main foyer, over two hundred café chairs, and "fine mahogany inlaid upholstered rockers and arm chairs."[28] *Furniture World's* report was similarly enthusiastic about the "massive, mahogany pieces, orna-

mented and gilded with all the Empire characteristics" that Stickley & Simonds made for the hotel.[29] This was a distinguished and highly visible furniture order that must have given Stickley experience in handling major clients.

It was perhaps at this time that Stickley's Arts and Crafts consciousness—barely hinted at in the bamboo ensemble of 1897—first flickered with promise. In February 1898, a few months after the sumptuous furniture had been shipped to the Waldorf-Astoria, *The Upholsterer* published an extraordinary pair of two-page spreads showing photographs of sixteen Stickley & Simonds chairs. One spread, apparently reflecting Simonds's taste, featured reproductions of eighteenth-century English designs. The second spread was devoted to eight simpler chairs. Four had turned legs and stretchers and were described as copies of "early American cottage furniture." The other four were called "Flemish" or "Spanish," and were mostly straight-lined, chunky, stained nearly black, and upholstered in heavy leather fixed to the chair frames with decorative round-headed tacks. These photographs betrayed perhaps an uneasy new ambivalence within the Stickley & Simonds firm: was it a maker of revival-style Chippendale or of plainer, countrified chairs?

Growing between the partners was a rift that would soon widen into an unbridgeable gulf. In one of those retrospective musings he later published in *The Craftsman*, Stickley seems to have been looking back at that year, 1898, when he explained, "At first, in obedience to the public demand, I produced in my workshops adaptations of the historic styles, but always under silent protest: my opposition developing, as I believe, out of a course of reading, largely from Ruskin and Emerson, which I followed in my early youth. More and more did I resent these imitations which, multiplied to infinity, could not preserve a spark of the spirit, the vivacity, the grace of their originals."[30] Stickley did not literally write these words himself—his reliance on ghostwriters has already been mentioned—and the purpose of this passage was mainly promotional. Nor can it be said with absolute certainty that he read Ruskin and Emerson while he was a young man; he certainly read them, but perhaps not until his later, Craftsman years. These caveats aside, the impassioned thoughts were certainly his, and his frustration with Stickley & Simonds's furniture—and with Elgin Simonds—remained sharply fresh.

Stickley was approaching middle age, supporting a wife and six children in upstate New York. He was apparently earning a good income and managing a profitable firm, but he remained an obscure industry figure. The evidence of his later statements suggests that he felt dispirited and compromised by what he now saw as the gimcrack reproduction furniture coming out of his factory.

In March 1898, Gustave Stickley reached his fortieth birthday. Two months later, prompted apparently by his simmering discontent, Stickley acted. On 5 May 1898, the board of Stickley & Simonds held a meeting at which Stickley was present and Simonds was not. Stickley persuaded the board members to close the Stickley & Simonds Company and create a new enterprise, to be called the Gustave Stickley Company. He bought Simonds's shares of the old company's stock for $23,500, and then made two additional payments to him totaling $5,000. The dispute between the partners was public knowledge within a week: "Rumor gives different reasons for the break," reported *Furniture World*, "but there is little question of there being a difference of opinion regarding the policy of conducting the business."[31] It was not an amicable dissolution. Determined to make changes, Stickley banished Simonds from the firm; he literally fired the president. In his forceful behavior there is an early glimpse of the duality that would often lie just beneath the surface of his future Craftsman enterprise: a high-minded desire to do good work on the one hand, and an unsentimental, commercially minded decisiveness on the other. Seeing the approaching end, Simonds was frantically trying to raise cash for himself a few days before the Stickley-led board forced him out.[32]

Stickley later said that he began his "experiments" in Arts and Crafts furniture design in 1898. There is no way to confirm this, though he did completely change the nature of his firm's production within two years. Simonds was an affable man, experienced and well connected, and he quickly found new business partners. In the five remaining years of his life he continued to make furniture that varied little from the work of Stickley & Simonds—and of hundreds of other manufacturers active at the time.[33]

16 In 1897, Stickley & Simonds manufactured the "massive, mahogany pieces, ornamented and gilded with all the Empire characteristics" for the main foyer of the Waldorf-Astoria Hotel.

Following their break, the former partners went their separate ways, and through the summer and fall of 1898 the Gustave Stickley Company was born. Stickley was president and principal owner, and he alone controlled the enterprise.

16

Within weeks of the closing of Stickley & Simonds, Gustave Stickley was reassuring his customers that business would continue uninterrupted and his products would remain unchanged. During the first year of its existence the Gustave Stickley Company was careful to stress continuity, with all of its advertising and publicity repeating the phrase "Successor to the Stickley & Simonds Company."[1] A Stickley rocking chair made in 1898 was typical of the new firm's designs: it had an elaborate, machine-embossed crest rail, machine-turned acorn finials, and machine-turned stretchers. Its back and seat were upholstered with machine-woven "tapestry" purchased ready made from an outside supplier.

Stickley was, indeed, conducting business as usual. If he was experimenting with new furniture designs in his Eastwood factory, he kept his innovative thinking to himself. Publicly, he was focused on building up his firm's sales volume by offering low-priced chairs: "The company has designed a line that will sell in quantities," reported *Furniture World*, "and it is now looking for carload business."[2] In 1898 Gustave Stickley had an enterprise to run, a payroll to meet, a family to support. Such real imperatives—not his desire to produce Arts and Crafts furniture—determined his daily priorities.[3]

In January 1899 Stickley displayed his current wares at the American industry's major trade show, the Grand Rapids Furniture Exposition held twice a year in the midwestern state of Michigan. Colloquially referred to as the "Market," this show had begun informally after local manufacturers exhibited highly acclaimed chairs in Philadelphia at the 1876 Centennial Exposition. It became a regularly scheduled event in Grand Rapids in 1878, in response to the large numbers of buyers who began visiting the city to view the work of the region's furniture factories.[4] Although there were other furniture trade shows—for instance, in New York City—the Grand Rapids market remained the most influential, and that probably explains Stickley's decision to attend. Here his salesmen introduced the firm's latest offerings and solicited orders from retailers.

His furniture had become even more elaborate than his work of the year before, and he was now making the kind of over-ornamented hybrids he would soon repudiate. One of the firm's Morris chairs, for instance, featured Colonial Revival-like sausage-turned legs and side spindles rising uneasily from a machine-embossed seat rail. Another had machine-carved, griffin-shaped front legs with foliate embellishments and massive paw feet, and was meant, apparently, to emulate Empire designs of the 1820s and 1830s. In November 1899 Stickley boasted to a visiting reporter that business was very good, his factory was bustling, and he expected things to stay that way.[5]

By his own account, however, published four years later in *The Craftsman*, Stickley had grown weary by 1900 of mass-producing undistinguished, revival style furniture.[6] He had begun dreaming, if only vaguely and deeply within, of producing good, sturdy work. In the closing months of the nineteenth century, that half-formed wish took on a new urgency for Stickley as the American Arts and Crafts movement came to life around him.

1 Detail of Stickley-designed room divider, leather and green-stained oak, ca. 1902.

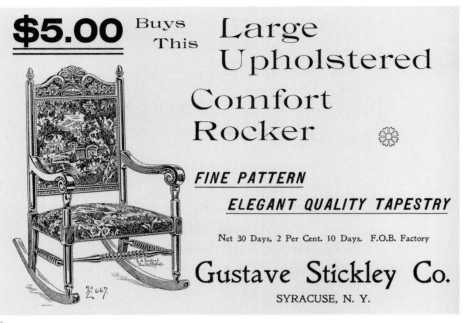

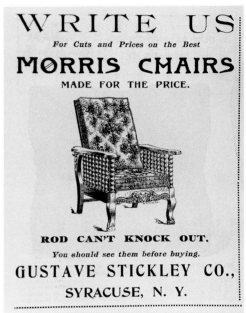

2   3

In the late 1890s, artisans, reformists, and aesthetically minded souls began banding together in Arts and Crafts societies in a growing number of American cities. References to the movement surfaced occasionally in the furniture trade journals that Stickley read, and, at the same time, new periodicals appeared on both sides of the Atlantic to advance Arts and Crafts ideals of skilled hand craftsmanship and honest design.[7] From November 1899 through February 1900, *International Studio* published Aymer Vallance's illustrated, 104-page review of the sixth exhibition of the Arts and Crafts Exhibition Society in London. This article marked the first time one of the society's exhibitions had been covered extensively in a magazine distributed in the United States and Stickley certainly read it. He must have examined its many photographs, carefully observing, for instance, the cabinet made to hold a copy of the Kelmscott Chaucer, exhibited by the English architect/designer C. F. A. Voysey (1857–1941). This quarter-sawn oak cabinet had a generally plain profile accented with a wide, beveled cornice and strap hinges on its door fronts. Vallance admired its simplicity, good proportions, and overall "restraint and refinement." This English work, and the language used to describe it, made an impression on Stickley. Several years later, when recalling his formative

2   Advertisement for a $5.00 rocking chair made by the Gustave Stickley Company, from *The Upholsterer*, March 1899.

3 Advertisement for a Morris chair, with sausage-turned legs and spindles, made by the Gustave Stickley Company, from *Furniture World*, 16 February 1899.

4 The "Bungalow" armchair of 1900. The conventionalized Gothic profile of its back slats identifies Henry Wilkinson as the chair's most likely designer.

period, he said, "The Arts and Crafts movement in England was more nearly in harmony with what I had in mind."[8]

The emergent handicraft revival and the accelerating trend toward reform in design represented compelling new ideas that flowed around Stickley and must have flooded his consciousness with liberating possibilities. Turning away from many of the precedents of the American furniture manufacturing meant risk for his firm; but it was a risk he was willing to take. The attraction of changing course was that it offered Stickley a chance to break free of the stereotypical production furniture made by his firm, and to begin, at last, to create vital and original work. In his embrace of the Arts and Crafts, Stickley's energetic idealism was ascendant. At the same time, his pragmatic, mercantile nature was engaged by the nascent American movement because it seemed to offer a potentially profitable new market.

Stickley's first furniture that can now be called Arts and Crafts appeared in 1900, at the turn of the new century. It evolved in part from the eclecticism of his earlier Stickley & Simonds productions and it drew as well on sources well-known to innovative late-nineteenth–century designers. There are suggestions, for instance, of Colonial Revival influence in the turned legs of the "Cottage" plant stands that Stickley made that year. (Identical turnings had appeared in 1899 on the Gustave Stickley Company Morris chair mentioned above.) The "Mikado," "Yeddo," and "Tokio" plant stands, both in their names and their forms—for instance, the "lift" stretchers of the "Tokio" plant stand—reveal that Stickley remained under the sway of Orientalism, as he had been

4

6   7   8

with the "bamboo" pieces of 1897.[9] Some of his small, floriform tables, for instance, the "Poppy," "Foxglove," and "Mallow," evolved partly out of European Art Nouveau, but they were more directly inspired by another New York State furniture maker, Charles Rohlfs (1853–1936). Rohlfs, who oversaw a small workshop in Buffalo, was a designer/artisan who had begun commercially producing his imaginative, flamboyant furniture in 1898, and whose flower-like tables anticipated Stickley's by perhaps a year.[10] Stickley's "Bungalow" armchair of 1900 hints at several sources, and is also quite innovative. It was one of his first slat-backed chairs. Unlike his later straight slats, however, the slats in this chair echo Gothic forms because they flare as they rise to the crest rail and define lancet-like spaces in between. The bottom edge of the seat rail evokes the "lift" motif or is perhaps meant to be a subtler rendition of the Art Nouveau whiplash. The shaped, two-dimensional front legs are the most significant development evident in this chair; they are harbingers of the flat board construction that would typify much of the firm's work for the next fifteen years.

Stickley was thus casting about for non-traditional visual elements to incorporate into his furniture, while at the same time inventing wholly new designs. The "Chalet" table is a good example of the originality and radical simplicity Stickley was capable of from the very beginning. It has a circular top and its legs and stretchers are crisp, straight planks; its three straight stretchers meet in a plain miter joint. Unlike many of Stickley's other 1900 designs, it is free of relief carving and molded edges, and its pure, unornamented geometry is saved from austerity by perfect proportions, good craftsmanship, and the appealing color and texture of its quarter-sawn oak. In its plainness and structural clarity it anticipates Stickley's finest work.

Most of Stickley's 1900 output was still limited to chairs. But there were also settees, small tables, plant stands, and a few modest cabinets. These pieces were constructed of lightweight wooden members and held together primarily with concealed joints. Tenon-and-key joints pushed their way through the surfaces of some pieces, but they vied for attention with the curved profiles, molded edges, turnings, surface carvings, and sawn out shapes that Stickley generally favored at this time. This work, like most Craftsman furniture in years to come, was made of American white oak. This native hardwood had great strength, and when planks were taken from logs that had been cut into quarters, this quarter-sawing revealed the attractive patterns of meandering lines—or "ray flakes" as Stickley called them—that occurred naturally within the grain.[11] Stickley's earliest Arts and Crafts furniture was offered in three matte tones: gray-brown, green, and gunmetal gray. To achieve these muted colors he applied what he poetically described as "unusual stains of silken luster, to which a wax finish gives a beautiful dull sheen."[12] He had rejected the highly polished, glass-like finishes then in common use because, to his newly opened Arts and Crafts eyes, they obscured the naturally beautiful grain and texture of the wood.[13] Just as he was now experimenting with design he was similarly experimenting with color and finishing techniques, and he was apparently not yet fuming

5 The "Chalet" table of 1900.

6 The "Cottage" plant stand of 1900, with an inset Grueby tile. Its sausage-turned legs are a carryover from the Gustave Stickley Company Morris chair made the year before.

7 The "Yeddo" plant stand of 1900, with inset Grueby tile.

8 The "Poppy" table of 1900, one of several floriform tables made by Stickley's firm that year.

Spanish Arm Chair
Number 2576
Made in Oak
Leather Seat

Piano Bench
Length,
Height,
Number 159

Manor Hall Seat
Single—No. 1?
Length, 25 inche?
Double—No. 1?
Length 36 inc?
Rush Seat

Piano Bench
Length,
Height,
Number 160

9

his cabinet wood with a solution of ammonia, a process he would later use to great effect.

Stickley left no record of what he thought of his 1900 furniture while he was making it. But looking back six years later he saw it as a kind of boyish indiscretion, a necessary digression as his understanding of Arts and Crafts design matured. "For about a year," he admitted, "I experimented with more or less fantastic forms."[14] In these experiments the Stickley firm had drawn upon both historic and recent precedents, and although some of the work was derivative, 1900 was equally a year of energy, exuberance, imaginativeness, and variety.

These startling new designs were created for Stickley by Henry Wilkinson (1869–1931), a young Syracuse architect who worked for the firm on a freelance basis during 1900 and was handsomely paid for his efforts. Late in the year, Wilkinson took his friend, the architect Claude Bragdon (1866–1946), to Eastwood to see the furniture he had designed for Stickley, and Bragdon mentioned it in a letter he wrote that evening. "This morning I walked...to the furniture factory where Harry [Henry Wilkinson was "Harry" to family and friends] is working. Harry gets one hundred dollars a week for his services. He has made a great success of his furniture and some of it is certainly very beautiful."[15] A native of Syracuse, Wilkinson graduated from Cornell University in nearby Ithaca in 1890 with a degree in architecture. He established a practice in Syracuse after graduation, specializing in domestic architecture and designing houses in a variety of styles. But his architectural education had been

steeped in Ruskin, Morris, and the Gothic Revival, and it was this background, as well as his considerable abilities as a designer, that led Stickley to choose him as his first creative collaborator in the development of the firm's Arts and Crafts furniture.

Stickley was back at Grand Rapids in July 1900. He prepared for this show as he always had, with advertisements and publicity in trade journals, and he dispatched four salesmen, including Leopold, to represent him. Part of the firm's display that year was prudently allotted to its "usual line of chairs."[16] These were the ornate, machine-carved, low- and medium-priced pieces that Stickley was then known for, the designs he could count on retailers to accept. This year, however, he also devoted space to his innovative new furniture that had little in common with those bread-and-butter chairs.

Stickley's first Arts and Crafts furniture, from the standpoint of design, was a true departure. But in choosing to introduce it at the Grand Rapids market he signaled his intention to distribute it through the same retail channels he had always used. It is important to mention here that he was not yet describing his new furniture as "Arts and Crafts." Instead, he used the phrase "furniture novelties," a bit of trade jargon applied to pieces that were unique or particularly out of the ordinary. Perhaps he adopted this term to help his customers accept what for many of them must have seemed

9 These two pages from the "New Furniture" catalog show the great variety in design and construction of Stickley furniture from 1900.
10 Henry Wilkinson, ca. 1908.

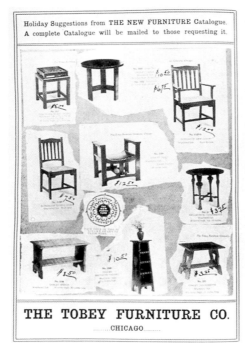

11

eccentric designs.[17] The response in Grand Rapids was mixed, and Stickley's salesmen wrote few orders for this furniture.

Yet press coverage at the time was favorable. *Furniture Trade Review* reported that Stickley's display had "attracted great attention at Grand Rapids."[18] What the trade journals admired most about Stickley's latest work was that he had found a new source of inspiration—plain, solid, mostly unornamented oak furniture—and adapted it to "practical production in a factory such as he commands."[19] He had brought along his established chair line to assure himself of orders at the Grand Rapids market, but he also showed convincingly that he was making a bold commitment to the new where others had been timid. As a writer for *Furniture Journal* said that August, "There have been examples... in the show rooms of Grand Rapids manufacturers for a season or two past, but no general display was made of these goods until July last, when the Gustave Stickley company showed a collection of about fifty pieces which met with instant favor."[20]

Whatever the industry consensus, the show was a success for Stickley. The firm made an unexpected sale that must have given him great satisfaction: he sold several pieces of furniture to Elbert Hubbard (1856–1915). In the midst of one of his frequent lecture tours, Hubbard, the head of the Roycroft Shops, an Arts and Crafts enterprise in East Aurora, New York, was apparently in Grand Rapids for a speaking engagement and decided to go through the exhibition. The Stickley furniture he bought was shipped to East Aurora for use in

Hubbard's offices and workshops, but at least one piece he took home for himself.[21] The most important result of the Grand Rapids show, however, was that Stickley's firm secured an order for about eight hundred pieces of its new furniture from the Tobey Furniture Company.[22]

Tobey was a major Chicago retailer and manufacturer with 143,000 square feet of selling space in its Wabash Avenue store, and it ran a successful mail order operation capable of reaching customers in every state in the union. This midwestern firm was headed by George Clingman (1857–1933), a former furniture designer and now a dominant figure in the American furniture industry. A *Furniture World* writer said of him, "He is manager of that mammoth establishment, the Tobey Company, which has the reputation of doing a million dollars annually in furniture."[23] Large and progressive, the firm was selling simple, handcrafted furniture by 1898, and in the spring of 1900, two months before that summer's Grand Rapids market, Tobey was advertising plain furniture that Clingman referred to as "Mission." This was a term that had gained currency since the New York firm of Joseph P. McHugh had begun promoting "McHugh Mission" furniture in 1898.[24] As he inspected Stickley's work on the convention floor, Clingman must have realized that here was a line ready made to meet the anticipated demand for simple furniture. Stickley and Clingman agreed that Tobey would take over its distribution.

By 1900, Tobey had reached a level of Arts and Crafts sophistication that Stickley could not yet match, and it was under Tobey's aegis that Stickley's

12

furniture was first presented as "Arts and Crafts." When Tobey advertised in the *Chicago Tribune* in October 1900, it headed its advertisement with the line "Furniture as an Educator," an allusion to Arts and Crafts notions about the character-shaping effect of the built environment. The copy defined the furniture as "*angular, plain* and *severe*," saved from starkness, however, by the sheen and color of the wood. And the advertisement drew a direct connection between this furniture and British Arts and Crafts: "The New Furniture belongs to a school of design almost unknown in this country.... Much of the furniture shown at the arts and crafts exhibition in England [i.e., the Arts and Crafts Exhibition Society]...finds its motive from the same source, and the late William Morris worked largely on these lines." Brought to the public's attention through the generally enlightened (if hyperbolic) merchandising acumen of Clingman, Stickley's furniture was no longer a mere upstart "novelty." It was "Arts and Crafts."

The Tobey Company was an astute and aggressive marketer. It gave Stickley's furniture a brand name—"The New Furniture"—and designed a circular, twig-enclosed trademark to give it a distinct and memorable identity.[25] During October, Tobey advertised The New Furniture in Chicago newspapers and placed an impressive two-page advertisement in the November issue of *House Beautiful*, a nationally circulated magazine devoted to art, craft, and domestic architecture.[26] The month before, almost certainly because of Tobey's prompting, the magazine published "Some Sensible Furniture," an essay by Margaret Edgewood that once again linked the furniture to British Arts and

Crafts. She praised the furniture's medieval quality as its "chief charm," and by evoking times past she imbued it with an aura of romance: "Around such tables knights of old might have sat in some dimly lighted Scottish hall and near the hearth of some huge fire the deep, high-backed chairs might have been placed." Another theme to emerge from Edgewood's article was her insistence that this furniture, admittedly a growth from European roots, was a vigorous and wholly up-to-date American phenomenon: "It is made of American wood," she wrote, "designed and executed by American artisans."[27] This same, emphatic nationalism—the insistence that these fresh new designs expressed the optimism and vitality of the American character—would later resound through Stickley's promotional materials.

In addition to its promotional campaign in local and national media, Tobey announced that it would issue a catalog, titled "The New Furniture," in mid-October. The catalog bore a stylish cover adorned with a very up-to-the-minute conventionalized floral motif, all Art Nouveau wiggles and whiplash. With this catalog, Tobey undertook a mail order campaign to sell these wares to out-of-town customers. Thus George Clingman and the Tobey Furniture Company launched Stickley's modest, hand-crafted furniture with a modern and well-coordinated campaign that combined advertising, publicity, direct marketing, and retail display.

11 The two-page advertisement for "The New Furniture" by the Tobey Company, *House Beautiful*, November 1900.

12 George Clingman, manager of the Tobey Furniture Company, from *Furniture World*, 28 April 1897.

13

Stickley shipped the bulk of the Tobey order over a three-month period, from December 1900 through February 1901. It was probably the largest single sale he had been involved with since the Stickley & Simonds Waldorf-Astoria commission three years before. By late 1900 or early 1901, Stickley's exclusive distribution agreement with Tobey was apparently unraveling in mutual disharmony. This relationship between Stickley and Clingman had been unequal from the start. Tobey was an industry giant, and Stickley was a little-known manufacturer trying to launch an innovative new product line. The Tobey deal gave his fledgling venture its first substantial order, and freed him from his reluctant reliance on his "usual line of chairs." It also gave him the means to bring his new furniture to a national market much more quickly and effectively than he could have done at the time on his own. And yet he had given up potential public recognition to achieve these benefits, and he was never more than one of Tobey's anonymous outside suppliers.

Apparently because of clashing egos, Stickley's dealings with Clingman came to a rancorous end. This experience was nevertheless decisive and taught him the valuable lesson of how to market Arts and Crafts furniture. He, too, issued a "New Furniture" catalog. Although enclosed in a different cover, it was essentially a twin of the Tobey version, and was the first of the many similar publications that would be issued by Stickley's firm during the next fifteen years. Stickley may have been overmatched by the Tobey Company initially. But his contact with Clingman taught him potent advertising, publicity, mail order selling techniques—as well as the importance of creating a memorable brand name—that he adopted and modified to suit his Craftsman purposes.

By September 1900, a few months after the Grand Rapids market, Stickley had added a full-time designer to his staff. This was LaMont Warner (1876–1970), an 1898 graduate of Pratt Institute, in Brooklyn, New York. Warner majored in design and studied under Arthur Wesley Dow (1857–1922), the artist, teacher, author of the widely influential book of art instruction *Composition* (1899), and ardent Japanophile. It was certainly while Warner was at Pratt that he acquired his life-long love of Japanese woodblock prints and textiles and, encouraged by Dow, began collecting examples he admired. Warner's knowledge of Japanese art and design was one of the assets he brought with him when he joined Stickley's firm.

In 1897, as Warner began his final year at Pratt, the English art journal *Studio* begun publishing an American edition, *International Studio*, and he became a regular reader. Starting in August 1897, and continuing for the next six years, he methodically clipped out photographs and drawings of furniture, decorative objects, and domestic interiors and kept them in his design files. Although he kept files of contemporary French, German, Austrian, and American design, most of the published images he clipped from *International Studio* pictured work by British architects and designers, among them Voysey, A. H. Mackmurdo (1851–1942), M. H. Baillie Scott (1865–1945), and Charles Rennie Mackintosh (1868–1928). Warner's files were very extensive by the time he arrived in Syracuse, and their significance lies in the fact that they became the everyday tools of a busy Stickley designer. These files were the conduits that often brought current design ideas to the firm, where Stickley and his designers Wilkinson and Warner seized on their lessons, sometimes simply

14

copying, but generally synthesizing them into convincing results. Warner was to remain with Stickley until late 1906, eventually becoming the firm's head designer, and it was in that capacity that this unacknowledged creative collaborator originated many of the important, precedent-setting furniture designs for which Stickley is known today.

During the first few years of the Gustave Stickley Company's existence, the Stickley family altered their living arrangements. They left their house on Walnut Avenue and, on 29 June 1900, Stickley paid $10,500 for a roomy but architecturally undistinguished Colonial Revival house newly built on a narrow lot at 416 Columbus Avenue in Syracuse.[28] Bought at exactly the time he was introducing his Arts and Crafts furniture, the house came to Stickley through his local furniture contacts.[29]

By December 1900, about six months after moving to Columbus Avenue, Stickley leased office space and large rooms to display his wares in the Crouse Stables at 207 South State Street in downtown Syracuse.[30] This red sandstone structure of 1888 had been designed by Archimedes Russell, who was also to be the architect of the Yates Hotel. It was the former home of a wealthy bachelor, D. Edgar Crouse, who lived in almost decadent luxury and kept his horses in prodigal style. A 1904 Craftsman booklet later tut-tutted that Crouse had

"literally lined the building ... with mahogany, carved minutely, but according to the false taste of the period, in meaningless designs.... [B]ut the climax of extravagance [was] devoted to the stabling of the horses. There, the animals drank from onyx bowls."[31] This ostentatious architectural folly had been converted into an office building after its free-spending owner's death. Its lavish Aesthetic movement interiors of marble, mahogany and rosewood were jarringly at odds with Stickley's new ideas about the beauty of plainness, but the building had advantages. It was just a block away from the Yates Hotel, it looked out on to a pleasant, tree-filled park, and, as the Stickley scholar Mary Ann Smith has observed, it was a locally prominent building in a fashionable part of town. By the spring of 1902 Stickley had taken over the entire building and remodeled its rooms to adapt them more to his liking. He covered the walls in "a plain green fabric," installed glass and iron Craftsman lanterns, added new woodwork of oak and chestnut, and built a substantial fireplace faced with matte green ceramic tiles made by the Grueby Faience Company of Boston. Outside the entrance he seems to have hung a discreet sign announcing that this building was now "The Craftsman Building," but otherwise he left the exterior unchanged.[32]

13 LaMont Warner, ca. early 1900s.

14 Crouse Stables shortly before Stickley leased the space and renamed it the Craftsman Building, ca. 1900.

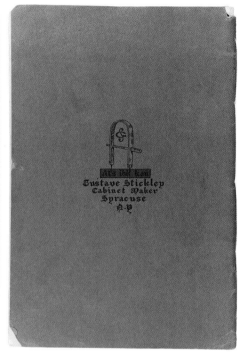

15   16

Stickley's move to the Craftsman Building was announced in December 1900. That same month he paid Irene Sargent $50.00 to write an essay for his first 1901 catalog, "Chips from the Workshops of Gustave Stickley." Her assignment, like Margaret Edgewood's in *House Beautiful* a few months before, was to create an aura of romance around his furniture. A professor at Syracuse University, Irene Sargent (1852–1932) was articulate, highly educated, possessed of a formidable intellect, and had a great gift for inspiring others. A writer for the *Syracuse Post-Standard* later praised "her ability to awaken latent powers in her students," adding, "her enthusiasm for beauty was conta-

15 Line drawing from "Chips from the Workshops of Gustave Stickley," 1901.

16 The joiner's compass and "Als ik kan" motto as they first appeared on the back cover of "Chips from the Workshops of Gustave Stickley," 1901.

17 Irene Sargent in front of Crouse College, Syracuse University, ca. 1922.

gious."[33] These words ring true: about 1900, Sargent awakened Gustave Stickley to a new world of aesthetic possibility. "She was really the one who discovered father," Stickley's daughter Barbara later recalled. "She saw his early work, his experiments, and she saw its great potential—perhaps even more than father did."[34] This "brilliant, peculiar, homely" woman nourished Stickley and became his Arts and Crafts muse and mentor.[35] He was good, solid,

American clay; but he needed the molding that Sargent could provide. Exactly how they met remains unknown.

"Chips from the Workshops of Gustave Stickley" was more than a mere catalog. It was a handsomely produced monograph, wrapped in a brown paper cover with a Gothic-inspired typeface printed in red and black. The inside pages were well laid out with handsome columns of type and line drawings of Stickley's furniture. Far from straightforward catalog copy meant simply to sell merchandise, the text of this booklet was at once a closely reasoned polemic and an aesthetic manifesto. It sought converts as well as customers.

In Sargent's unsigned "Chips" essay, titled "A Revival of Old Arts and Crafts Applied to Wood and Leather," Stickley and his workers were said to be inspired by "the extant examples of the household art of medieval Germany and the Tyrol, of France and Flanders, of the England of the Puritan...[and] American colonial furniture." They were equally inspired by the example of William Morris, who was invoked, by quotation and paraphrase, throughout the text but oddly never named.[36] And they aligned themselves with Morris's followers, "those English art-artisans of the last quarter century," whose work offered "the promise that the old order of things hostile to beauty should never

again return." As he was portrayed in "Chips," Stickley was rejecting both eclectic Victorian taste and the historic styles: they were unsuited to contemporary life and did not meet the needs of "the middle class individual" that the firm saw as the most likely buyer of its goods. For all its insistent medievalism, Sargent's text equally proclaimed Stickley's "modernity"—his identity as a twentieth-century man. The world had changed, said Sargent, "All things have become new," and therefore America needed a new style of furniture.

Sargent's "Chips" essay sounded familiar Arts and Crafts themes with many references to the joy of hand craftsmanship, the moral basis of good design and construction, and the reformist impulse: "we are working for a definite and high purpose; that is, the improvement of public taste." This essay, as noted, exuded true idealism. But it was urgently commercial as well: Stickley meant to improve his readers' taste in order to sell them his furniture. Because it introduced many of the ideas that would drive his enterprise for the next fifteen years, "Chips from the Workshops of Gustave Stickley" is a crucial document. It was Stickley's first attempt to put his new thinking onto the printed page, but once he decided to publish the first "Chips," this passionate but unlettered Arts and Crafts partisan did not write it himself. He had turned instead to Irene Sargent.[37]

It was in "Chips" that Stickley introduced his famous motto: "Als ik kan."[38] He explained the significance of his choice on the cover of another publication a few months later:

> In the Middle Ages, that golden period of the arts and crafts, each master-workman adopted some device or legend which, displayed upon every object of his creation, came finally to represent his individuality as completely as did his face, or his voice.... Among the legends so employed, the one assumed by Ian van Eyck, the early Flemish painter, has retained its force and point down to our day. Als ich kanne (if I can) appears written across the canvases of this fourteenth century chef d'ecole.... William Morris...used it, in French translation, first in tapestries designed for his own dwelling, and finally it became identified with him.... The same legend in its modern Flemish form, Als ik kan, has been adopted by the Master of the United Crafts. It here forms an interesting device with a joiner's compass, which is the most primitive and distinctive tool of the worker in wood.[39]

In June 1901, Stickley published "Chips from the Workshops of the United Crafts," a revised version of the earlier "Chips" catalog, with photographs of his most recent furniture now tipped into its pages. His name had been dropped from the title and the designation "United Crafts"—used here for the first time—appeared in its stead. With their self-conscious medievalism, the intent of these publications was to transform the Gustave Stickley Company—at least rhetorically—into an entity called the United Crafts, "A Guild of Cabinet Makers, Metal and Leather Workers."

Stickley was now publicly referring to his factory workforce as a guild, and styling himself "Master of the United Crafts." Except for the rudimentary profit-sharing plan he adopted at this time, there is no evidence that he made any organizational changes when he started labeling his firm a guild.[40] The place he

18 The curved mullions and Gothic forms of the #510 bookcase designed by Henry Wilkinson are characteristic of Stickley's 1901 furniture.

now called the "Workshops of the United Crafts" was in truth his Eastwood factory, little changed from its Stickley & Simonds days, and fully equipped with a battery of up-to-date, power-driven machinery.[41] He had begun the process of constructing his Arts and Crafts persona, while at the same time attending to the routine, though important, affairs of furniture manufacturing. The day-to-day demands of managing the enterprise remained a constant, and in addition to his public role Stickley's attention was often diverted to the various financial and legal matters that arose in the normal course of business.[42]

The furniture Stickley began making in 1901 had changed almost completely from his work of the year before. He continued to produce small tables and chairs, but only a few of his 1900 designs remained in production. Stickley was now working on a larger scale: substantial Morris chairs, dining tables, and cabinets, strongly constructed of plain, slab-like planks of quarter-sawn oak or ash, became staples of his production. These massive new pieces exemplified the firm's developing sense of good design. Big, plain furniture appealed to Stickley's eye. He introduced such work, however, not just to please himself but also in response to those trend-sensing retailers who believed that bigger furniture was what American consumers now wanted to buy. "Mr. Stickley," a local newspaper reporter wrote in March 1901, "says the trade wants large pieces of furniture."[43]

All of this new work was designed by LaMont Warner and Henry Wilkinson. Warner was then Stickley's sole in-house designer. Wilkinson remained a freelancer, and Stickley paid him $500 for the five weeks he spent in the firm's design studio in January and February 1901.[44] During this period Warner and Wilkinson created the massive, furniture that Stickley introduced in the first "Chips" catalog early in the year.

According to "Chips" Stickley was still achieving color effects solely with wood stains, but by the end of the year he had begun coloring his oak furniture by fuming it.[45] This process involved subjecting the untreated wood to the fumes of a potent ammonia solution that penetrated its surface and gave it the deep, rich, subdued hues Stickley was fond of. He also achieved this effect by applying a solution of aqua-ammonia directly to the wood with a sponge or a brush; the evidence of his furniture suggests that that this was in fact his preferred method. Stickley's adoption of fuming was also in part promotional, because it allowed his firm to stress the "romance" and "mystique" of its exotic finishing methods.[46] But the real point of fuming was that it yielded rich color: Stickley's finishers added gray or green tints to the fumed cabinet wood to create subtle gray-brown or green-brown hues.[47] With few exceptions, time and sunlight have reduced the dual tones of Craftsman furniture to simple browns, and Stickley's contributions as a colorist have consequently been underappreciated.

It was apparent to Stickley that he needed to moderate the austere lines of his furniture, and, as he later stated, "I felt that the solution to this question lay largely in the proper use of color." He was under some constraints, he said, because "as a cabinet-maker, I was bound to achieve my color-effects largely from wood."[48] Yet from the first year of his Arts and Crafts furniture production he was able at times to overcome this limitation by accenting the surfaces of some of his smaller pieces with the more intense greens and blues of inset Grueby tiles. Other materials—textiles, leather, and metal hardware—were also employed to add their colors to the furniture.

19

20

Some of Stickley's 1900 motifs were carried into 1901. For instance, the curve mimicking the pointed Gothic arch, first seen on Stickley's 1900 Bungalow chairs, was more in evidence in the new year, and began appearing as well on settles, cabinets, and chests. Although curvilinear profiles and, in a few instances, molded edges, were still incorporated into the furniture, they were rarely the focal points of Stickley's 1901 designs. His aesthetic emphasis now shifted to prominently revealed joints. He had arrived at what he called "the structural style of cabinet making." This was a combination of honest craftsmanship and visible construction, guided by the idea that "structural lines should be obtrusive rather than obscured."[49] As Stickley explained, "such elements as mortise and tenon, key and dovetail can be made very decorative, providing they appear only where needed and actually do the work for which they are intended.... The practical use of such features is the reason for their existence; the fact that they are ornamental is merely an instance of the natural growth of ornament out of construction."[50] Structure could also be expressed in subtler ways. The mullions that framed the panes of glass in cabinet doors, for instance, fit together with plain miter joints. Stickley was equally rigorous about structure that did not show. The backs of his case pieces were constructed of substantial, vertically aligned, bevel-edged planks fastened to one

another with internal splines; his avowal of "honest craftsmanship" included a refusal to skimp on labor or materials.

Stickley linked his decorative use of structure to the practices of the medieval craftsman. Irene Sargent first spoke of this connection in her March 1902 *Craftsman* essay, "The Gothic Revival." Two years later a retrospective piece in the magazine's October 1904 issue, published under Stickley's by-line, enlarged on this theme: "From the ... careful examination of the Gothic cathedral," said Stickley, "I first learned the relation between construction and decoration: finding the best examples in the great medieval style ... ornamented by features, which, like the flying buttress, gave them strength and support."[51] Stickley's view of structure as decoration may have had a medieval inspiration, but there was a more recent intermediary, the combative advocate of Gothic Revival, the English architect A.W.N. Pugin (1812–1852). As early as the 1840s Pugin had decreed that "all ornament should consist of enrichment of the essential construction of the building."[52] And it was Pugin's formulation—wholly embraced by Stickley and perfectly apparent sixty years later in every stick of his early Arts and Crafts furniture—that Gothic "does not conceal her construction but beautifies it."[53] In his argument for honest construction, Pugin infused the furniture he designed with moral purpose—it was good furniture made by good men for good people. He further saw his domestic furniture as a means to reforming popular taste.[54] And, anticipating one of the central themes of Sargent's "Chips" essay, Pugin suggested that the middle class was the most likely market for such simple, structural designs.[55]

By the time Stickley began making Arts and Crafts furniture Pugin's ideas had become common wisdom within the movement, though they were by no means

19 The shaped top rail, chamfered vertical boards, and molded shelf fronts of this plate rack are identifying elements of Stickley's 1901 furniture.

20 The spaces between the corbeled legs of this 1901 taborette form a truncated Gothic arch and are evidence that this piece is a Henry Wilkinson design; the top has an inset Grueby tile and is relief-carved with a conventionalized floral motif.

21 This ca. 1902 oak and leather room divider is a rare surviving example of the color effects Stickley achieved with his favored, but fugitive, green stains.

22

23

universally observed. It is impossible to say how much of Pugin's writings Stickley knew first hand and how much he had taken in through the works and writings of others. In 1901, for instance, Stickley's firm first made the #407 library table clearly influenced by a similar table designed nearly fifty years before by the English architect George Edmund Street (1824–1881). Street's table had straight stretchers terminating in bold tenon and key joints and legs that were simple, shaped planks; these were basic components of the vocabulary adopted by Stickley. He is unlikely to have realized, however, that Street's table derived from an earlier design by Pugin.[56] Yet Stickley certainly knew who Pugin was. Irene Sargent had written briefly about Pugin in "The Gothic Revival," but it was Ruskin and Morris whom she placed at the heart of that revival. She dismissed the influential Pugin— whose reputation at the time of Sargent's essay remained in eclipse—as an architectural copyist who sought merely to reproduce the Gothic cathedral rather than create new work inspired by its example.[57]

22 A Pugin-inspired structural table designed by G. E. Street, ca. 1854.

23 The similar #407 library table first made by Stickley's firm in 1901.

24 Now referred to as the bow-arm Morris chair, this chair has curved arms that are echoed in the curves cut into the lower edges of the front and side seat rails; early versions of this chair, such as this example, have subtly tapered legs.

The influence of another English architect, M.H. Baillie Scott, was also evident in some Stickley furniture of 1901. One good example is the Eastwood chair, first made late that year. This chair is overscaled, almost primitive, a distillation of Stickley's thoughts about the design of

furniture. But its genesis lies partly with Baillie Scott. The legs of the Eastwood chair are substantial oak posts. Its back is composed of three wide horizontal slats, and, below the seat rails, four boards form a visually continuous stretcher bracing the legs. In the first year that it was made, it had a rush seat wrapped over round rails to support a leather cushion. These elements were apparent in Baillie Scott's chair #32 of 1901. With the Eastwood chair, Stickley made the sides of the front legs parallel, widened the arms, added a Tudor arch beneath each arm, and raised the seat to standard height. By making his chair more rectilinear and constructing it on a much more massive scale, and by adding a cushion as a welcome concession to the sitter's comfort, he changed the design enough to make it unmistakably his own.

Like LaMont Warner, Stickley must have seen Baillie Scott's work in international art journals and the American furniture trade press.[58] And he had to have owned a copy of "Furniture Made at the Pyghtle Works," a catalog of the architect's designs issued in 1901 by John P. White, a manufacturer with a factory in Bedford and showrooms in London.[59] Besides the armchair discussed above, it included illustrations of several other pieces that would later be echoed in Stickley's work. Baillie Scott wrote an introductory essay for this catalog, which he began with his most provocative statement, inviting "those who are interested in furniture and decoration to realize the absurdity of filling their houses with mechanical reproductions of the furniture of other times or other countries." His plain, soundly constructed furniture, he contended, was the best and most sensible alternative. In language that was to be echoed in

24

Craftsman publications, he enumerated his furniture's virtues: simplicity; good proportions; the unobtrusive brown or green stains that added color to the oak or ash used in its construction. Most of the furniture in this catalog was offered with or without inlays of pewter and tinted woods. This was a means of adding color to furniture that Stickley would briefly incorporate into his own work, but not until two years later. There is no evidence that Stickley and Baillie Scott ever met, but at some point Stickley began sending copies of his *Craftsman* magazine to Baillie Scott. This was a puzzling gesture. Baillie Scott was perhaps the greatest single influence on Stickley's furniture designs, and he certainly realized the extent of his influence as he leafed through the magazines that arrived from Syracuse in his mail. The well-bred Baillie Scott responded to these mailings with a sincere, appreciative, if somewhat cool, thank-you note.[60]

For all his attention to design in 1901, Stickley was equally focused on the distribution of his furniture. He would never again cede control of his sales as he had with Tobey. During the summer and fall the United Crafts exhibited its latest furniture at the Pan-American Exposition in Buffalo, New York. Stickley shared his space with the Grueby Company, and Charles Rohlfs was across the aisle. The exposition offered one way for Stickley to bypass retailers and offer his wares directly to the public, and it was in every way a successful occasion.[61] In addition to winning a silver medal and reaching new customers, his display received flattering publicity in three periodicals. The Buffalo exposition prompted the writer Clara Ruge to write about the American Arts and Crafts

movement in the Austrian art journal *Kunst und Kunsthandwerk*. She discussed three furniture makers whose work she had seen in Buffalo: Charles Rohlfs, whose "artistic fantasy" greatly appealed to her; Joseph P. McHugh, whose mission furniture she deemed too "monastic" but well made; and the United Crafts. She admired the harmonious green and brown hues of the firm's furniture, and approvingly noted that the "furniture forms are based on the simple English style, and the influence of the English movement through Morris is acknowledged." Ruge reproduced three line drawings of Stickley furniture earlier published in "Chips," and her article brought him his first international recognition.[62] *The Art Interchange*, a New York City-based magazine read by artists and craft workers, published an article about Stickley furniture in November 1901 that praised it as "an embodiment of comfort and convenience, of simplicity and harmony, of stability and honesty.... Mr. Stickley insists on good design [and] sound construction."[63] In the same month, a writer for Chicago-based *House Beautiful* remarked succinctly that "[t]he furniture of Gustave Stickley, a member of the United Crafts, is exceedingly good."[64] And at least one exposition visitor, the young California architect Charles Greene, was to be profoundly influenced by the Stickley furniture he saw there.[65]

Stickley was also making sales in the display rooms of the Craftsman Building in Syracuse and reaching customers via his catalogs. He was thus repeating the pattern—now in Arts and Crafts form—that he had established nearly twenty years earlier in Binghamton, and he was once again a furniture

25

manufacturer and wholesaler, and a retail merchant. By 1901 Stickley was selling his Arts and Crafts wares through a few congenial retailers in key markets, for instance, Marshall Field & Co. in Chicago, the Cobb-Eastman Company in Boston, George C. Flint in New York City, and a handful of others. By the close of the year, Stickley furniture was being sold in New York City by the retailer James McCreery, and a news item mentioning McCreery in the December 1901 *Upholsterer* said, "we believe that the United Crafts propose to establish an associate craftsman…a co-worker or distributor of their goods—in every city and town of the United States."[66] This notice marked the beginnings of the group of Stickley-selected retailers (he called them "Associates") that at its peak a decade later would carry his products nationwide in fifty American cities.

In the same December 1901 issue of *The Upholsterer*, the journal's editor expressed admiration for the bravery of Stickley's venture: "We have the greatest respect for Gustave Stickley, for unlike a large number of manufacturers, he is a believer in his ideas and is willing to rise or fall by them. We have had considerable to say about the work of the Arts and Crafts societies, who for the past eight or ten years have endeavored to break away from the accepted schools of cabinet work, but none of them have had the courage to make anything more that a few experimental pieces."

Stickley's most ambitious undertaking that year, and certainly the one that grew most important to him, was *The Craftsman* magazine. It was launched modestly in October 1901. Stickley had begun making plans for it earlier that year. On 18 May he mentioned it in a letter he sent to Henry Turner Bailey (1865–1931), a prominent Massachusetts arts educator who lived near Boston. He told Bailey that the United Crafts "will shortly proceed to publish a magazine, to be known as 'The Craftsman,' and to be devoted to the furtherance of sound artistic principles and ideas among the middle classes."[67] Stickley's earliest published reference to his magazine, in the summer of 1901, called it "an illustrated brochure of designs, single drawings, and examples of finish in both wood and leather." He also said that it was to be "devoted to the interests of labor, considered in its relation to art and life."[68] Like the "Chips" essay published earlier that year, *The Craftsman* had a promotional purpose and a reformist agenda, and pursued

both with utmost seriousness. The first issue included a foreword and three brief articles stating the firm's intent to use the magazine to make its simple household furnishings known to the public. Most of this issue, however, was devoted to discussions of the life and work of William Morris. The second issue interspersed furniture promotion with substantive essays on John Ruskin, and the third, a monograph on medieval guilds, continued in the same vein, setting the pattern the magazine would follow through its first year. These three issues were entirely written by the first editor of *The Craftsman*, Irene Sargent, and she was to remain its dominant voice for nearly four years. It was Sargent's erudition and literary skill, along with Stickley's energy, ambition, and his attraction to the role of teacher that made the magazine possible.

In addition to its photographs of individual pieces of furniture, the initial issue of *The Craftsman* also featured two interiors. They were both in Syracuse and both connected to Ernest I. White (1869–1957). The first was the interior of the Onondaga Golf Club, of which White had been a founding member, and the owner of the land it was built on. The second was the billiard room in his home. In 1901, White was a wealthy young man whose name often appeared in local papers, and who had recently embarked on a career as an attorney with "diversified business affairs including banking, and…various important industrial and commercial enterprises."[69] He was exactly the kind of person Stickley wanted to know. They probably met at the Onondaga Country Club or the Century Club, to which both belonged. White now became one of Stickley's earliest patrons.

He bought furniture from Stickley when he built his Craftsman-like billiard room, and there was a sympathetic melding between the furniture and this interior. Its walls were paneled with wooden wainscoting and framed with substantial wooden posts that supported massive ceiling beams; it had deeply recessed window bays with built-in seating and leaded glass lights in the windows. The vocabulary of this room clearly anticipated those more ambitious Craftsman interiors—the Craftsman Building in Syracuse and Stickley's own remodeled house—of the following year. Stickley later asked White to act as a judge in *Craftsman* design contests. White's early importance to the new enterprise—as an individual client and as an influential friend—is underscored by his visibility in the first issue of *The Craftsman*, and again in September of the following year. And, in another apparent gesture to the golf-loving White, Stickley named one of his firm's chairs "Thornden." With its strong vertical and horizontal lines and its interplay of solid and void, the Thornden armchair is one of Stickley's most assured early chair designs. What White probably appreciated

25 Designed by Baillie Scott and cataloged in 1901 by John P. White, this diminutive, almost child-sized chair is the apparent precedent for Stickley's Eastwood chair.

26 Built on a large scale, the substantial and very comfortable Eastwood chair is one of the Stickley firm's most uncompromising expressions of its early design vocabulary. This example dates to 1901, the first year this model was produced.

27a

29

30

most, however, was its name: In 1896, Thornden—a palatial private estate that later became a public park—had been the site of the first golf game ever played in Syracuse.

The Craftsman magazine gave Stickley a monthly platform from which to communicate his Arts and Crafts ideals and promote his Arts and Crafts wares to a national audience. It was primarily in its pages that he reinvented himself as "Gustav Stickley – The Craftsman," and created his compelling Craftsman persona. Admiration for *The Craftsman* quickly spread, and in October 1902, at the end of its first year of publication *Furniture Journal* noted, "The Craftsman, the clever magazine originally established to exploit the furniture of the United Crafts... has grown into a magazine of much literary and artistic merit... even though its primary purpose undoubtedly was to exploit the products of a very modest furniture factory in a manner entirely original."[70] The magazine became influ-

27a, b Previous: The Stickley firm's exhibit space, shared with the Grueby Faience Company, at the 1901 Pan-American Exposition in Buffalo, New York, from *The Craftsman*, November 1901.

28 The Thornden armchair, first made in 1901.

29 Ernest I. White's billiard room, from *The Craftsman*, September 1902.

30 Ernest I. White, ca. 1900.

ential and widely read, by far the most important periodical to come out of the American Arts and Crafts movement.

Eda and the children assembled the early issues of the magazine by hand, sitting at the kitchen table in their Columbus Avenue home.[71] By December 1901 the Stickleys had been living in this house for a year and a half, and they were looking forward to the season's holidays. On Christmas Eve, the family was together in the dining room when Barbara smelled smoke. Her father checked the fireplaces and decided the problem was just damp logs.[72] In fact, a fire had broken out, and flames spread quickly throughout the house. Some of Stickley's neighbors helped him hurriedly pull "valuable articles of furniture... antique silverware... [and] expensive rugs" from the burning structure. City fire companies poured water into the house for three hours, destroying the furniture and other possessions that remained inside but finally subduing the blaze. The year thus ended in a wrenching personal loss for Stickley and his family when fire reduced their home to a roofless, burnt-out shell. The loss, however, was more emotional than financial, because the ever-prudent Stickley had insured the house and its contents. Sensing a chance to learn where others might have despaired, he would rebuild his Columbus Avenue home.

The Eastwood chair had been one of the designs that signaled a new direction for Stickley's furniture at the beginning of 1902. He was still building with massive oak planks bound together by strong, visible joints, but the joints were less insistent now. Stickley's "structural style of cabinet-making" had at first signified visible construction. Now there was a subtle shift in the meaning of that phrase, and it stood increasingly for unadorned, geometric form. The idiosyncratic, dynamic outlines that had once engaged Stickley's eye disappeared from his catalogs. The firm's newest designs—for instance, a double-bay bookcase first made in 1902—were emphatically rectilinear.

One reason for this shift was straightforward enough. American furniture manufacturers of this era routinely introduced a new line every year; it was not uncommon to devise two new lines annually, one for the January Grand Rapids market and another for the market in July. During his firm's most prolific period as an originator of new furniture designs, Stickley may have been following one of the industry norms he had accepted years before. This change was sales-driven as well: Stickley was certainly shrewd enough to know that a constant flow of innovation was one effective way to keep the attention of the buying public. But the essential fact about this shift is that it rose out of the everyday creative efforts of his studio; with experience, Stickley furniture designs became more assured and more consistently good.

This evolution was evident in "Things Wrought by the United Crafts," a new catalog issued by the firm in January 1902. Its text, apparently written by Irene Sargent, stressed this heightened plainness. "The purpose of the United Crafts in producing their distinctive cabinet work is to conform to what may be called *the primitive structural idea*. That is: the form that would naturally suggest itself to a workman, were he called upon to express frankly and in the proper materials, the bare essential qualities of a bed, chair, bench, table, or any other object of this class. In this way, imitation or even reminiscences of 'style' are avoided, and the provision for practical needs becomes the requisite of design."[1]

In the first month of 1902, holding up the "bare essentials" as his ideal, Stickley was stressing his "modernity" and rejecting the recent Victorian past. He often couched this conflict in nationalistic terms: the dead hand of decadent Europe suffocating the vital American spirit. In "Things Wrought," Sargent warned against "Shapes of exaggerated slenderness; sofas and chairs adapted from the furnishings of palaces…more or less cheaply produced…. [T]hese are the objects which make their foreign presence felt today in a large proportion of American middle-class homes."[2] Yet the reality of the firm's latest furniture was never as simple as Stickley made it out to be; it far transcended his rhetoric of a stark, stripped-down functionalism. Stickley's full-time staff designer, LaMont Warner, and his occasional freelancer Henry Wilkinson, had mastered the art of creating perfectly proportioned, geometric designs, such as: the massive, strap-hinged #967 sideboard; the #962 serving table, its modest hardware a new development that year; and the #188 settle.[3] The settle had a back made from one-and-a-half-inch-thick oak boards, and the straight, rhythmically spaced, vertical slats on its sides were to become familiar elements of Stickley's furniture. He was making highly sophisticated simple furniture, the ultimate and most compelling realization of the "structural style" that he was to achieve.

This furniture was finished in deep, rich colors evocatively described in Craftsman promotional copy: "As to the oak itself, the sturdy wooden

1 Detail of the rhythmically spaced vertical slats of the Stickley-designed #188 settle, oak, ca. 1902.

2

quality of it can be brought to its highest development only by treating it so that there is no trace of anything applied. It must rather be ripened...and this can be done only by a slow and laborious process that...gives it the appearance of having been mellowed by age and use.... In the process that I speak of...the color effect gained is the soft brown of old oak which has been long exposed and much handled."[4] The reality of his Finishing Room—where Stickley's workers followed the "process" he alludes to—was more prosaic. Factory inventories from 1902 show that as many as forty-five gallons of ammonia were kept on hand. The Finishing Room also maintained large stocks of shellac, varnish, and "banana liquid," an alcohol-based lacquer so named because of its strong, fruity odor, along with ebony stain and yellow, blue, and green aniline (i.e., synthetic) dyes. While Stickley romanticized the natural beauty that fuming brought out in his cabinet wood, at the factory he was the pragmatic professional who knew exactly how to achieve superb colors using standard stains—sometimes combined with fuming and sometimes not.

The new rectilinear furniture designs that appeared in January 1902 were followed in February by the first house and plan to be published in *The Craftsman*. The house was designed by Henry Wilkinson, now in practice in New York City, and it was the first, tentative step toward formulating an architecture compatible with Stickley's furniture and bringing together harmonious colors appropriate to a Craftsman interior. The unsigned article accompanying Wilkinson's renderings merely glanced at this notion, stating only that the furniture "must appear to be a part of the house." Discussion of color was confined to a cursory mention of "soft melon green" Grueby tiles, and woodwork and plaster in "a grayish tone."

The Craftsman published its second house plan—by an unknown hand—in August 1902. In the accompanying text, Irene Sargent called this house "simple, convenient and beautiful," but in truth it was a rudimentary

2 This double-bay bookcase shows that Stickley's 1902 furniture was massive, rectilinear, well-proportioned, and intricately constructed.

3 The #188 settle, first made in 1902.

3

4

5

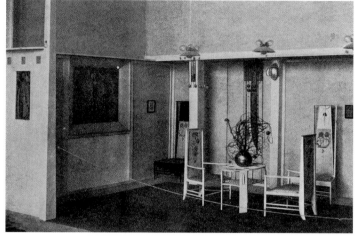

6

structure, dreary and uninviting. Stickley's eye for furniture had yet to carry over into architecture. Compared to Wilkinson's handsome house design in February, the August house was forbiddingly spartan. Only the descriptions of the suggested colors brought it to life. Where Stickley had earlier concentrated on subtly blended browns, greens, and grays, he now began to conceive a lighter and more varied color palette. The woodwork was brown chestnut, but the walls above the wainscoting were covered in blue burlap panels. In the living room there was a plaster frieze of "Naples yellow" and the ceiling between the chestnut beams was a "lighter and paler shade of yellow, creamy and soft." The rugs had patterns of "brown, blue and yellow," and the yellow tones were repeated in the draperies and seat cushions. In her description of the interior, Sargent wrote that the "colors, tints and shades are no less to be noted than are [the] skillfully adapted features of construction." Harmonizing color was thus becoming as important as structure, and this house, despite its flaws, signaled the beginnings of an important new stage in the evolution of Craftsman design.

In the summer and fall of 1902, the furniture press and art periodicals carried illustrated reports on the International Exhibition of Modern Decorative Art that had opened that April in Turin, Italy. The Scottish section, and in particular the exhibit by Charles and Margaret Mackintosh, called "The Rose Boudoir," was widely published. The Mackintoshes chose white, pink, silver, and

green for The Rose Boudoir, and the furniture they placed in it was light and graceful, with stylized, softly colored rose motifs stenciled onto the canvas backs of the chairs. These designs were the absolute antithesis of the massive, proudly plain furniture Stickley was then producing, and he and his designers noticed.[5] The Mackintoshes' work was to be a new influence that would become evident when Harvey Ellis arrived at the Craftsman Workshops the following year.[6] The publication of The Rose Boudoir offered a second, greater lesson for Stickley. In August 1902, in its report on the Scottish section in Turin, International Studio praised the space designed by the Mackintoshes for its success as an ensemble, saying: "To use materials rightly, to scheme the rooms to a definite idea, to have their proportions and spacings and colours complete in themselves...is to create harmony."[7] This was the kind of coherence that Stickley had sought but not achieved in the house published by The Craftsman in August 1902.

During the second half of 1902 Stickley's firm became increasingly ambitious. His cabinetmakers, for instance, produced the first Craftsman clock cases. He opened a metal shop about May 1902. Stickley also began a book binding operation, although that initiative was to have little success. And it was at this time that he hired

4 The #967 sideboard of 1902.

5 Interior of the house designed for The Craftsman, August 1902.

6 The Rose Boudoir, designed by Charles and Margaret Mackintosh for the Turin exhibition, from International Studio, August 1902.

N° 962

8

Louise Shrimpton (1870–1954) as a designer and delineator of Craftsman furniture and interiors; she was to stay with the firm until 1906.[8] Shrimpton was an 1893 graduate of the School of the Museum of Fine Arts in Boston, where she studied painting and drawing the human figure. The school also offered courses in decorative design that included instruction in "proportion, the elements of architectural and decorative form, the composition and application of ornament…line drawing, the use of color and perspective."[9] The instructors and guest lecturers who spoke on decorative art approached their subject from an Arts and Crafts perspective (all would later be founder-members of the Society of Arts and Crafts, Boston) and Shrimpton's education in art and design ensured her readiness for the work she was to do for Stickley.

There was another important development at the firm in 1902. In September, Stickley's brother Leopold resigned as a stockholder of the Gustave Stickley Company. Leopold had left his job as the firm's foreman the previous January, and in February 1902 he founded the L. & J. G. Stickley Company, in nearby Fayetteville, New York, with another brother, John George. It was the modest beginning of a furniture manufacturing business destined—fourteen years in the future—to have an unimagined importance for Gustave Stickley.

7 Factory photograph of the #962 serving table of 1902.

8 Louise Shrimpton, undated photograph.

In October 1902, the first anniversary of *The Craftsman*, the magazine published "A Visit to the Workshops of the United Crafts at Eastwood, New York," a promotional article written by the English émigré architect and journalist Samuel Howe (1854–1928). Howe's apparent assignment—like Sargent's in "Chips" the year before—was to place Stickley's enterprise firmly within the Arts and Crafts tradition. He therefore linked Stickley to "the great craftsmen…of the Middle Ages [and] William Morris and his followers in England." Howe further stressed this connection with a rhapsodic evocation of the beautiful, rural setting where Stickley's workers were said to be contentedly practicing their crafts. The dream of exchanging the enervating stresses of city life for the freedom of healthy country living was a familiar Arts and Crafts theme, a response to the harshness of rising industrialization and urban squalor. Stickley and Howe certainly knew of the gardens at Morris's Merton Abbey Works, and they are likely to have known that C.R. Ashbee, that very year, had led his Guild of Handicraft out of the East End of London and resettled it in the rural Cotswolds. The following year, *The Craftsman* would reprint Morris's "Work in a Factory as it Might Be," an 1894 essay in which the English master had written that factories "might be beautiful after their kind, and surrounded by trees and gardens…. Our factory, then, will be in a pleasant place."[10] The photograph of Stickley's factory that illustrated Howe's essay presented the building as a little rectangular block set amid wide fields, tall trees, and the low, rolling hills of central New York State. By publishing a photograph taken at some distance, Stickley offered a pleasant Morrisian vision of his factory.

9

9 Stickley's factory,
"The Workshop of the
United Crafts," in Eastwood,
New York, from *The
Craftsman*, October 1902.

10 The flower garden in front
of the main workshop at
the Guild of Handicraft in
Chipping Campden, England.

11

11 Stickley leather workers in the factory, from *The Craftsman*, October 1902.

12 Cabinetmakers at work on the third floor of Stickley's factory, from *The Craftsman*, October 1902.

13 Workers making rush seats at the Stickley factory, from *The Craftsman*, October 1902.

12

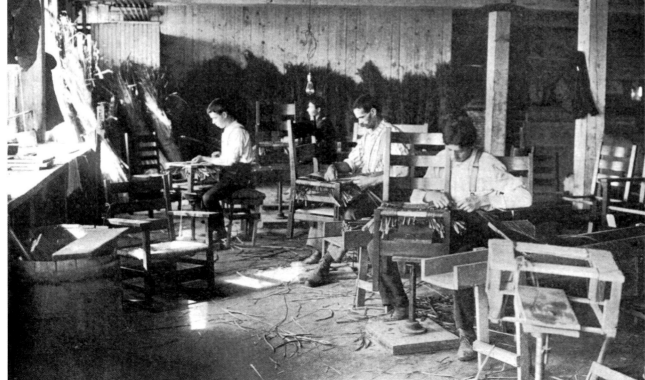

13

14

15

16

Howe's *Craftsman* article also praised the furniture made by the United Crafts. Reflecting on Stickley's favorite cabinet wood, American white oak, Howe hinted at the possibility of a new phase in the work of the firm. Oak, he said, "is so willing to be shaped...that one is greatly tempted to...test the addition of some quaint inlays of metal, ivory or bone, as used by the early guilds." At the time this article was published, Stickley was fully engaged with his structural style—at its peak in 1902—and inlay should have been briskly dismissed as unworthy "applied ornament." But with the example of Turin shimmering before him, and with his magazine's growing emphasis on domestic architecture, he was seeking new ways to enrich his work with color.

That fall, Stickley's structural style began to attract press attention that was largely but not unreservedly favorable. In October 1902, he exhibited his furniture at the Mechanics Fair in Boston, and an anonymous writer in the November issue of *Handicraft*, the journal published by Boston's Society of Arts and Crafts, was impressed by the "admirable workmanship and finish of this furniture." This judgment was followed, however, by the comment that "[s]ome of the armchairs [e.g. the Eastwood chair] suggest sitters of abnormal size and bulk, and...in the present exhibition, the more delicate pieces are by far the more satisfactory, and we should be glad to see the excellent work of the 'United Crafts' tending toward greater delicacy and appropriateness." [11] Writing in *House Beautiful*, Oliver Coleman admired the perfect workmanship and finish of Stickley's furniture, but then added: "Some of [the] furniture is heavy—heavy to see and very heavy to move."[12]

Stickley defended himself against such critics by granting the merits of their arguments but drawing a different conclusion. Responding to one complaint about the massiveness of his furniture, Stickley said, "It is true that our severe and simple style now errs upon the side of crudeness. But it suggests vital force and progress."[13] With such statements, Stickley and Sargent seemed almost to be paraphrasing a sentiment from Ruskin's essay "The Nature of Gothic." "[I]mperfection is in some sort essential to all that we know of life," wrote Ruskin. "It is the sign of life in a mortal body, that is to say, a state of progress and change."[14] And yet Stickley would increasingly leave this sort of Ruskinian thinking behind, and he was soon to renounce—for a time—the fundamentals of the structural style and launch in a new direction.

14 The remodeled living room of Stickley's Columbus Avenue house, from *The Craftsman*, December 1902.

15 The second-floor hallway in the remodeled house, from *The Craftsman*, December 1902.

16 The house on Columbus Avenue in Syracuse, New York, that became the Stickley family's home in June 1900.

17

In December 1902, *The Upholsterer* published a photograph of the "Arts and Crafts room...recently erected in James McCreery & Co.'s store by the Gustave Stickley Co."[15] Stickley was gradually expanding the roster of retailers where he would sell Craftsman furniture, and, aided by his friend Charles Coutant, the manager of McCreery's East Twenty-third Street store, he had arranged the first major display of his goods in New York City. Built with wooden wainscoting, heavy ceiling beams, and, at one end, a band of mullioned casement windows, this model room was furnished with a Craftsman dining table and chairs, a sideboard, and two settles. Gleaming pieces of copper and brass added color to the predominant brown and buff tones, and the hanging copper light fixtures were fringed with what must have been a jarring "bright red beading." Although Stickley's promotional materials emphasized his factory's rural setting, he knew that to sell his furniture successfully he needed to exhibit it in cities. So in the fall of 1902 he set his work before the buying public by creating handsome model rooms in Boston and New York. His use of model rooms to merchandise his furniture would become increasingly sophisticated in the years ahead.

Exactly one year after the Christmas Eve fire in Stickley's home, *The Craftsman* published the renovated interior as an exemplary domestic design. "A Visit to the House of Mr. Stickley," another promotional article by Samuel Howe, appeared in the magazine in December 1902. Although there are no photographs accompanying this article, the perspective views seem based on photographs, suggesting that the remodeling was complete, or at least close to complete, at the time of the article.[16] Stickley never identified the architect who did this work, but Howe is a likely candidate. The unsigned drawings of the rebuilt

17 Exhibit of Stickley living room furniture, hanging light fixtures, and Grueby pottery at the Boston Mechanics Fair, from *The Craftsman,* November 1902.

18 The Stickley model room in the James McCreery store on East Twenty-third Street, New York, from *The Upholsterer,* December 1902.

Stickley house were wonderfully executed. They were, in fact, the most convincing architectural illustrations to appear in *The Craftsman* before the arrival of Harvey Ellis.

The floors were now wide chestnut planks fumed a dark brown. The walls, like those of the Craftsman house published in August, were wainscoted in brown fumed chestnut, and massive chestnut posts supported heavy oak ceiling beams. The furniture, too, was predominantly brown fumed oak. The walls above the wainscoting and the panels between the ceiling beams were covered with textured plaster and painted off-white. Two new downstairs fireplaces were made of "common red brick," and one, on the evidence of the drawing, was fitted with andirons designed by George Jack.[17] The upstairs fireplaces were now faced with Grueby tiles. Except for these minor passages of subdued color, and the few hand-worked copper or brass vessels set out on the dining room sideboard, the first fully realized Craftsman domestic interior was a somber composition of rich browns and occasional touches of white.

Howe admired this interior for its Craftsman virtues: "Quiet harmony is the prevailing note of the composition, characterized by singular uprightness and sturdy independence." Despite his enthusiasm, even Howe seemed a little uncertain about the scale and plainness of the structural timbers and the unrelenting brown that, apparently, had been required by his client. "This severe treatment is truly...welcome.... I like Mr. Stickley's house because it is strong, robust, wholesome, free from affectation, vagaries; yet it might be...softened with the addition of furnishing details." Swinging the pendulum against the eclectic polychromy and opulence of high Victorian taste, Stickley, at first, chose assertive plainness, and pushed perhaps too far.

This Craftsman residential interior was realized with a somewhat heavy hand, but it was also thrillingly new. Its wooden structure suggested Japanese timber construction, but it was otherwise not quite like anything that had been built

before. Stickley had inserted a bold, uncompromising, unified—even radical—interior into his conventional, undistinguished Colonial Revival house and created a whole new world within its walls. (The exterior, unmentioned by Howe, was barely changed.) The reinvention of the interior made a sincere and unambiguous statement about Stickley's integration of Arts and Crafts precepts into the fabric of his daily life: "[W]hen you look at the house," Howe observed, "you view the man." It also suggested Stickley's ever-present set of contradictory impulses. The new interior was about domesticity, a shrine to the values of family, hearth, and home; it was also about commerce, an example to *Craftsman* readers of how they might use Craftsman principles and Craftsman products in their own homes. Its open planning and visible structure could be read as metaphors for candor, but they equally served the purpose of furthering Stickley's image-making campaign. He had created a comfortable family home that was equally a kind of stage setting where he could act out his role as "The Craftsman." Stickley's Columbus Avenue house blended artifice and utter sincerity in equal measure.

On 1 December, 1902, Stickley opened the new Craftsman Building lecture hall by bringing in a guest speaker to deliver a talk on "The Gothic Churches of France."[18] Two weeks later, on 13 December, Stickley invited his workers and their families to an evening of dancing and dining at the Craftsman Building, and he and Eda received them in the main hall. Before those festivities began, the guests were entertained by musical selections played by a local orchestra and Edward Schirmer—one of Stickley's office workers—sang for them. They were then offered several brief, improving lectures on "economic and social questions": a talk by a local architect, E.H. Gaggin, who spoke on "The Ideal Relation of the Craftsman to His Work," and another by Samuel Howe, titled "Five Minutes in the Life of a Craftsman." With such events, Stickley again showed himself to be a follower of Morris, who had envisioned that "a factory will surely be a center of education" combining library, school room, and dining hall, and a congenial place for "social gatherings, musical or dramatic entertainments."[19]

The *Syracuse Post-Standard*, in an article headlined "Gustave Stickley Entertains Before Going to Europe," recorded the event:

> A very enjoyable evening was afforded the United Craftsmen last night in their handsome rooms in the Crouse stables [the Craftsman Building] in South State Street by Gustave Stickley, who leaves for Europe tonight.... Some very interesting addresses were made, especially by Dean McChesney of the College of Fine Arts, who complimented both employer and employees on the spirit of good will which characterizes their relations socially and commercially.... The object of Mr. Stickley's visit to Europe is to procure some displays for the exhibition which is to be given in the rooms of the Craftsman in the near future.[20]

The next evening, 14 December, Stickley set out on his journey. As far as is known, this was his first trip since 1896, when he had gone to England and France for Stickley & Simonds.[21]

19 Stickley left Syracuse from the New York Central Railroad Station on 14 December 1902, traveling by train to Manhattan, where he boarded a passenger ship ultimately bound for Europe.

In the intervening years his life had greatly changed. He had met Irene Sargent, he had begun reading art journals, and he was becoming well known as an Arts and Crafts furniture maker. Stickley went this time to select "fine specimens of the most recent industrial art work" for his planned Arts and Crafts exhibition, but he also went in search of direct inspiration from the recent European designs he had hitherto only read about. The objects Stickley chose while on this trip reveal his evolving eye. In Paris he visited *La Maison de l'Art Nouveau*, the shop owned by Siegfried Bing, the merchant-entrepreneur who since 1895 had been the leading promoter of the emerging Art Nouveau style. From Bing, Stickley bought an Edward Colonna-designed Limoges porcelain dinner service decorated with a delicate tracery of plant forms on a cream-colored ground. The price was reportedly $700, a staggering sum if correct, the equivalent today of about $12,000.[22] He acquired other Art Nouveau objects from Bing as well, and in the shop of René Lalique he bought a silver and gold belt buckle that Lalique had designed and made.[23] The "bare essentials" perhaps no longer exerted quite the hold on him that they had the year before.

Stickley also went to London, and this proved to be the most decisive part of his trip. His visit coincided—as Stickley certainly intended—with the opening of the Arts and Crafts Exhibition Society exhibition at the New Gallery, on Regent Street, on 16 January 1903. This was the seventh exhibition the Society had held since its founding, and these events had become essential showcases where English Arts and Crafts designers, architects, and artisans could place their work before the public. Stickley had probably become aware of this Society by reading about it in *International Studio* during the winter of 1899–1900. Now, in January 1903, he was no longer limited to thumbing through magazines; he had steamed across the Atlantic to see for himself the handicrafts on display (and for sale) at the Arts and Crafts Exhibition Society's show.

What did Stickley see at the exhibition? According to a later item in *The Craftsman*, he returned from England with examples of metalwork made by three Birmingham firms: the Faulkner Bronze Company, the Art Fittings Company, and the Birmingham Guild of Handicraft. He also sought out English Arts and Crafts textiles. (These subjects will be taken up in a later chapter.)

At the New Gallery, Stickley bought an upholstered oak wing chair, with a geometric inlay pattern worked into its front legs, made by the firm of Walter Scull & Son. He also admired furniture designed by the English architects who were already influencing Craftsman design. C.F.A. Voysey exhibited several pieces of his furniture and household objects, including a side chair with a tall back made of vertical slats, and a small, inlaid, fall-front writing cabinet. The sole Baillie Scott piece in the show was a low settle with wide vertical slats inlaid with circular, biomorphic shapes, made at John P. White's Pyghtle Works in Bedford. Although one reviewer dismissed these pieces, Stickley, the savvy American furniture man on reconnaissance in London, apparently lingered over them and savored the designs.[24] He did not buy any of the Voysey or Baillie Scott furniture at the exhibition, but he looked at it with care, and later he and his designers read the journals that published illustrated articles on this show. Before the year was out his factory would be making Craftsman versions of both the inlaid writing cabinet and the tall-backed side chair he had seen in Voysey's exhibit, and also the Baillie Scott settle.

In addition to going to the Arts and Crafts exhibition, Stickley visited the London shop of J.S. Henry, a maker of "art furniture" who sold primarily to

20

21

the trade. Stickley bought several pieces of Henry's inlaid furniture designed by G. M. Ellwood (1875-1960 ca.).[25] He also bought a small, inlaid Voysey cabinet; it was nearly identical in form to Voysey's writing cabinet at the Arts and Crafts Exhibition, but its inlay was more elaborate. Henry is known to have executed some of Voysey's designs, so it is likely that Stickley bought this piece from him.[26] With criticisms of the massiveness of his 1902 furniture fresh in his mind—the *Handicraft* and *House Beautiful* reviews had appeared six weeks before he left on this trip—it is not surprising that Stickley was drawn to the Voysey, Baillie Scott, and J.S. Henry furniture he saw in London. It was built on a lighter scale and was more overtly decorative than his own, and may have recalled for him the furniture displayed in Turin that he had read about the year before. He was seeking change, a next step in the evolution of Craftsman design.

Stickley's growing focus on domestic architecture and interior decoration—that is, not just furniture—was increasingly evident in early 1903. His architectural quest led him to Ernest George Washington Dietrich (1857–1924), a New York City architect who was a talented delineator and had great facility with watercolors. Dietrich contributed two house designs to *The Craftsman* in February and May of that year.[27] They were competent efforts with heavy stone walls and gambrel roofs, but they were little different from houses Dietrich had published twenty years before. The interiors quoted ideas Baillie Scott had earlier conjured with greater verve; Dietrich, when Stickley met him, certainly knew Baillie Scott's extensively published work, and was very much under the English architect's sway. Nevertheless, the houses Dietrich contributed to *The Craftsman* were crucial to Stickley's emergent architectural ideals of color harmony and design unity. Describing the house published in February, Dietrich wrote, "It is much to be desired that the furniture complete the scheme which has its inception in the house itself."

Writing about his project for the May issue—the first house to be called a "Craftsman House"—Dietrich proposed "a harmonious color scheme" of "soft, deep, velvety" greens, olives, yellows, and beige, accented with "high notes of color...in pillows of brilliant orange, yellow and green designs." The first floor woodwork was to be fumed chestnut, chosen for its texture and natural brown tones, and on the second floor Dietrich specified woodwork painted ivory white. He told *The Craftsman* readers that "color effects...should conform to a general scheme of which each separate room should be an integral part."

Dietrich's house designs reveal the direction of Stickley's thinking in late 1902 and early 1903. He was seeking a coherent Craftsman architecture and searching for shapes, colors, and textures with which to create interiors that were unified ensembles of furniture and decorative objects. These were not startling new ideas. Although Victorian taste celebrated the eclectic, the exotic, the hyper-elaborate, Pugin, in the 1840s, had memorably proposed a unity of architecture and interior design in which everything "spoke the same language."[28] For decades his plea was almost universally ignored. Interiors unified by harmonious decorative elements, however, had begun to be realized—at least for wealthy patrons—by the 1870s and 1880s.[29] The American writer Clarence Cook helped popularize this approach to interior decoration in a series of articles he wrote for *Scribner's Monthly* and subsequently gathered together in his popular book, first published in 1877, *The House Beautiful*. "[T]he carpets, walls, and ceilings of a room," according to Cook's prescription, were to be "treated as a whole, and brought into proper harmonious relation."[30] In a

20 Advertisement for J. S. Henry, "Artist in Furniture," from *Academy Architecture*, 1903.

21 The inlaid Voysey writing cabinet bought by Stickley while he was in London in January, 1903, from *The Craftsman*, August 1903.

22 The exhibit of Voysey designs, exactly as Stickley must have seen it at the Arts and Crafts Exhibition in London, from *Kunst und Kunsthandwerk*, 1903.

23   24

perhaps more rarefied sphere, Voysey and Baillie Scott had mastered this mode by the mid-1890s, and Mackintosh raised it to an even higher art a few years after that. In 1903, the ideal of architectural unity was not only not new, it was not even completely new to Stickley; he had made rudimentary steps in this direction with the house pictured in the August 1902 *Craftsman*, and also in the remodeled house where he lived with his family.[31] To see this ideal so fully realized in Dietrich's Craftsman house, however, was something new. If he had continued to work with Stickley they might have developed it even further, but, after May, Dietrich disappeared from the pages of *The Craftsman*.

Stickley returned from Europe in February 1903, the same month that *The Craftsman* began publishing Dietrich's house designs. In the midst of this intensely active period, Stickley undertook one of the most ambitious projects of his new career. On Monday evening, 23 March, he opened an Arts and Crafts exhibition with a festive reception at the Craftsman Building. It began with informal but high-minded talks delivered to an audience of about two hundred. Following these generally earnest lectures, refreshments were served, a local orchestra played waltzes, and the guests strolled through the exhibition. Later in the week, Theodore Hanford Pond (1873–1933) lectured on "The Arts and Crafts Movement: Its Origin and Relation to Modern Life." He was a designer, the new head of art instruction at the Mechanics Institute in Rochester, and the organizer, with Stickley's financial backing and guidance, of this landmark exhibition. Pond had chaired the "arrangement committee," and with the committee's members—Irene Sargent, Blanche Baxter, LaMont Warner, and others—had planned the exhibition, designed its installation, and redecorated the Craftsman Building in spring-like greens and yellows.[32]

At Stickley's Arts and Crafts exhibition, objects were displayed individually as well as in room settings combining furniture, textiles, ceramics, and metalwork. The range and quality of the work Stickley and his co-workers assembled was extraordinary, for instance: Grueby, Rookwood, Newcomb, Van Briggle, and Robineau ceramics; plaques, lanterns, lighting fixtures, candlesticks, and other metalwork by Robert Jarvie, Jessie Preston, and Art Fittings Limited; designs for book covers and bookplates by Claude Bragdon and others; and finely bound books, including a copy of Daniel Berkely Updike's *The Altar Book* (1896), illustrated by Robert Anning Bell and with type and decorative borders by Bertram Goodhue. The exhibition also included handwrought jewelry, American and English needlework, tapestries, rugs, and Native American crafts, including fine Indian baskets from the collection of George Wharton James.

One area was arranged as a model dining room, with a sideboard, corner cupboard, linen chest, table, and leather-covered chairs typical of the Craftsman Workshops' structural style of the past eighteen months. The sideboard was for sale for $190, an amount equal to nearly $3,300 today, and the corner cupboard was priced at $100, the equivalent today of over $1,700; Stickley's catalogs hymned the middle classes,

23 Part of the Colonna-designed porcelain dinner service that Stickley bought in Paris from Siegfried Bing.

24 The inlaid and upholstered Scull & Son armchair, from *The Craftsman*, June 1903.

25 The first house to be called a "Craftsman House," designed by E.G.W. Dietrich, exterior perspective from *The Craftsman*, May 1903.

26 The library of the "Craftsman House," hand-tinted by Dietrich to show its harmonious colors.

27 The model dining room, with Craftsman furniture, Grueby pottery, Bing porcelain, and a Donegal carpet, at Stickley's 1903 Arts and Crafts exhibition in Syracuse, from *The Craftsman*, May 1903.

25

26

27

Arts and Crafts EXHIBITION

Under the Auspices of The United Crafts

CRAFTSMAN BUILDING

March Twenty-three to April Four

OPEN DAILY, EXCEPT SUNDAY, 10 A.M.—10 P.M.

SHOWING EXAMPLES OF

METAL WORK
CERAMICS
GLASS
TEXTILES
EMBROIDERIES
RUGS
BASKETRY
DESIGNS
BOOKBINDING
CABINET MAKING

A TEA ROOM will be opened in connection with the Exhibition, where light luncheons will be served each day from 12 until 5 o'clock

General Admission, 25 cents. Season Ticket, $1

A CORNER OF THE ARTS AND CRAFTS SHOW

A PANEL OF RUGS, TEXTILES AND METAL WORK.

but the prices of his early furniture put it beyond the reach of many. The dining table was set with the champagne glasses and Colonna-designed porcelain that Stickley had bought from Bing, arrayed on pale yellow embroidered table runners. The table and chairs were on a woolen Donegal rug of deep green ($190), another token of Stickley's recent travels; he was now importing these carpets.[33] The J.S. Henry desk that Stickley had brought home from London, diminutive in this setting, was exhibited in *The Craftsman* editorial office. With fine French porcelain and elegant English Arts and Crafts furniture amid the frankly structural Craftsman pieces, these two rooms signaled the dramatic shift that was taking place in Stickley's mind.

During the two weeks of the exhibition, Stickley opened a tea room on the top floor of the Craftsman Building. Overseen by the head of his textile department, Blanche Baxter, it was a cozy retreat where light refreshments were offered every day. Stickley commissioned fine china for the tea room; it was decorated with delicate green bands and Stickley's joiner's compass logo. The Craftsman furniture here was stained dark green, and the room was softly lit with hand-hammered copper, brass, and silver light fixtures that Stickley had bought in England and France. Vases of yellow tulips, jonquils, and daffodils filled this space with spring-like color. The *Syracuse Evening Herald* proclaimed it "most artistic." Stickley's tea room suggests that he was already aware that shopping and eating were complementary pleasures. This was a lesson he would apply ten years later, on a much vaster scale, when he opened the Craftsman Restaurant at the top of the Craftsman Building in New York City.

The Scull & Son wingback armchair, the inlaid Voysey cabinet, and other inlaid pieces made by J.S. Henry were also on view at Stickley's Syracuse exhibition. The inlays on the Henry pieces were conventionalized floral motifs executed in dull brass and pewter, a form of ornament not yet seen on Stickley's furniture because, until now, it would have so overtly violated his strictures against applied ornament. When photographs of the Voysey cabinet were published in the August *Craftsman*, readers were assured that this inlay was acceptable to the Craftsman canon because—echoing Pugin—it was ornament that emphasized the lines of construction. Here was the argument that Stickley would later adduce as he began making inlaid furniture of his own.

Stickley's Arts and Crafts exhibition closed on Saturday, 4 April. The following month, Irene Sargent published a long piece about it in *The Craftsman*, and her pleasure in the exhibition's success was evident throughout the essay: "For a fortnight The Craftsman Building glowed with subtle, enchanting color, and abounded in objects of good and beautiful design."[34] Stickley had spent a substantial $5,000 to mount this exhibition, which had a twenty-five cent admission charge. Although it was very well attended—"Crowds Flock to Crafts Exhibition" announced a headline in the *Syracuse Post-Standard*—it does not seem possible that it could have been financially profitable on the basis of ticket sales alone. Yet it brought the Arts and Crafts movement to life for many of the area's residents. Local newspaper coverage was uniformly favorable.

"The Craftsman Building," said a writer for the *Evening Herald*, "has the appearance of a magnificent home." Although sponsored by a business enterprise, and certainly meant to publicize the Craftsman name and Craftsman products, the exhibition was not simply a commercial undertaking. It was equally idealistic, a part of the much larger campaign, pursued by Stickley and other Arts and Crafts partisans, that sought to reform public taste.

Stickley held a grand, celebratory banquet at the Craftsman Building on the Monday after the exhibition closed. The next day, the exhibits were loaded into freight cars and shipped ninety miles west to the city of Rochester. The exhibition, with some additions, reopened on April 15 in the Eastman Building of the Mechanics Institute (now the Rochester Institute of Technology). In its new venue, this show added further substance to Stickley's reputation as a sincere maker of Arts and Crafts wares. Sensing the central truth about Stickley's Arts and Crafts enterprise, an astute writer in the *Rochester Post* saw that it was a commercial venture guided by earnest idealism: "Gustave Stickley, editor of the 'Craftsman,' has been the guiding spirit in the choice of work to be represented at the exhibition. Mr. Stickley is not disinterested; nobody ever is; he is a craftsman and wishes to have his furniture in houses all over the country. But he wishes to gain this end [by deserving it], and that fact differentiates him from the grasping trader whose one and only end is gain."[35] Some of the city's newspaper reporters were initially startled by the massiveness of Stickley's furniture; one thought the Craftsman settle in the exhibit was "as substantial as a man of war."[36] Most of the press coverage was complimentary, with one newspaper reporting that "the Stickley furniture has made many converts" and another saying that the furniture was "plain and simple in its construction, but beautiful in its simplicity, its finish and materials."[37] By 25 April, closing day, Stickley had sold a considerable amount of furniture to Rochester patrons.

The Rochester Arts and Crafts exhibition was a great success for its organizers—exhibition rooms packed with visitors; healthy sales for the exhibitors; good, often glowing, reviews. It also brought Stickley into contact with Harvey Ellis, the designer/architect who had laid out the exhibition's much-admired installation in the Eastman Building.

The closing months of 1902 and the first half of 1903 were, then, the time of gradual redefinition of Stickley's ideas about design. Stickley was clearly seeking some sort of new visual synthesis, yet neither he nor his designers had thus far been able to draw these several threads together. Then in May 1903 he hired Harvey Ellis and brought him to Syracuse. The following month, Ellis began dramatically to redirect the course of Craftsman design.

28 Previous: The Craftsman editorial office, arranged for public view, as it appeared during Stickley's Arts and Crafts exhibition in March and April 1903, from "What is Wrought in the Craftsman Workshops," 1904.

29 Advertisement for Stickley's exhibition, with a few lines of copy announcing his Tea Room, from *The Syracuse Journal*, 18 March 1903.

30 Two photographs of the exhibition installed in the Craftsman Building, from *The Syracuse Sunday Herald*, 22 March 1903.

31 The Rochester, New York, installation of Stickley's Arts and Crafts exhibition. Except for the andirons and fireset in the center right of the photograph, the metalwork visible here was made in England by Art Fittings Limited. The large rug is a Donegal carpet manufactured under the direction of Alexander Morton.

32 A second room of the Rochester installation: Stickley furniture exhibited with Grueby, Newcomb, and other American art pottery, an Art Fittings Limited circular plaque and a Donegal carpet hang on the wall. Linda Parry suggests that the Donegal rugs Stickley exhibited were designed by C.F.A. Voysey or Lindsay P. Butterfield, both of whom were under contract to Morton at this time.

Harvey Ellis (1852–1904) is a central figure in this narrative because he was the one transcendent creative collaborator of Stickley's Craftsman career.[1] On 2 April 1903, Ellis traveled from his home in Rochester to Syracuse and spent the day at the Arts and Crafts exhibition in the Craftsman Building.[2] His mission was to inspect the exhibits, measure the rooms where the objects were on view, and estimate how much space would be needed when the exhibition traveled to Rochester. He probably spent a considerable part of that day in conversation with Gustave Stickley.

In April 1903, Stickley and Ellis were essentially complete opposites. Stickley at forty-five was a prosperous furniture manufacturer and magazine publisher energetically building his enterprise. Ellis was fifty-one, short of funds and in need of work, a superbly talented but obscure architect and delineator who had spent much of his career toiling in anonymity for a succession of midwestern architectural firms; his best days were now seemingly behind him. A vigorously healthy middle-aged man, Stickley was to live another thirty-nine years; Ellis, who had suffered from a chronic illness, a dependence on alcohol, through much of his adult life, was now in fragile health and only nine months remained of his life.

For all their differences the two men had much in common, and they must have quickly discovered their mutual enthusiasm for British Arts and Crafts. Stickley had recently returned from his visit to London, where he had gone to the Arts and Crafts Exhibition Society show. Ellis had carefully studied the coverage of that exhibition in the English architectural press. Around the time Ellis visited the Craftsman Building Stickley was collaborating with E. G. W. Dietrich on an unsatisfactory attempt to invent harmonious interior designs integral to Craftsman domestic architecture. Ellis, however, had already achieved that synthesis in his own work. In the promotional article Samuel Howe had written for the October 1902 *Craftsman*, Stickley had mused about introducing lighter, more graceful furniture, but that too had eluded him. Ellis, in contrast, had been dexterously designing such furniture for at least three years. In the spring of 1903, Ellis and Stickley shared so much common ground and were thinking along such similar lines that it almost seems inevitable that they should find a way to work together.

When Stickley invited Ellis to join his firm, the promise of regular work as a designer, illustrator, and architect—with salary and an expense account—must have been irresistible. On 30 May, the *Syracuse Herald* reprinted this brief item from the *Rochester Herald*: "Harvey Ellis, a well known architect and artist of this city, has accepted a position with Gustave Stickley of Syracuse, who will hereafter control Mr. Ellis's designs and work. The work of the Stickley shops was conspicuous at the recent arts and crafts exhibition held at the Mechanics Institute, and the products of the Syracuse institution are quite familiar to Rochesterians."[3] Ellis rented a room in a private home in Syracuse, and by early June he was at his drawing board in the Craftsman Building and, if not literally coming under Stickley's "control," at least having the benefit of his steadying influence.[4]

In addition to innate talent and a mastery of design and draftsmanship acquired during decades of architectural experience, Ellis brought two other valuable assets to the Craftsman Workshops. He had been active in Arts and Crafts circles for over six years; in this he was ahead of Stickley. And he possessed

1 Detail of pewter, copper, and wood inlay on an Ellis-designed screen, 1903.

4

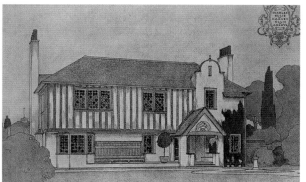

5

design files filled with clippings from art journals and architectural periodicals that he could dip into for inspiration.

The founding of the Rochester Arts and Crafts Society was announced on 13 March 1897, and Ellis was its first president.[5] M. Louise Stowell (1861–1930), a teacher and artist who painted in Ellis's style, was named vice-president, and another Ellis protégé, the young architect Claude Bragdon, took the post of treasurer. Like similar societies in England and America, the Rochester Arts and Crafts Society meant to shape public taste with lectures and exhibitions, while also promoting the work of its members. In May 1897, it held an exhibition, with an accompanying catalog, of Japanese prints and recent Japanese-influenced French posters. The anonymous writer of the catalog reminded readers that during the two preceding decades Americans had become avid collectors of Japanese decorative objects but that "few people except artists perceive the beauties of the paintings and prints." The exhibition's aim was to reveal those beauties and to show how "the extraordinary quality of the composition of line and mass" of Japanese art had influenced not just modern French poster artists, but an entire generation of European and American painters.[6] As the society's president, Ellis was instrumental in arranging this exhibition. The stylized, essentially two-dimensional qualities of Japanese prints affected his own vigorously drawn posters of this period, and would later influence many of the designs he created at the Craftsman Workshops.

In 1900 and 1901, as the pioneering Ellis scholar Jean France has written, Ellis was designing houses in an Arts and Crafts manner, including an addition to the Rochester home of Joseph Cunningham and an unexecuted house design published in the "Catalogue of the Fourteenth Exhibition of the Chicago Architectural Club." The Cunningham interior had an angular fireplace hood— apparently formed from hand-hammered metal—flanked by tall, tapering

posts with saucer-like caps. A circular repoussé metal plaque hung on one wall, and to the right of the fireplace Ellis drew a high-backed chair with vertical back slats rising to a shaped crest rail. The Cunningham house shows that Ellis had been paying close attention to English Arts and Crafts architecture, particularly the small, artistic houses by Voysey and Baillie Scott that were then often illustrated in architectural journals and *International Studio*. The unbuilt half-timbered house published by the Chicago Architectural Club led Baillie Scott's biographer to see Ellis as "a highly creative American architect" who was "the most responsive and poetic of the Americans who emulated Baillie Scott and Voysey."[7]

Although Ellis's surviving files and architectural papers are incomplete, they, too, reveal how much the Arts and Crafts increasingly drew his attention. He read Ruskin. His copies of *The Stones of Venice* and *The Seven Lamps of Architecture* are among the few extant volumes from the H. & C.S. Ellis office library. He also owned Ruskin's less well known *The Poetry of Architecture*, a poetic contemplation of the picturesque first written in serial form while Ruskin was still an Oxford undergraduate. The youthful writer's plea for a domestic architecture in harmony with its natural surroundings must have had a sympathetic reader in Ellis.[8]

Ellis clipped articles and pictures from the American and British architectural journals that he read. His files still hold a seemingly unending selection of published drawings and photographs of the medieval cathedrals that filled his imagination and were the sources often evident in his

2 Ellis's 1898 poster for Bausch & Lomb.

3 Harvey Ellis, from *The Brochure Series of Architectural Illustration*, 13 November 1897.

4 The library and conservatory designed by Ellis for the Joseph T. Cunningham house, 1900.

5 The unexecuted half-timbered house that Ellis designed in 1901, from *Architectural Review*, December 1908.

7

8

9

designs, paintings, and drawings. In addition to these romantic images, there are also pictures of the contemporary American work that was such an important influence on him: stone structures by H. H. Richardson and Louis Sullivan (about whom Ellis would write admiringly in the December 1903 *Craftsman*), and Gothic Revival churches by Ralph Adams Cram and Bertram Goodhue. Ellis also kept photographs of Henry Wilkinson's Uptegrove Building that had been published in the *Brickbuilder* in 1902 (this building is discussed on p. 217). Most of Ellis's clippings, however, are British.

He kept, for instance, every drawing of Mackintosh's entry in the Liverpool Cathedral Competition published in the March 1903 issue of the *British Architect*. He also kept a published photograph of the partly half-timbered "Cressington" (1899), a house by the Birmingham architectural firm of Crouch and Butler.[9] Although he was not to make use of half-timbering in his Craftsman houses, Ellis may have kept this photograph because of its pertinence to designs he submitted to the Chicago Architectural Club exhibition. From the *Builder* in February and March 1903 he clipped four pages of photographs taken at the Arts and Crafts Exhibition Society exhibition. These photographs pictured entries designed by several English architects: furniture by Ernest Gimson, Ernest Barnsley, Sidney Barnsley, and others. Nothing in these pictures specifically anticipated Ellis's Craftsman designs, but the fact that he kept them—most of his filed pictures are not of furniture or decorative objects but of buildings—suggest that shortly before he met Stickley Ellis was growing more attentive to architect-designed Arts and Crafts furniture. He also filed an illustration of a schoolroom, published in the *Building News* in March 1903, by the architect, designer, and teacher Wickham Jarvis.[10] Jarvis's arch-enclosed inglenook, his somewhat stiff, upright tall-backed chairs, and the two-dimensional quality of his wash rendering influenced illustrations Ellis was to create for Stickley's *Craftsman* magazine in July and August of that year.

While the British Arts and Crafts movement gave Ellis some of his favorite decorative motifs, Japan's impression on him was similarly strong. His files include a two-part article on Japanese ornament published by the *Builder* in January 1903. In the photograph of Ellis most familiar today he is wrapped in a kimono (while wearing a starched, white collar and stout laced-up shoes and, on the table before him, there is a copy of the *Rochester Post-Express*!). Writing after Ellis's death, the architect Hugh Garden said, "His love for things Japanese (at a time when most of us had never seen a Japanese print) influenced all of his later work, and particularly his color."[11] Claude Bragdon made the same point more emphatically: "The key to understanding Harvey Ellis's evolution as an artist, as it is to Whistler's, is the Japanese color print.... When I knew him Harvey was just succumbing to the spell of Japanese art. He studied his little collection of prints to such purpose that he came to see things *à la Japonais*.... What Japanese art really did for Harvey was liberate his color-sense."[12]

In July 1903, the shared sympathies of Gustav Stickley and Harvey Ellis bore their first fruit in the pages of *The Craftsman*. In the early, pre-Ellis months of 1903, Stickley had gradually enhanced the graphics of his magazine. He first tried handsome—but bland—covers with blocks

6 Previous: Early members of the Rochester Arts and Crafts Society: Claude Bragdon, architect; George Humphrey, antiquarian bookseller; John Dumont, photographer; Harvey Ellis; James Constable Hillman, architect.

7 Liverpool Cathedral competition design by C. R. Mackintosh, from *The British Architect*, 13 March 1903.

8 School room by Wickham Jarvis, from The *Building News*, 13 March 1903.

9 "Cressington," a house near Birmingham by Crouch and Butler, from *The Architect*, 6 March 1903.

10 Furniture at the London Arts and Crafts Exhibition designed by: (1) Sidney Barnsley, (2) Ernest Gimson, made by Peter Waals, (3) Ernest Barnsley, large chest; Sidney Barnsley, small cabinet, (4) W. Curtis Green, made by A. Romney Green, (5) Ernest Gimson, made by Peter Waals, from *The Builder*, 28 February 1903.

11 Harvey Ellis, undated photograph.

2

3

4

5

11

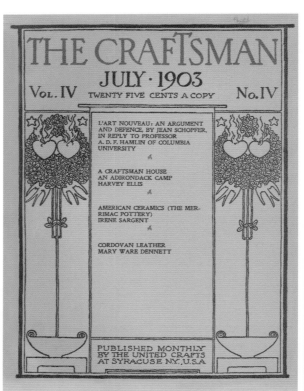

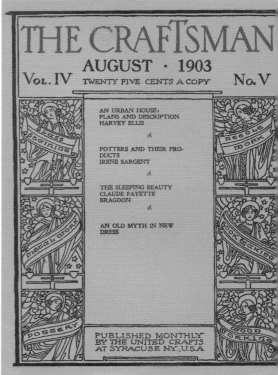

12 13 14

15

of black and red type printed on beige stock, and then in May shifted to a pictorial approach. The cover of the issue coming off press just as Ellis arrived — the June *Craftsman* — was illustrated by an anonymous artist with a competent drawing of a torii gate, a suitable image, by coincidence, to welcome the Japanophile Ellis to the firm. Then, the following month, everything changed. In July, Stickley's *Craftsman* magazine was transformed by Ellis's mastery of sophisticated linearity and sense of two-dimensional design.

Ellis created a new cover format, replacing the magazine's stolid typography with a more stylish typeface and jauntily raising the "T" in the title *Craftsman* above its surrounding letters.[13] Ellis subdivided the cover into well-proportioned rectangular panels. The vertical central panel, with its suggestion of a wide slab top, was an echo of the furniture forms he was now beginning to create for Stickley. To illustrate his first *Craftsman* cover Ellis drew two symmetrically composed bay trees with conventionalized birds and hearts that recall motifs favored by Voysey and Baillie Scott. But Ellis's hearts were visibly aflame. Ellis, who had become a Catholic in the mid-1890s, often incorporated religious iconography into his later paintings, and he continued to do so in some of the graphics he created for Stickley.[14] His intensely personal, mystical imagery feels subtly out of place on the cover of this magazine, although few readers were likely to have noticed anything beyond the charming decorative effect.

12 *The Craftsman* cover by an unknown illustrator, June 1903.

13 *The Craftsman* cover by Harvey Ellis, July 1903.

14 Ellis's second *Craftsman* cover, August 1903.

15 Claude Bragdon in his studio, 1896.

With the July 1903 *Craftsman*, Ellis burst fully into print. For this issue alone, in addition to the new cover, he contributed two articles, "A Craftsman House Design" and "An Adirondack Camp," and illustrated a third article, "A Child's Bedroom." Because the inside pages of the magazine were printed in black and white, readers had to content themselves with written descriptions of the colors Ellis chose. Nevertheless, he supplied this issue with at least twelve fully realized illustrations, and they were by far the best yet seen in *The Craftsman*.

Claude Bragdon, his Rochester architectural practice temporarily slowed by strikes among the building trades in New York State, spent several weeks in Syracuse that July and August. He and his wife, the former Charlotte Wilkinson, stayed with her family in the house that Charlotte's brother Henry had designed ten years before. Bragdon worked often that July in *The Craftsman* office and produced two articles for the magazine, "The Sleeping Beauty" in August and "A Simple Dwelling" in September.[15]

A good son and faithful correspondent, he also wrote several letters to his mother that summer, and they provide the few surviving glimpses of Ellis during his time with Stickley: "Yesterday I had old Harvey up to lunch … [he] is working very hard and looks worn and old, but he's doing great stuff, as good as he has done in his life. The influence of Stickley is just what it should be — it subdues and chastens Harvey's naturally riotous fancy. He's designing a series of covers for The Craftsman. The next number [August], containing my article and 22 of Harvey's drawings (badly reproduced) will be out Tuesday or Wednesday."[16] Bragdon wrote that same week to his brother-in-law Henry Wilkinson, then traveling in Germany. As Bragdon reported, "Harvey is here, working hard for Stickley. I don't know how long it will last, but the Craftsman and the furniture are both vastly better by reason of his ministrations….

17

18

19

Harvey I see much of and learn much from. Four of his lovely water-colors hang above this desk where I write, and he is at work at others upstairs"[17] Bragdon also collaborated on some unspecified creative projects with his friend: "Yesterday," Bragdon told his mother, "I worked at Stickley's with Harvey all the forenoon."[18] A few weeks later he wrote that, "I saw old Harvey, who was working on a stunning poster for the Craftsman."[19] He was almost certainly referring here to Ellis's idealized painting of craft workers published by the magazine that October; it was perhaps Ellis's most glorious *Craftsman* illustration, and Stickley had it printed in full color on heavy coated stock. The Ellis who emerged in Bragdon's letters was, as would be expected, a greatly gifted artist and designer; he was also the complete professional who worked hard, coped with his employer's magazine deadlines, and was reliably productive.

Ellis's perspective drawing for "A Craftsman House Design," in the issue for July 1903, revealed a compact structure with a sailing ship weather vane balanced atop a tall, thin spire that seemed to fix the house to its site like a pin holding a butterfly. The exterior walls were of white roughcast and the windows were small paned casements drawn in the manner of Richard Norman Shaw.[20] There were shaped gables on either side of the house, and two diminutive, unmatched gables perched atop the crisp two-story bay that rose from the terrace at the front. In vivid contrast to the white walls, the roof was Venetian red. Ellis's design for this house brings to mind one of his favorite maxims, later quoted by Bragdon: "Not symmetry, but balance." This was an imaginatively conceived house with a sense of playfulness and delight in variety that was quite new to *The Craftsman*. It was very English, with echoes of Voysey and Baillie Scott; but it also recalled some of the architectural vocabulary Ellis had adopted in the late 1880s.

16 Previous: Ellis's idealized craft workers, from *The Craftsman*, October 1903.
17 Dining room by Harvey Ellis for "A Craftsman House Design," from *The Craftsman*, July 1903.
18 Living room by Harvey Ellis for "An Urban House," from *The Craftsman*, August 1903.
19 Ellis's exterior perspective for "A Craftsman House Design," from *The Craftsman*, July 1903.

Ellis described the colors of this dining room as golden yellow and olive green, with a frieze of bright Venetian red and curtains of creamy white, old rose and gold.[21] Above the built-in sideboard, he placed a tripartite leaded-glass window with a pronounced central arch (evoking Shaw's "Ipswich" window) and a field of milk-colored glass streaked with turquoise. Six gray-blue martins, their heads encircled by bright yellow Baillie Scott-like halos, flew in a swirling pattern across the opaque surface. These birds were reminiscent, too, of the *mon* birds—medieval Japanese family crests—that Ellis, like Bragdon, must have known from Thomas Cutler's 1880 book *A Grammar of Japanese Ornament and Design*. The room's minimalist design, and its flat areas of color, were Japanesque, while the quadrat motif in the carpet and table runners and just below the frieze, recalled Mackintosh and other Glasgow Style designers. The magazine tuned this acutely aestheticized interior to an even higher pitch by recommending that "two or three Japanese prints of a good period and by approved masters" should be matted in parchment, framed in dull ebony, and artfully arranged on the walls of the downstairs hall.

The living room of Ellis's house for the August issue, in his article "An Urban House," was a large space with separate functional areas—hall, sitting room, music room, inglenook—defined by changes in floor level, a means of spatial organization favored by Baillie Scott. The floors were ebonized cherry, the woodwork Stickley's rich brown, and the walls were covered in plum-color linen rising to a slate-blue linen band. The stylized swirl of the stenciled rose bush on the wall to the left, the sprouting spade shape on the frieze above the fireplace, and other lesser details, were borrowed from designs by the Mackintoshes. Above the linen band, the plaster walls were painted yellow and the ceiling tinted a complementary pale cream. Olive green portieres, with indigo and ivory appliqués that were outlined in dark brown and yellow stitching, were hung at one end of the room (not visible in Ellis's rendering). These elegant, highly aestheticized, Whistlerian color schemes were not meant to be read as literal prescriptions. The magazine offered them instead as inspiring

20

examples of "unity and delicate harmonious beauty" intended primarily to suggest new and liberating ways of thinking about domestic interiors. It seems unlikely that many of the magazine's middle-class readers tried to duplicate this room's subtle pastel palette. As an index of Ellis's creative prowess, however, it is worth remembering that only eight months had gone by since Stickley published the remodeled interior of his home on Columbus Avenue and suggested it as the paradigmatic Craftsman house. Still, for all their apparent differences, both this Ellis interior and the Columbus Avenue interior relied upon the post and panel construction that was to be one of the defining features of the Craftsman houses designed in the following decade.

Harvey Ellis left behind a lucid, matter-of-fact argument for the kind of architectural coherence he created for Stickley. In his December 1903 *Craftsman* article, "How to Build a Bungalow," he wrote, "If, after having been built with great respect for harmony and appropriateness, the bungalow should be filled with the usual collection of badly designed and inadequate furniture, the *ensemble* would be distressing, and the thought involved in the structure of the building thrown away. The ... furniture ... should be conceived by the designer.... Unity between the furniture and structure," in Ellis's view, was simply a necessity.[22] Ellis's message blended easily with the demands of commerce: to create harmonious interior ensembles readers were to avoid "badly designed and inadequate furniture," and, it was implied, buy Craftsman furniture instead.

Drawings of Ellis's newly conceived furniture first appeared in the July 1903 *Craftsman*. There were probably no finished pieces to photograph yet, although Stickley's cabinetmakers were working on them by this time. This issue also carried Stickley's first advertisement for his new, inlaid furniture, describing but not showing the delicate color effects and chaste shapes that were "Lighter in Effect and More Subtle in Form than any former productions of the same workshops." The inspiration for these designs, according to the advertisement, lay in a "deep study of the principles of the new art movement"; that is, in the contemporary decorative arts (for the most part British) known to Stickley and his designers.

These influences were evident in the inlaid furniture Ellis drew for the July and August issues of *The Craftsman*. The front of a cabinet he designed for "A Child's Bedroom" in July, for instance, was inlaid with a large spade shape enclosing a disk, with three conventionalized sprouting plant forms rising through it. (This pattern was to be modified by Ellis for the living room frieze in "An Urban House.") In 1897, a similar motif, created by C.R. Mackintosh and Margaret MacDonald to adorn the front of a linen press, had been published in *International Studio*; this was certainly Ellis's source. The Ellis child's cabinet was not

20 The inlaid Baillie Scott settle seen by Stickley at the London Arts and Crafts Exhibition, January 1903.

21 The inlaid Craftsman settle designed by Harvey Ellis in June or July 1903. The pillow is a modern reproduction of an Ellis design derived from Native American motifs and originally published in *The Craftsman*, October 1903.

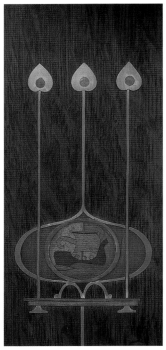

22

23

produced, but the inlay appeared on the legs of a library table he designed for Stickley. In August, in one of the interiors he drew for "An Urban House," Ellis rendered another Mackintosh-influenced piece. This was a bow-sided music cabinet adapted from a similar cabinet, published in *Dekorative Kunst* in 1899, that Mackintosh had designed for his client Hugo Bruckmann. Ellis's sole Craftsman settle design, with wide, inlaid slats at the back and sides, also appeared in "An Urban House." It was based in part on a child's settle that LaMont Warner had drawn for the magazine in June.[23] Both the Warner and the Ellis settles were indebted to the Baillie Scott settle exhibited at the London Arts and Crafts Exhibition the previous January, where Stickley had seen it. The inlay on Ellis's Craftsman settle, however, was wholly unlike the abstract, biomorphic inlay pattern devised by Baillie Scott. Ellis invented a linear and symmetrical inlay design, centering on roundels containing flat, stylized landscapes. The source that shaped these scenic inlays was not British; it was instead the Japanese woodblock prints that both Ellis and Warner collected.

Ellis's drawings in the July and August issues of *The Craftsman* brought a new vocabulary to Craftsman furniture that is now widely recognized: wide, overhanging cornices; bowed sides; arched aprons; simple geometric drawer and door pulls; and cabinet backs of lightweight frame and panel construction. Veneer was rarely seen on Stickley furniture prior to Ellis's arrival. But Ellis effectively used quarter-sawn oak veneer to give his pieces their sleek appearance and to serve as a smooth, neutral ground for his linear, two-dimensional, symmetrical inlays of pewter, brass, and tinted woods. The sources of this vocabulary are for the most part the British and Japanese motifs that Ellis adapted to the robust Craftsman idiom. In the process he reimagined them and made them his own. And he created wholly new Craftsman furniture designs as well.

Although Ellis had no peers as a Craftsman furniture designer, he did not work entirely on his own. Stickley certainly suggested ideas to him, and Claude Bragdon and LaMont Warner collaborated on some of the designs now attributed solely to Ellis. But arguably his most important collaborator during his months with Stickley was a man virtually unknown today, George Henry

22 A Mackintosh-designed linen press with applied metal decoration, from *International Studio*, August 1897.

23 Detail of Ellis-designed inlay, first published in *The Craftsman*, July 1903. Its shape is derived from the applied metal decoration on the earlier Mackintosh cabinet, but it is on a wholly different scale and its center roundel is inlaid with a storybook Viking ship, a favorite Ellis motif.

24 An inlaid, bow-sided music cabinet first drawn by Ellis for *The Craftsman*, August 1903.

24

JONES! THE
MARQUETERIE
.. MAN.

Estimates
and Designs
Furnished.

407 Second Ave. (N. W. Corner 23d St.), New York City.

26

27

Jones (1865–1927). He was the owner of an inlay and marquetry firm who styled himself "Jones the Marqueterie Man," and it was in his New York City workshop that Stickley's inlay was made.[24] Lacking workers skilled in this craft, and without the requisite equipment to produce it profitably himself, Stickley subcontracted this specialized task to an outside supplier and thus assured himself of consistent, high-quality workmanship and materials. In addition to making inlay and marquetry to order, Jones was also an accomplished designer.[25]

In July 1903, Ellis's inaugural month in *The Craftsman*, the magazine published "George H. Jones as a Craftsman," a brief, unsigned article in praise of Jones's skills. It presented him as "a young craftsman," an enlightened Arts and Crafts artisan reviving a lost handicraft. He "unites in himself the designer and maker.... As a designer he is capable and original, a follower of l'art nouveau...adopting the...plant form with excellent decorative results." His designs were also said to arise "under Japanese inspiration," a comment that underscores the shared visual sympathies of Stickley, Ellis, Bragdon, Warner, and Jones.[26] The *Craftsman* article criticized the garish, commercialized, machine-made marquetry of the late nineteenth century, and then described the ideal: "The real art is a true veneer: the design being completed independently of the object...and then applied to the construction." Jones was praised for his subtle color effects and his masterful handling of the exotic woods stockpiled in his workshop, among them "pear, apple, plum and satin woods,

amaranth, figured maple, woods stained carmine-red, olive and other greens, saffron, blue, and violet." Nothing in this article suggested Jones's role in Craftsman inlay. But Stickley received his first shipment of inlay from Jones on 9 July 1903, and a steady flow of these parcels continued to arrive throughout the remainder of the year.[27]

Stylistic evidence makes it possible to attribute some Stickley inlay patterns to Jones. The fairly naturalistic grapevine design on an inlaid Craftsman music cabinet, for instance, lacked the free-flowing yet symmetrical linearity of Ellis inlay; it was apparently one of Jones's conventionalized plant forms. Whatever designing he may have done, however, Jones's main value to Stickley was as a *maker* of inlay, and this is how the process worked: Stickley's designers created the inlay motifs and their design sketches were sent to New York City. Jones and his workers executed the panels of inlay and shipped them back to the Eastwood factory, where Stickley's cabinetmakers used them to construct the inlaid Craftsman furniture. Harvey Ellis was the most prolific and most imaginative designer of Craftsman inlay, and he is rightfully the most celebrated.

25 With rhythmic, shaped top rails and inlays of pewter, copper, and tinted woods as seen on this three-panel screen, Ellis gave Stickley's furniture a gracefulness and delicacy that it had not possessed before.

26 Advertisement for Jones the Marqueterie Man, from *Furniture Trade Review*, 10 February 1895.

27 This conventionalized grapevine inlay pattern on the front of a Stickley music cabinet was apparently designed by George H. Jones.

28

29

30

But Warner, Bragdon, and Jones, to an extent that it is no longer possible to gauge, were creators of this work as well.

As 1903 ended and 1904 began, a heavy snowfall drove across northern New York State, and the temperature dropped to twenty-five degrees below zero. Although Syracusans were inured to fierce winter weather, the arrival of the New Year saw the city locked in snow. Ellis had become seriously ill in December, and after several days in the hospital, he died on Saturday, 2 January 1904.[28] His body was taken to John McCarthy & Son, undertakers, and as Coy L. Ludwig has discovered, it was not until the following Friday that friends were able to travel from Rochester to claim Ellis's remains.[29] Ellis was buried on Monday, 11 January, in St. Agnes cemetery in Syracuse, and Claude Bragdon and Gustav Stickley paid for his funeral.[30]

The next day, the *New York Times* printed a brief obituary on its front page.[31] Stickley's magazine eulogized Ellis in its February issue: "In the death of Mr. Harvey Ellis…The Craftsman lost a valued contributor to its department of architecture. Mr. Ellis was a man of unusual gifts; possessing an accurate and exquisite sense of color, a great facility in design and a sound judgment of effect. These qualities were evidenced in his slightest sketches, causing them to be kept as treasures by those fortunate enough to acquire them.… Mr. Ellis was, further, a connoisseur of Japanese art, the principles of which he assimilated and practiced. Altogether, he is to be regretted as one who possessed the sacred fire of genius."[32]

Harvey Ellis, indeed, had extraordinary gifts. He was a fluent graphic artist who brought visual sophistication to *The Craftsman* magazine. He designed some of the most superb furniture ever to emerge from Stickley's firm. A deft, imaginative architect and delineator, his architectural drawings for the magazine created a convincing vision of what a Craftsman house could be. He brought to Stickley a new color palette and new color harmonies, and the interiors of the Craftsman houses he designed were integral to the architecture. He was thus the first of Stickley's designers to create interiors as coherent works of art. This was the synthesis that Stickley had sought in late 1902 and early 1903, but until he found Ellis this pursuit had had little success. Its realization was Ellis's single most important contribution to the aesthetic development of Stickley's firm. In turn, as Bragdon astutely observed during the summer of 1903, it was thanks to the healthy "influence of Stickley" that Ellis was finally thriving.

The Ellis era at the Craftsman Workshops did not quite end with his death. Although Ellis's influence quickly faded from *The Craftsman* magazine and Craftsman architecture, Stickley continued to produce Ellis-designed inlaid furniture until perhaps June 1904. Stickley exhibited an inlaid settle and an inlaid music cabinet at the Art Institute of Chicago in December 1903, and this work was praised in the local press.[33] As a writer in Chicago observed, "In these pieces the flat surfaces are not disturbed by ornament, except the slight traceries, made of insertions of copper and white-metal lines, combined with limited tints of wood-marquetry. There is almost nothing to the ornament; but it so restful and so well chosen that everyone will be grateful. On the whole, this is one of the most satisfying exhibits in the galleries."[34] In February and March 1904 Stickley's firm shipped seven inlaid pieces to retailers in Dallas and Washington, D.C., and examples are known today with store labels from several other cities. Stickley had in fact regularly promoted inlaid furniture in his magazine throughout Ellis's tenure, culminating in the *Craftsman* article that formally launched it in January 1904. Perhaps, however, it was too "artistic" and too expensive for the middle-class customers Stickley sought, and inlaid Craftsman furniture was not a commercial success.

Stickley occasionally made inlaid furniture in the decade following Ellis's death, although this work was neither shown in catalogs nor published in *The Craftsman* magazine. The examples that can be dated to those years are Stickley production pieces that were inlaid, apparently, only on special order. This later inlay—almost always on a ground of maple veneer—was supplied by George H. Jones. The inlaid chairs that filled the dining room of McCreery's Pittsburgh store, for instance, were manufactured during the post-Ellis era. These later pieces, of course, were not designed by Harvey Ellis.

Even while Ellis was working for him, Stickley was already turning to his other designers to apply Ellis's ideas to furniture that Ellis had not designed. This adaptive process had begun by October 1903, when a complete Ellis-like dining set, apparently drawn by LaMont Warner, was published that month in *The Craftsman*. For the June 1904 *Craftsman*, Warner drew a bedroom with an inlaid dressing table and an inlaid chest of drawers, and a bed with bow-sided head- and footboards. Within months of Ellis's death, complete suites of bedroom and dining furniture with arched aprons, bowed sides, and wide, overhanging tops—but without inlay—had been added to the Craftsman line. Today these production pieces are routinely attributed to Ellis, but they did not appear until after his death, and there is no evidence that he ever drew them. They were created by LaMont Warner, now the firm's senior furniture designer, and by Louise Shrimpton. Ellis had acted as mentor to them while he was at the Craftsman Workshops, and although they were never to equal him, both learned to mimic his manner. The Stickley firm rationalized the defining characteristics of the Ellis vocabulary and incorporated them into the basic repertoire of Craftsman catalog furniture. By mid-1904, it had begun making "Standard Stickley" furniture. This was the high-style line of production furniture that came into being throughout that pivotal year.

28 This dining set, apparently drawn by LaMont Warner, was inspired by the designs of Harvey Ellis and was published in *The Craftsman* in October 1903.

29 A bedroom with Craftsman inlaid maple furniture drawn by LaMont Warner for the June 1904 issue of *The Craftsman*.

30 This Ellis-designed secretary/bookcase combines a wide, overhanging top and arched apron with vigorous hand-hammered metal hardware and wooden pulls characteristic of Stickley's 1901 and 1902 furniture.

31 Following: The countless inlaid chairs in the dining room of James McCreery's Pittsburgh department store were manufactured by the Craftsman Workshops during the post-Ellis era.

After beginning bleakly with the death of Harvey Ellis, 1904 would turn out to be a pivotal year for the Craftsman enterprise. This year Stickley completed the process of shedding his sometimes self-conscious medievalism, and abandoned the fiction that he was the master of a "guild." By June 1904 he had dropped the name United Crafts and picked up the more modern-sounding banner, Craftsman Workshops, that he was to follow for the next ten years.[1] Hereafter the firm would be less quirky and personal—less *experimental*—than it had been in the preceding four years. Its products and publications were increasingly standardized, expressing a new status quo. By the end of the year, Stickley was overseeing a well-established Arts and Crafts enterprise. It is perhaps an indication of his increasing success and influence that in December his former associate, George Clingman of the Tobey Furniture Company, took the very unusual step of criticizing an industry colleague—Stickley—in the normally sunny pages of a trade magazine, *Furniture Journal*. "The trouble with Gustav Stickley and his followers," said Clingman, "is that they expect the furniture suited to a modest $5,000 home to serve in the mansion of a millionaire."[2]

In the January 1904 *Craftsman*, the first issue with a four-color cover, Stickley published plans for Craftsman House #1, the design of a still-unidentified architect.[3] This house has low, hipped roofs covered in unglazed red ceramic tiles, white roughcast exterior walls, and an arched entryway. These are components of mission architecture, although the article never alludes to that connection. With Craftsman House #1, Stickley launched the Craftsman Home Builders' Club, a venture that he hoped would boost subscription sales of his magazine. Membership was available at no charge to any *Craftsman* subscriber who wanted to join, and the benefits offered by this "Club" included free plans and specifications for any Craftsman house published by the magazine that year. With the new Club needing a monthly supply of

Craftsman houses, and his star architect Ellis dead, Stickley had little choice but to find replacements quickly. By February he had brought in George R. Nichols, a New York City-based architect, to design houses for him, and he also turned to members of his in-house design staff, among them LaMont Warner and the young architect Oliver J. Story. Stickley's firm drew on a number of creative people throughout 1904. In addition to Warner and Story, another young architect, Harry L. Gardner, was on his staff, as were the designer/illustrator Louise Shrimpton and the "draughtsman" Ruth Anne Williams. At least two more architects, Carl Sailer and Alfred T. Taylor, worked for Stickley that year on a freelance basis. All of them had talent and the ability to respond creatively to Stickley's direction; none equaled "the sacred fire of genius" granted to Harvey Ellis.

From their debut in January 1904, the magazine's Craftsman houses followed the philosophy of integrated design that Stickley, aided by Dietrich and Ellis and the example of British Arts and Crafts, had embraced the year before. The development of the Craftsman house was a natural, perhaps inevitable, step for Stickley: like his furniture, it was intended as a vehicle for reforming public taste. It held out the prospect of comfortable suburban or rural living that middle-class families could afford. The sturdy, unpretentious Craftsman house embodied the "plain living and high thinking" ethos of the Arts and Crafts movement, and it was, for Stickley, an idealistic undertaking. By making the Craftsman house a monthly feature of his magazine, and the basis of his subscription-boosting Home Builders' Club, he would exploit its commercial potential as well.[4] A Craftsman house, as Stickley certainly understood, was a big, empty box that his customers would want to fill with Craftsman products.

1 Detail of the massive, strap-hinged #967 sideboard, oak, ca. 1902.

THE CRAFTSMAN

VOL. V   JANUARY·1904   NO. 4

COPY 25 CENTS	PUBLISHED MONTHLY BY THE UNITED CRAFTS SYRACUSE·N·Y·-·U·S·A·	YEAR 3 DOL LARS

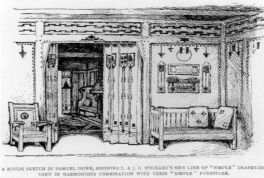

A ROUGH SKETCH BY SAMUEL HOWE, SHOWING L. & J. G. STICKLEY'S NEW LINE OF "SIMPLE" DRAPERIES USED IN HARMONIOUS COMBINATION WITH THEIR "SIMPLE" FURNITURE.

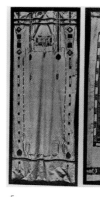

3   4   5

At the beginning of 1904 domestic architecture was only one of Stickley's interests. Commenting later that year on "the large business he has built up," *Furniture Trade Review* told readers that "Mr. Stickley's ideas...radiate in a hundred directions"[5] This was perhaps never more true than in 1904, when Stickley's radiating ideas shone from the pages of *The Craftsman* and the furniture trade press. Ever energetic in pursuit of business opportunities, he began methodically to promote his Craftsman furniture, metal work, and textiles with a series of advertisements in twelve consecutive issues of *Furniture Trade Review*. He was looking to expand his sales beyond the consumer markets where he was already having success, and one goal of this campaign was to sell Craftsman goods and services to other manufacturers and to the furniture and decorating trade as well. He was also seeking more retailers to carry his wares. Since his abortive venture with the Tobey Company, Stickley had kept tight control of his retailing, selling for the most part through a few large department stores and through the catalogs his firm mailed to retail customers. But this apparently proved too limiting, and as 1904 began he was making a concerted effort to expand the number of affiliated retailers—his Associates—that sold his wares in major cities across the country. One of those associates was the giant Chicago retailer Marshall Field and Company, which, in 1904, was featuring a model dining room with Craftsman furniture and fireplace tools, oak wainscoting, Japanese grass cloth wall

2 The first four-color cover of *The Craftsman*, January 1904.

3 Trade advertisement for The Craftsman Workshops, from *Furniture Trade Review*, 10 August 1904.

4 An L. & J. G. Stickley model room, with echoes of both English Arts and Crafts and Native American motifs, designed by Samuel Howe, from *The Upholsterer*, February 1905.

5 L. & J. G. Stickley embroidered and appliquéd "peasant embroideries" designed by Samuel Howe, from *International Studio*, March 1905.

coverings, Tiffany lighting, and textiles and a wallpaper frieze imported from England. The predominant tones were greens and browns, accented with touches of heliotrope. This handsome model room was put together to help customers see how Stickley furniture could fit into their own homes; it also typified the inventive merchandising practiced by Stickley and his associates.

It may be that his quickened commercial pace in part reflected competitive pressures from members of his own family. Although his brothers Leopold and John George had formed their L. & J.G. Stickley Company in February 1902 in the Syracuse suburb of Fayetteville, it was not until early 1904 that they began actively to court the retail trade. In January of that year, L. & J.G. Stickley exhibited at the Grand Rapids furniture market for the first time. They incorporated their firm in February. By April they had adopted a new, Arts and Crafts-like brand name, Onondaga Shops, and had issued a catalog of furniture designs that were substantial, straight-lined, and unequivocally structural, much as Gustav Stickley's furniture had been two or three years before. Late in the year L. & J.G. Stickley opened what Leopold called the "Stickley Crafts Shop." There they made their first metalwork and textiles, recruiting Samuel Howe, still a frequent contributor to *The Craftsman* magazine, to direct this new undertaking. Gustav Stickley had initially been supportive of his brothers' efforts: according to Stickley family tradition he lent them money to help them start their business. But by 1904 he was certainly aware that they were making metalwork, textiles, and plain oak furniture very like his, and promoting their wares determinedly to the same retail trade.[6]

Despite the intensifying demands of his enterprise, Stickley took time off to travel. He left Syracuse about 5 March—a late winter day of snow and light rain—for a seven-week transcontinental journey to the West Coast with Eda

6

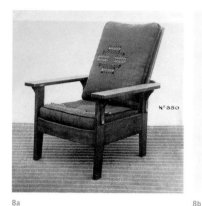

8a

8b

8c

and their daughters Barbara and Mildred, both then in their late teens. For him it was a working vacation, business mixed with the pleasures of touring and sightseeing. George Wharton James (1858–1923), a California writer who would soon become associate editor of *The Craftsman*, acted as the family's traveling companion and tour guide.

English by birth, James was a writer, editor, lecturer, photographer, tour guide, collector, activist for Native American rights, and, at one time, a roving Methodist minister. Perhaps his true calling, though, was as a public relations man, and over the course of his career he publicized tourist-carrying railroads, California real estate, fellow writers, and "Captain, the Horse with a Human Brain," with equal enthusiasm. A Pasadena resident, he was a founder of the Arroyo Guild of Fellow Craftsmen, a short-lived cooperative association of artisans and designers, based in nearby Garvanza. James's character had its share of flaws, and it is true that he was an inveterate booster and self-promoter; and yet, as a kind of bi-coastal Arts and Crafter, he occupied a position that remains practically unique. He is one of the few figures of the American Arts and Crafts movement who worked for both Elbert Hubbard, helping him run the Roycroft summer school in East Aurora, New York, in about 1901–1903, and Gustav Stickley, as associate editor of *The Craftsman* in 1904–1905. James was a man of admirable enthusiasms and he was a diligent, prolific writer; today his books are collectable and flood rare book sites on the Internet. But, by his own admission, his prose was often "cut and paste."[7]

It is worth mentioning James's literary shortcomings because they probably rule him out as the ghostwriter of the two wonderfully lush and evocative California essays—published by *The Craftsman* magazine in 1904 and signed by Gustav Stickley—that will be quoted frequently in this chapter. The first, "The Colorado Desert and California," appeared in June, and the second, "Nature and Art in California," in July. James took notes for these articles while he and Stickley traveled through the state, but he was apparently not their author.[8] The narrative voice of these essays generally suggests a writer who is urbane, widely traveled in Europe, and highly educated, especially about art history. That describes neither Gustav Stickley nor George Wharton James. It does, however, describe Irene Sargent, and it is likely that Sargent, working with James's notes and direction from Stickley, was Stickley's California ghost. She had been writing similarly discursive essays for him, sometimes signed by her and sometimes not, since 1901.

In the months leading up to this trip, Stickley's magazine had been paying an increasing amount of attention to the American West. George Wharton James wrote his first article for *The Craftsman*, a piece on North American Indians, in November 1903, followed in December by

6 Exterior perspective of Craftsman House #6 by LaMont Warner, from *The Craftsman*, June 1904.

7 The Craftsman model room at Marshall Field and Company, from *The Upholsterer*, June 1904.

8a, b, c Factory photographs of Onondaga Shops furniture—a low chest, Morris chair, and corner cabinet, first made by the L. & J. G. Stickley Company ca. 1904.

CALIFORNIA

For pleasure, for recreation, for health and for education, a trip to California is an investment that pays a handsome interest on a small capital. There you can pick flowers and enjoy outdoor life all the year 'round. California is quickly and comfortably reached by the through train service of the

CHICAGO, MILWAUKEE & ST. PAUL RAILWAY

The Overland Limited runs via this line, is electric lighted throughout and offers the best of service and equipment. Choice of routes going and returning. Booklets free. Ask the nearest ticket agent of this company for additional information, or write to

F. A. MILLER, *General Passenger Agent,* CHICAGO

9

10

"Sermons in Sun-Dried Bricks," Harvey Ellis's essay on missions of the Southwest. Ellis saw the missions from an Arts and Crafts perspective, admiring their frank expression of purpose, their adaptation to the local climate, their forthright construction, and the simplicity and dignity of their designs. He called them proper models for modern domestic architecture; other Craftsman architects would later design houses guided by this insight.

James's series on the California missions began in the January 1904 issue of *The Craftsman* and continued through most of the year. Also, beginning in that same January issue, the magazine began regularly carrying full-page advertisements for railroad lines that took passengers to the Pacific Coast. Westbound railroads had advertised in *The Craftsman* before, but these large advertisements became a constant presence throughout 1904. On other occasions, James is known to have traded his publicity services for free railroad passes, and Stickley may

have been doing something similar here—exchanging advertising space for free or reduced fares to California.[9] Two full pages of railroad advertisements appeared in the March 1904 issue, the same month the Stickleys headed west.

Although their trip had a serious purpose, the Stickley family took time to enjoy themselves as tourists. The family visited Palm Springs, then a tiny desert settlement, with two hundred residents, that had risen up around the old Indian spring, Agua Caliente.[10] There Stickley and James, two serious-minded, middle-aged men, momentarily abandoned their comportment, stripped off their dust-laden clothes, and plunged into the hot springs, an experience, said James, that "makes the heart leap." This brief, boyish and uninhibited moment was the euphoric peak of Stickley's vacation.[11] Leaving Palm Springs, the party went on to the Mission Inn in Riverside, and later made stops in Los Angeles, Pasadena, and Santa Barbara. After visiting and photographing Mission San Miguel, the Stickleys and James cruised up the San Joaquin River, pausing along the riverbank to look over a herd of Holstein cattle. In the San Francisco area they took automobile jaunts up Mt. Tamalpais and Mt. Diablo, and then returned to Southern California before heading home.[12] The Stickleys were giddy sightseers up and down the state.

9 Railroad advertisement beckoning tourists to California, from *The Craftsman*, February 1904.

10 *Furniture World* reported on Stickley's California trip on 30 June 1904. In a gesture that could not have pleased him, the magazine illustrated the cover of this issue with a drawing of a monk sitting amidst mission furniture.

11 George Wharton James, the English-born humorist Marshall P. Wilder, and Elbert Hubbard, on the Roycroft campus in East Aurora, New York, ca. early 1900s.

It is difficult to verify more than these glimpses of Stickley's personal time in California, but the public dimension of this trip is fairly well documented in the two *Craftsman* articles and in news items published by industry trade journals.[13] *Furniture Journal* reported that "Gustav Stickley, the pioneer in the introduction of Mission furniture...has been spending time in Southern California studying Mission models to be found in that part of the country."[14] This news item may have been good publicity but it could not have pleased Stickley: he hated the term "mission furniture." In all of his publications he was careful to differentiate his Craftsman furniture from the popular "mission-style" furniture mass-produced by East Coast and midwestern furniture factories. As he once declared at the start of an interview with a trade press reporter, "Don't say 'Mission' or I will stop right here. I am not trying to make Mission furniture. I am making simple things in a simple way."[15] And, while he admired the furniture found in the California missions, he wanted to be quite clear that he was not imitating it. As he patiently explained to the writer from *Furniture Journal*, his Craftsman furniture was sometimes confused with furniture from the missions because of their shared traits of plainness and frank adaptation to purpose.

Furniture World reported on Stickley's trip in June, and the illustration chosen for the cover of that issue—a drawing of a monk seated on a mission chair at a mission desk—must have dismayed Stickley as well. His emphasis in these trade journal articles, however, was not on furniture, but on California. He praised the state and said it would make a perfect site for the cooperative community he planned to build there. His western visit had inspired a revelation: "In talking with my friend here, George Wharton James, I find we have almost similar ideas. We intend to start a community where we shall live the simple life. Here in California you have ideal conditions for such a community. Here are the climate, the pure air, the scenery, the fruitfulness of soil, the conditions which render outdoor life easy and make such a community practicable." Like other visitors from the industrialized east, Stickley responded expansively to the natural beauty and fertility—the heady sense of promise and possibility— of California.

Discussing his California craft community, Stickley set forth specific plans: "We shall take pupils and educate them practically, as the old guilds of Europe used to do, in blacksmithing, carpentering, stone masonry, bricklaying, silverworking, weaving of all kinds of textiles, gardening and the like.... We shall have an ideal community as far as possible, where music of all kinds, art of all kinds and craftsmanship of all kinds will be practiced and taught." Although he had not originated these compelling ideas, he had become their ardent spokesman. In his *Craftsman* magazine he advocated them to a sympathetic national readership, and, in California in the spring of 1904, he searched for a way to put them into practice.

12 The eucalyptus pergola that Stickley enjoyed while staying at the Mission Inn, Riverside, California, from *The Craftsman*, June 1904.

Of course he had to pay for this plan, and his idealistic vision was necessarily tempered by mercantile considerations. As he stressed to *Furniture World*, "it will be an essentially practical affair. There will be a sterling business basis to everything. It will have a definite, practical, commercial value." Stickley understood that his rural community of artisans and students needed more funding than he could personally supply, and he also understood the role that publicity could play in attracting that funding. This was one of the reasons he publicized his California trip in the trade press and then recorded it in such exquisite detail for *Craftsman* readers in June and July. It also helps explain why he chose James, the consummate publicist, as his traveling companion.

In the first article, "The Colorado Desert and California," Stickley and his party traveled by train and horse-drawn wagon to Palm Springs, which seemed to him the perfect site for his craft-based community: "[A]s we neared the valley-oasis, great buttresses of the mountain range stretched out their walls to offer protection against the elements. Orange, lemon, fig, almond and apricot trees were in full bloom; the air, of a caressing softness, was laden with mingled perfumes; the eye was intoxicated with the beauty of the sky, foliage and flowers, and the outside world seemed a troubled dream." Stickley was enchanted by California, but this ecstatic language was certainly meant in part to inspire the recruits needed to populate and pay for this West Coast utopian community. As Richard Guy Wilson has written, "The sentiments expressed by many of the California Arts and Crafters were both profound and commercial; they strove to find meaning in life and at the same time were unabashed real estate promoters."[16] This insight applies equally well to Stickley. To his *Craftsman* readers he summoned up irresistible pastoral images of "men and women working in groves, vineyards, orchards, or at handicrafts in their own dwellings; leading no idyllic existence but free, at least, from the more depressing anxieties...than if they had remained in the crowded cities...of the East."

Stickley never realized this vision of a craft-based settlement flowering in the California desert, but he did pragmatically think it through. He intended to capitalize this venture by raising a million dollars through a public offering of 100,000 shares of stock to be sold at $10.00 each. Then he could buy land and begin to develop it. He planned to attract four hundred colonists, to whom he would sell parcels of land ranging in size from one to five acres. He also expected to engage artisans who would set up workshops and give instruction to the tuition-paying students.[17] "Yes, it is a big plan," Stickley boastfully told an interviewer from the *San Francisco Call*, "but this is an age of big things, and nothing can be accomplished by attempting to work on a small scale. We shall plan large, begin small and work up to a full achievement of all we have planned and more."[18] But it was only a dream, really, and after 1904 nothing more was heard about it. Yet the vision stayed alive in his mind. Four years later, as he was buying the New Jersey land that would become Craftsman Farms, his plans for the site included not just a house for his family, but a school, an artisan colony,

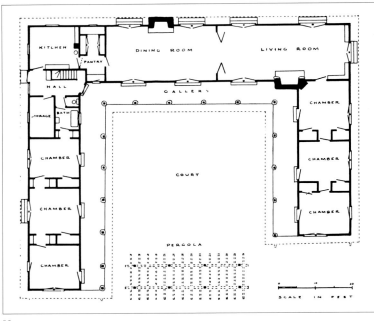

13

and a close-knit community of home owners farming their own small plots of ground. There would even be a herd of grazing Holsteins.

The Stickleys jaunted on to Riverside and checked in to the Mission Inn, a mission revival resort hotel decorated with Native American artifacts and mission-style furniture, as well as Craftsman furniture made by Stickley's firm.[19] Like those railroads mentioned earlier, the Mission Inn was advertising in *The Craftsman* magazine in March 1904, and its owner, the promotionally minded businessman Frank Miller, was a good friend of George Wharton James. In the June *Craftsman* article Stickley enthused over the simplicity of the Inn's design, and stressed that this grand structure was "perfectly adapted to climatic and local conditions." He admired the roof tiles salvaged from an old mission and the rough textured plaster walls, but he was particularly taken by the eucalyptus pergola that flanked the court-yard entrance; reworked and adapted by Oliver J. Story, it would soon appear in the drawings of a Craftsman house.

The Stickleys traveled on to Pasadena, where they stayed at La Pinteresca, a hotel recommended by James.[20] The second *Craftsman* article set in California began with the party having arrived in

13 The U-shaped plan of Charles and Henry Greene's Arturo Bandini house, 1903, a house probably seen by Stickley when he visited Pasadena in 1904.

14 Stickley furniture filled the living room of the Greenes' James Culbertson house, 1902–1910.

this city. The writer, Stickley's ghost, offered the unremarkable thought that the state's domestic architecture should follow nature and be in accord with the region's cultural heritage, and then cited Pasadena and Los Angeles as two places that failed to do this. The inhabitants, so the indictment ran, favored a Colonial Revival style of architecture suitable to New England but not southern California. There was *some* truth to this comment, but it still seems a little odd.[21] The month before Stickley went west, for instance, *The Craftsman* published a full-page photograph of a substantial mission revival house built six years earlier in Los Angeles. Several more photographs of mission revival houses in California—illustrations for an article by George Wharton James—appeared in the same issue. And, in May 1904, the *Los Angeles Examiner* commented that "every street in Pasadena had a bungalow."[22] As James took him around Pasadena in March and April 1904, Stickley could not have failed to notice those bungalows.

Stickley certainly saw some of the Pasadena houses designed by Charles Greene (1868–1957) and Henry Greene (1870–1954). As Mildred Stickley recalled nearly seventy years later, she and her parents "went to see the Greenes."[23] They probably visited the Greenes' Culbertson house of 1902. It was no more than a minute's walk from Charles Greene's home on what is now Arroyo Terrace, and Stickley would have immediately seen its kinship with the houses he had been publishing for the past two years in *The Craftsman*

14

magazine. Its decor mixed Japanese and Native American decorative objects with early Stickley furniture, and this combination created a handsome ensemble in the Greenes' architectural setting. In a contemporary article about the Culbertson house, the writer Una Nixson Hopkins said of the living room, "The furniture and the woodwork of this room give a feeling of having been designed simultaneously, or one with the other continually in mind. The heavy wood shelf of the mantel has the same stability as has the library table, and the lines of the wood on the ceiling and those making friezes, as well as those running at right angles, have the actual feeling of the real furniture."[24] The Culbertson living room combined muted grays and deep browns, and the dining room was predominantly brown and soft matte blue, relieved with an occasional spot of pale yellow. The Greenes' rich and subtle color harmonies paralleled the kinds of color combinations recommended by *The Craftsman* magazine. The shapes and colors of the Culbertson interior—and all that Stickley furniture!—must have made Stickley feel that although he was three thousand miles away from home he had alighted on familiar ground.

Stickley probably also saw the Greenes' Arturo Bandini house of 1903. This was a single-story, U-shaped house enclosing a central courtyard and a small pond. The courtyard was bounded on three sides by covered verandahs, and the plan, responsive to the mild southern California climate, allowed easy circulation between indoor and outdoor living spaces. The Greenes sheathed the

Bandini house with rough redwood boards, and they expressed its structure by leaving the wooden roof trusses visible inside the house. Two large cobblestone fireplaces, one in the living room and one in the dining room, gave the house its evocative Spanish name: "El Hogar," the hearth. Four years after Stickley's California vacation, a *Craftsman* article would single out the Bandini house as "an excellent example of the wooden patio house."[25]

The Greenes' domestic architecture would become a staple of *The Craftsman* within a few years of Stickley's trip. Stickley's magazine admired these two California architects for designing houses that made decorative use of structural timbers and existed in harmony with "the land as nature made it." And it recognized the evident influence Stickley exerted on their work.[26] Charles Greene, as mentioned earlier, had seen Stickley furniture at the Pan-American Exposition in Buffalo, New York, in 1901, and he was an early and faithful reader of *The Craftsman* magazine. As Edward R. Bosley has written, "At what point Charles Greene began to clip illustrations from *The Craftsman* is unknown, but his work soon began to reflect an intimate awareness of its aesthetic message."[27] Some of Charles Greene's earliest furniture designs, for the Mary Reeve Darling house of 1903 and the Edgar Camp house of 1904, were derived from drawings of Craftsman furniture in a Craftsman brochure issued about May 1903 that is still among his papers.[28] His personal copy of the July 1903 *Craftsman*, the first Ellis issue, survives in a private collection today.

15

16

Following Stickley's journey west, however, the polarity of influence started to shift. In July 1904, just five weeks after his return from California, *The Craftsman* published plans and perspective views of a single-story house for the article "Cool and Quiet Days." This house shows early evidence that even though Stickley had criticized the inappropriate Colonial Revival houses he had seen in Pasadena and environs, he did find local architecture that he could emulate. It is awkwardly drawn, but the U-shaped plan, the enclosed courtyard bordered on three sides by covered verandahs, and the central decorative pond are elements of this house that unmistakably echo the Greenes' Bandini house. Designed by Oliver J. Story, this modest Craftsman house has five massive fieldstone fireplaces, an allusion perhaps to "El Hogar." And these fireplaces implicitly acknowledge that a southern California structure reincarnated in a different region of the country — a northeastern state — would need to be amply heated. There is an additional California influence on this house. The projecting roofs around the courtyard are supported by tree trunks stripped of branches and bark, a not uncommon handling of natural materials seen in late nineteenth- and early twentieth-century rustic houses. In this instance, however, the design recalls nothing so much as the eucalyptus pergola that Stickley, a few months before, had happily strolled through at the Mission Inn.

"Cool and Quiet Days" appeared in the July 1904 *Craftsman*, the same issue that carried the second installment in the magazine's account of Stickley's western travels. In that article, which began with Stickley in Pasadena, he and

his party headed north to visit Charles Frederick Eaton at his home in Montecito. Eaton was a worldly, wealthy man who pursued his twin passions for landscape design and handicrafts, making richly ornamented objects in the private workshop he set up on the grounds of his estate. His daughter, Elizabeth Eaton Burton, was his equal as a designer and artisan, and Stickley and James stopped at her Santa Barbara studio on 2 April 1904. Eaton and Burton seemed to Stickley to be living the Arts and Crafts ideal that he had long pursued. They were skillfully handcrafting beautiful objects from natural materials, and with their workshops set amidst informal but dramatically landscaped gardens, they practiced their crafts in an inspiring setting.

After traveling through southern California, Stickley and his party went to San Francisco, staying at the St. Francis hotel. He almost certainly visited Paul Elder, a bookseller, publisher, and Arts and Crafts retailer who advertised his firm's books in *The Craftsman* magazine. It was probably while Stickley was in San Francisco that he met the talented young metalworker who was then making objects for sale in Elder's store.[29] His name was Victor Toothaker, and within a few years he was to become one of Stickley's key artistic collaborators.

15 The U-shaped Craftsman house designed by Oliver J. Story for "Cool and Quiet Days," from *The Craftsman*, July 1904.

16 The courtyard of the house Story designed for "Cool and Quiet Days" contains clear echoes of the Bandini courtyard and the eucalyptus pergola at the Mission Inn, Riverside.

17 "Cool and Quiet Days," plan, from *The Craftsman*, July 1904.

17

Gustav, Eda, Barbara, and Mildred Stickley returned to Syracuse from the West Coast on 22 April 1904. Stickley was soon traveling again, arriving in St. Louis in June to see the Louisiana Purchase Exposition. Although his magazine could not countenance the rampant commercialism of this world's fair ("There is no educative value…in a pile of carpet sweepers reaching to the ceiling"), Stickley was entranced by the displays of German decorative arts. In the August and October issues of *The Craftsman*, two long articles, signed by Gustav Stickley, vividly described the furniture and interiors he had seen in the German section of the Varied Industries Building.[30] He praised the "chaste, dignified" German model rooms for their decorative use of structure, subdued colors, and sympathetic handling of materials; he valued them exactly as he wanted Craftsman furniture and interiors to be valued.

When Stickley did venture a criticism, his comments followed a discernible pattern. Assessing a music room by the architect Bruno Paul, for instance, he remarked that it contained "the most charming details…but provok[es] the question as to whether it offers a unified whole." Thus the ideal of unity of design had been so totally absorbed by Stickley that it now became the basis of the critical standards he applied to the work of others. It is somewhat of a surprise, then, that the October issue of his magazine published drawings of German and Austrian interiors with the disharmonious addition of Craftsman furniture. Despite their shared ideological roots, a self-consciously modest

Craftsman chair was never going to look at home in one of Josef Hoffmann's (1870–1956) stylish, urbane interiors, and these rooms fail to convince.[31] But this aesthetically unsuccessful experiment did show the extent to which Stickley was leaving behind the strong, structural Craftsman forms of 1901 and 1902 as well as the sleeker Ellis models of 1903 and early 1904. The pieces of Craftsman furniture placed in these Continental settings were in fact early intimations of the Standard Stickley designs the firm was then developing, and that would be introduced the following February with the publication of "Catalogue D."

While Stickley was at the St. Louis fair he certainly visited the California State Building. It must have looked familiar to him because its architects, the San Francisco firm of Newsom and Newsom, had modeled it after Mission Santa Barbara, which he had seen a few months before. His reason for this visit, however, was not just to admire the architecture, but to see his own work. *Furniture Trade Review* reported in June that "Mr. Stickley has fitted up the California Building at the World's Fair."[32] This furniture—all of which was ordered through his Los Angles associate Niles Pease and shipped directly to the fairgrounds—was used in three public rooms, a handsome assemblage of chairs, settles, library tables, and one tall case clock. So, at the Louisiana Purchase Exposition in St. Louis in the summer and fall of 1904, California continued to be important to Stickley, with his Craftsman furniture in daily use in the mission-style California Building.

Stickley's views on design reform were evident in the 1904 *Craftsman* articles about his California travels as well as in the essays on German and Austrian decorative arts. *The Craftsman* published two other reformist statements this year, and both were sharply pointed: "A False Effort to be Fine," in March, and "From Ugliness to Beauty" in December.[33] These articles are sincere statements of belief, but they are also partisan attacks on those who cling to what Stickley saw as the perilous dishonesty of historically based design. They break the usually smooth verbal surface of his magazine with flurries of invective, and they make for lively reading.

"A False Effort to be Fine" is Stickley's plea for sanity in the decorative arts. He advocates forthright design and construction, sensible proportions, and sound craftsmanship, and he does this with words and images that show his readers what pitfalls they must avoid. He preaches reform of design by offering extreme examples of bad design, analyzing their failings, and in the process subjecting them to ridicule. Although a maker of plain furniture himself, it is not ornament per se that Stickley criticizes; he acknowledges, for instance, the great merit of the masterfully handmade, hand-carved Chippendale furniture of the eighteenth century, and refers to Thomas Chippendale as an "artist-craftsman" and a "delightful artist." The special objects of Stickley's scorn are those later imitators who jumble together period motifs, and, driven only by their desire for profits, produce ostentatious, shoddily made designs "which can be multiplied to the million by the machine, for the degradation of art and of the public taste."

Stickley breathes real fire into his argument with drawings of "false" furniture witheringly described. He calls one example, a Morris chair, a "chaos of construction," and directs the reader's eye to its front legs: "The animal forms so effectively used in mediaeval, the Renascence and the First Empires styles are here travestied and degraded. The line of the body—so attractive when treated by the old craftsmen...here become almost revolting, through a clumsy touch of realism. Then the hoofs of the animals are shod with casters, while all other details are equally commercialized to the limits of vulgarity.... This chair has no excuse for being."

In "A False Effort to be Fine," Stickley campaigns to improve public taste, and his argument is clear and memorable. It is worth noting, however, that the examples of "false art" Stickley chose for this article were not merely concocted by *The Craftsman*. They were actual pieces of furniture made by other manufacturers, and all of them had been published a few months before in *Furniture World*.[34] The Morris chair singled out by Stickley, for instance, was made by the firm of S.A. Cook & Co. The targets of this criticism, Stickley's erstwhile furniture industry colleagues, must have resented it, and he perhaps tactlessly brought it to their attention by placing a condensed version, called "Bad Art is Bad Business," in a trade journal, *The Upholsterer*.[35] Many of *The Upholsterer's* readers must have remembered that just five years earlier the Gustave Stickley Company had been proudly promoting its own machine-carved Morris chairs, chairs that anyone, then or now, would find hard to differentiate from those marketed in 1904 by the unfortunate Mr. Cook.

18 A Morris chair offered as an example of "false" furniture and subjected to devastating verbal attack in *The Craftsman*, March 1904.

19 A Morris chair manufactured by S. A. Cook & Company, from *Furniture World*, 7 January 1904.

Stickley's December 1904 polemic, "From Ugliness to Beauty," was a more measured performance. He began it with a straightforward declaration of principles that most Arts and Crafts practitioners could accept, defining his quest as a return to "the old frankness of expression, the primitive emphasis upon structure, the natural adaptation of ornament to material." Despite these by now familiar sentiments, "From Ugliness to Beauty" revealed something new in Stickley's thinking. In this article he no longer invoked as his models the idealized medieval craftsmen he had learned to revere through the influence of Ruskin and Morris. He turned instead to the sturdy American past, recalling "our forefathers of the Colonial and early Federal periods" who had "labored strenuously to produce good work...whether it appears in the Constitution of the United States or yet in a chest, or a chair." He would soon adopt the stance that Craftsman furniture was the first "distinctively American style of furniture," and leave his medievalism behind.

Stickley structures the argument of this article with a series of Pugin-like "contrasts," offering paired examples of "before" and "after" rooms. The "befores" are extreme, almost comically incoherent, but they legitimately reflect the fashion of the day. As Stickley tells his readers, the furniture in these rooms was drawn from actual examples of American cabinetmaking that had recently been exhibited at the Louisiana Purchase Exposition. He had seen them firsthand. The "after" rooms have been stripped down, simplified and made soothing and unified with a few chaste pieces of tasteful furniture, some of it Craftsman and some not. Colors now harmonize. In one room, for instance, the walls are covered in a warm blue-gray paper, and the stenciled frieze is deep blue picked out with contrasting orange and rich green. The rug has a gray-green ground and a border pattern that repeats the colors of the frieze, and the curtains are pale green silk with a few woven strands of yellow. The leaded glass window is yellow and green. These model rooms, the "afters," integrate architecture and interior design to create pleasing, modest spaces that have been recast as complete ensembles. They recall little of the aestheticized interiors that Harvey Ellis had designed for *The Craftsman* the year before, but they nevertheless reflect the lessons in coherence that Stickley and his designers had learned under Ellis's inspired tutelage.

Freeing these rooms from their enslavement to "fashion" and creating simple, honest interiors was not merely a matter of aesthetics, or even taste. Arts and Crafts earnestness makes itself felt here, and Stickley is equally concerned with the moral effects of the home environment. The admonitory caption for one of the "before" rooms reads, "Gilt and glitter are the factors of restlessness." Reincarnated as a Craftsman room, it becomes "A place of contentment and beauty conducive to good work." In this article Stickley is acting as a manufacturer and merchant unobtrusively promoting his wares, but he is also exercising his idealistic Arts and Crafts impulse to reform design and thereby improve his readers.

Stickley stayed close to home during the fall of 1904, and there he entertained an important guest. He invited Charles Wagner (1854–1918) to Syracuse. Wagner was a French Protestant minister, an apostle of modest living guided by quiet faith, and author of the book *The Simple Life*. He was then on a lecture tour of the United States, having been invited to this country by President Theodore Roosevelt. *The Simple Life*, Roosevelt had written, "contains so much

18

19

20 Stickley furniture in the California Building at the Louisiana Purchase Exposition, St. Louis, 1904.

21 A Craftsman adaptation of a Josef Hoffmann workroom, from *The Craftsman,* October 1904.

22 A "before" room, where "gilt and glitter are the factors of restlessness," from *The Craftsman*, December 1904.

23 As re-envisioned by Stickley's designers, the "after" room becomes "a place of contentment and beauty conducive to good work," from *The Craftsman*, December 1904.

that we of America ought to take to our hearts."[36] Wagner's appeal for a progressive businessman like Stickley is clear. He preached the centrality of family life, a recurrent Craftsman theme, and, as David Shi has written, "By emphasizing that simplicity had more to do with one's perspective than one's income, [he] had implicitly sanctioned the prevailing capitalist system."[37] Wagner spoke at the Craftsman Building on the evening of 11 October, for which Stickley paid him a handsome $300 lecture fee.[38] It was not difficult for the empathetic Wagner to see that Stickley's calling had parallels with his own, and in a later book, *My Impressions of America*, he said of his generous friend and host:

> Besides the Western languages into which "The Simple Life" has been translated, it has had the honour to be put into Japanese...and Hebrew.... But a still more unexpected translation has been made of it, that has given me acute pleasure; it has been interpreted in oak. The man to achieve this work, Mr. Stickley...is at once the editor of a magazine, The Craftsman, and an artificer who himself works out the ideals it upholds. The aim Mr. Stickley has set for himself, is the realisation of home-like simplicity and honest durability in furniture.... To build houses worthy to be the social centre of the family [and] to furnish them with objects at once useful, practical and capable of speaking to the heart—such is Mr. Stickley's high ideal.[39]

Wagner's insights into Stickley's idealism, his need to pursue a course that was morally and ethically correct, capture the very essence of the character of Gustav Stickley; they miss, however, his taste for commerce. In 1904 Stickley's idealistic and mercantile impulses were equally ascendant, and although that fact may not be readily apparent today, his contemporaries saw it. *Furniture Trade Review*, for instance, published an assessment of Stickley mid-year that accurately took his measure:

> The trend of the efforts of the United Crafts, of Syracuse, the unique establishment presided over by Gustav Stickley, is worth examining.... The theory of management runs from the strong, simple, noble elements of mind and life as exemplified by Ruskin and Morris and others, right down without wavering to the time when cash is taken in payment for the goods. It is the advocacy of the four-square life and the four-square furniture, the elegance of simplicity, the absence of ostentation, the use in ornamentation only of things that are necessary.... Mr. Stickley has founded a large business and a successful one, which is based on a theory of life. It is a combination of the ideal and the practical.[40]

The editors of trade journals have perennially been eager to write flattering pieces about their regular advertisers. Although meant as puffery, the brief article published by *Furniture Trade Review* remains perhaps the most cogent statement about Stickley that has yet appeared. It captures him at a moment of professional redefinition: "Early Stickley," in all of its untrammeled manifestations, is coming to an end; "Standard Stickley," in its carefully calibrated sobriety, is emerging in 1904. The Craftsman Workshops has branched out from furniture making into several related fields, built up its wholesaling and retailing capabilities, and become an enterprise of national scope.

24 Charles Wagner, seated in a Craftsman Morris chair and, standing left to right, a man named Xavier Koenig, apparently Wagner's traveling companion, George Wharton James, and Gustav Stickley, at the Craftsman Building in October 1904, from *The Craftsman*, November 1904.

In February 1905, Gustav Stickley published an extensive catalog of new or modified furniture designs, the 128-page "Cabinet Work from the Craftsman Workshops – Catalogue D." Both in its format and its contents it was an unmistakable sign of the changes the firm had made the year before.

Stickley's earlier catalogs and promotional booklets had been bound in stout brown paper covers with Gothic display type and Morrisian decorative borders, and carried Irene Sargent's reform-oriented essays linking Stickley's furniture to medieval antecedents and to the inspiring example of William Morris. The furniture catalogs of 1901 and 1902 were evocative documents, palpably wrought by hand; although meant to make sales, they were equally tokens of Arts and Crafts earnestness.

In 1904, however, Stickley had peeled away the patina of medievalism that had heretofore colored the whole of his Arts and Crafts enterprise, and "Catalogue D" was a much more straightforward affair than anything he had published before. The cover was gray and rather industrial looking, and the furniture photographs on the inside pages were crisp and clear. But these black and white images failed to convey any sense of the hues and textures of the actual wood; the furniture sketches in the earlier catalogs had done that much better. The proselytizing agenda of Sargent's essays was gone, supplanted by a brief promotional foreword delivered in what had become Stickley's habitual first-person singular. With the publication of "Catalogue D," Stickley left behind his vigorous, varied, though in some instances derivative early work, and began

making furniture more consistent with the Craftsman virtues of unity and refined simplicity.

This shift in emphasis toward plainness and standardization enabled Stickley to streamline his production processes. His workers had always used power-driven machinery to cut and shape the cabinet wood, but much of the early furniture making was laboriously done by hand. The evidence of the furniture is that from 1904 onward Stickley turned increasingly to the more orthodox dictates of machines. In the words of a 1906 *Craftsman* catalog: "To say in this day of well-nigh perfect machinery that anything that is good must be done entirely by hand is going rather far. There are certain purely mechanical processes that can be accomplished much better and more economically by machinery, giving the craftsman prepared materials to work with instead of taking his time for their preparation."[1] After 1910 he simplified his designs even further. According to one of his grandsons, Stickley bought new furniture-making machinery for his factory "as soon as he could afford it." The evolution of Craftsman furniture design, in this too-narrow view, was less a matter of ideology or aesthetics than it was of advancing technology and increased capital.[2] Stickley *liked* furniture-making machines, and in the decade following 1904 he invested in them heavily.[3]

Stickley's newly simplified and regularized construction methods were evident throughout "Catalogue D." The mitered mullions once

1 Detail of LaMont Warner designed #804 sideboard, oak, 1905–1909, first drawn in the May 1904 *Craftsman*.

New England
People ......
are showing great
interest in the new
Craftsman Sales-
rooms in Boston
These rooms are most at-
tractively arranged to
show the many pieces of
Craftsman Furniture, as
well as the electric lighting fixtures and other
copper and iron work,
which lend interest to the
decorative scheme of a
room. You are invited to
call at 470 Boylston street
and see the new pieces
which we have not, as yet,
illustrated.

THE CRAFTSMAN COMPANY OF BOSTON
470 BOYLSTON STREET

FREDERICK KEER'S SONS 917 Broad Street NEWARK

MANY additions to the well-
known Craftsman furniture
have been made lately and
some pieces that are remarkably interesting in form and finish have
been added to the familiar designs.
This settle is one of them, and, while
intended primarily for a piece of hall
furniture, it is equally at home in
either living room or dining room,—
especially where a comfortable fire-
side seat is desired. This is one of a
number of Craftsman pieces that
have a look of old-world comfort and
solidity, even while entirely express-
ive of the tastes and needs of modern American life.
     Special attention is called to our Picture and Framing Departments. Hav-
ing our own shop and machinery we are able to execute satisfactorily any
orders entrusted to us.
     Exclusive agents for Newark for Tiffany Glass and Lamps, Rockwood
Pottery and Lenox China.

3

found on the doors of Craftsman bookcases and china cabinets were replaced by simpler, lap-jointed mullions. The backs of case pieces were now in most instances constructed of lightweight panels. Seams, where wooden members butted together on cabinet doors or the sides of cases, were now hidden beneath sheets of quartersawn oak veneers. Exposed tenons were still much in evidence, but few pieces with tenon-and-key joints remained in production. The most recent designs lacked the characteristic massiveness of the early furniture, and the timber used in their construction was generally thinner than the stock used before. Stickley's wood finishes retained their beautiful, subtle luster and durability but, like his furniture, they were increasingly standardized.

To assure uniformity within the revamped Craftsman furniture line, while maintaining good quality control, Stickley introduced a template system for use by the workers in his factory. An employee first drew the outlines of the individual structural members to exact size on pieces of scrap wood. Then, after the actual wooden members were sawn and bored, they were matched against the pencil-drawn master outline to assure that they were, first, correctly configured (with, for instance, their mortises properly placed) and, second, that they were exactly the right shape and dimension. These templates simplified the sawing and boring of cabinet wood, but their main purpose was to assure the consistency of parts from one cutting to the next. They also made it possible for less skilled workers, and not only the higher paid cabinetmakers, to complete some of the steps required in building Craftsman furniture. These templates were followed in much the same way that a dressmaker cutting cloth follows a preprinted pattern.[4]

With "Catalogue D," and with the "Supplement to Catalogue D" issued about six months later, Stickley fused the sturdiness of his 1901 and 1902 furniture with the more refined Ellis creations from 1903 and 1904, and created designs that were admirably plain, modest, and coherent. These new designs were tangible proof that he felt confident enough in his own powers to make the kind of simple, functional furniture that he had espoused from the first but not always achieved. And they were well adapted to efficient, profitable factory production. The Craftsman Workshops was making "Standard Stickley."[5]

2 A #804 sideboard (variant size), first drawn by LaMont Warner in The Craftsman, June 1904, and then photographed for "Catalogue D" issued in February 1905.

3 Two advertisements for Standard Stickley, from The Craftsman, November 1908. The metalwork, textile, and ceramics on the #814 sideboard were meant to show customers the kinds of accessories the Stickley firm considered appropriate.

4

5

4 A #220 Craftsman
daybed and the factory
template that assured
the consistent configuration
of its legs.

5 Detail of the factory
template for the leg of a
#220 daybed.

6 A maple #915 chest
of drawers, first drawn by
LaMont Warner in
The Craftsman, June 1904.

7

8

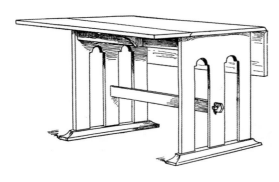

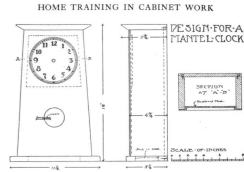

HOME TRAINING IN CABINET WORK

DESIGN·FOR·A MANTEL·CLOCK

9

10

11

Placed one beside the other, nearly any example of early Stickley furniture is a more visually compelling object than nearly any example of the generally muted and unassuming Standard Stickley. By late 1904 and early 1905, however, the Craftsman Workshops was less interested in creating stunning, stand-alone pieces. The designs now created for Standard Stickley furniture were regularized and free of visually competing elements. They were consistent in and of themselves, and with one another. A roomful of Standard Stickley produced a visually unified ensemble. To achieve this totality of effect, the designs of individual pieces of furniture were necessarily subordinated. This was a decided change of emphasis, consciously arrived at and reflected not just in the furniture but also in the manner of its promotion. The illustrations for a 1907 catalog, for instance, showed not single pieces but "groups of furniture, so

7 A #964 china cabinet, cataloged by Stickley in 1902 for ninety dollars.

8 A #815 china cabinet, first cataloged by Stickley in 1905 for forty-eight dollars (This example is from 1912 or later).

9 Furniture designed by W. J. Neatby, from *International Studio*, August 1903.

10 "Home Training in Cabinet Work" table by Louise Shrimpton, based on Neatby's table design, from *The Craftsman*, April 1905.

11 "Home Training in Cabinet Work" mantel clock by Louise Shrimpton, from *The Craftsman*, December 1905.

arranged as to give an idea of the relation of one piece to another."[6] The new concern for integrated design also led the firm, in March 1905, to issue its first metalwork and textile catalogs and to introduce new cabinet woods. According to one of the promotional booklets of this time, "The wood best adapted for Craftsman furniture is quartered oak...but many of our pieces are also made in maple and mahogany, to suit interiors where these woods would be more harmonious than the sturdy oak."[7]

The plain, lighter forms of Standard Stickley answered those critics who had complained that Craftsman furniture was too heavy and substantial, and built on too large a scale. These new designs also made the furniture more affordable.

The introduction to the "Supplement to Catalogue D" faced these interrelated issues head on: "These pieces are as handsome and as durable as the more massive furniture, but are suited to smaller rooms. Some...are built after our familiar models, but on rather lighter lines, so that they are easier to handle and are also somewhat less expensive." Stickley had been emphasizing since 1901 that his furniture was meant for "the middle-class individual." Despite such statements, the retail prices of his labor-intensive early furniture were fairly high. For instance, the 1902 #964 china cabinet with leaded glass doors was priced at $90.00, the equivalent of about $1,600 today. The #815 china cabinet, introduced three years later in "Catalogue D," was a handsome though more simply constructed piece of furniture. It sold for $48.00, an amount that translates today to about $850.[8] Thus, while not inexpensive, Standard Stickley was affordable to many households that could not have paid the higher prices charged for early Stickley.[9]

To make his furniture available in an even less costly form, and with an eye toward widening his market, Stickley devised a way for his customers to circumvent retail prices altogether. In March 1905, the month after the release of "Catalogue D," *The Craftsman* magazine began the "Home Training in Cabinet Work" series. Although initially presented as entirely Stickley's work, it was in fact anonymously drawn by Louise Shrimpton. Some of the "Home Training" designs were created solely for the series, some were simplified renditions of Stickley production furniture, and others were inspired by furniture published in international art journals. According to the first article, the series' purpose was therapeutic, offering satisfying recreation to the tired office worker at the end of a stressful day, and also educational, providing manual training that would "fit a boy, by practice, to become a skilled workman, builder, or designer." It had the additional effect of getting low-cost Craftsman or Craftsman-like furniture into the homes of those readers willing

13

14

to make their own. The firm may have derived some income from "Home Training" by selling Craftsman wood finishes and Craftsman hardware to amateur cabinetmakers. There was perhaps another benefit: *Craftsman* readers who had made a few pieces of "starter" Stickley might in time be induced to buy the actual product.

The "Supplement to Catalogue D" also saw the first examples of Stickley's spindle furniture, the designs of which he patented in August 1905.[10] Although this form of construction unmistakably suggests the influence of spindle designs created earlier by Frank Lloyd Wright, Wright's name was never mentioned in *The Craftsman*. According to the catalog's introduction, the spindle pieces were slender and graceful and "rather more ornate" than the heavier furniture, but "in reality quite as structural and simple." His spindle furniture gave Stickley elegant forms that, unlike the more costly to produce inlaid pieces, were readily accommodated to his factory's mechanized production capacities and did not require the services of an outside contractor. It gave him a cost-effective way to bring a measure of "quaint refinement" to Craftsman furniture, and was thus one line of defense in his campaign to counter the earlier criticisms that his work was too massive. The spindle line was to flourish only during the first four or five years of the Standard Stickley era, and by the end of the decade it would be dropped from production.

Stickley also added lightness to the Craftsman line when, in the spring of 1904, his firm began working in willow. This woven furniture was not offered as a substitute for his wooden pieces, but was meant instead to complement them by providing "exactly the relief that is necessary to lighten the general effect of the darker and heavier pieces."[11] The geometry of Craftsman willow chairs and settles generally followed stylish Viennese wicker models designed by Hans Vollmer, a student of Josef Hoffmann; this Continental wicker work had earlier been published in *Dekorative Kunst* and *International Studio*, where Stickley and his designers certainly saw it.[12] The willow furniture was most likely first made at the Eastwood factory, but in time Stickley established a willow manufacturing site in New York City.

Most Craftsman furniture, of course, was made not of willow but of hardwood. With the introduction of Standard Stickley the firm was using less wood in each piece of furniture, and yet its consumption of cabinet wood now dramatically increased. On 1 January 1901 (when Henry Wilkinson was still designing Stickley furniture and LaMont Warner had recently joined the firm), there was just under $10,000 worth of wood stacked up at the Eastwood factory. As of 1 January 1904 (the day

12 A mahogany #286 spindle settee, first made in fall 1905.

13 A German willow chair designed by Hans Vollmer, from *International Studio*, February 1904.

14 A Craftsman willow chair, 1904 or later.

15   16

before Harvey Ellis died), that amount had more than doubled: Stickley had over $23,000 worth of cabinet wood on hand.[13] Much of this wood was supplied by William E. Uptegrove & Brother.[14]

With an office and lumberyard on East Tenth Street in New York City, the Uptegroves were Stickley's chief source of cabinet wood. William Uptegrove (1852–1935) and his brother Jerome Uptegrove (1856–1932) dealt in mahogany, mahogany veneers, and Spanish cedar (for cigar boxes), and they were also a large-scale wholesaler of hardwoods, including American white oak. Following a catastrophic fire that destroyed an entire block of East Tenth Street on Thanksgiving Day, 1901, they erected a new office building on this site in 1902, designed by the recently formed architectural firm of Henry Wilkinson and his partner H. Van Buren Magonigle. Stickley apparently enjoyed close professional and personal ties to the firm that was his principal supplier of oak, maple, and mahogany, and it is likely that he introduced William and Jerome Uptegrove to these architects.

When Standard Stickley was introduced, Wilkinson had left the Craftsman Workshops, and Harvey Ellis was dead. LaMont Warner and Louise Shrimpton, however, had stayed in Stickley's studio, and, under his direction, they were the designers who created this new line. In 1906, however, the year after "Catalogue D" was issued, Warner left to join the art department of Columbia University's Teachers College, and Shrimpton became a journalist. New designers arrived at the Craftsman Workshops to take their places.

One was Peter Heinrich Hansen (1880–1947), who apparently worked for Stickley in 1906 and 1907, during a year or so of the Standard Stickley era.

Born in northern Germany, Hansen left his native land for America and arrived in New York City in November 1905. He was a highly skilled young cabinet-maker, carver, and furniture designer who shared with Stickley a German heritage, a love of working with wood, and a boyhood on a farm. Designs that were first made during Hansen's time with Stickley, and may therefore by attributed to him, included the Josef Hoffmann-inspired #730 desk, the #391 spindle "cube" chair, and the #291 spindle settle, all of 1907.

It must have been at the Craftsman Workshops that Hansen met Louise Shrimpton's friend, the "draughtsman" Ruth Anne Williams (1876–1956). Hansen and Williams were married in October 1907. A former art student, Williams became a Stickley "draughtsman" in 1904, first on a freelance basis and then as a member of his studio. She stayed with the firm when it moved to New York City, but left after her marriage. In early 1907, Hansen had moved to Fayetteville, New York, and begun working for the L. & J.G. Stickley Company. He was to stay there until he retired in the 1940s. It is as the creator of its classic designs—among them the trapezoidal mantel clock (reminiscent of one of Shrimpton's earlier "Home Training" clocks) and the low-slung "prairie" settle—that he is best remembered today. As that firm's sole designer, he was also responsible for creating the "Handcraft" furniture—Leopold's retort to Standard Stickley—made by L. & J.G. Stickley after Hansen's arrival in Fayetteville.

15 Stickley's chief source of cabinet wood, William E. Uptegrove, 1896.

16 One of the Uptegrove firm's New York City lumber-yards, from The Craftsman, January 1905.

17 The first version of the #730 desk was cataloged by the Craftsman Workshops in January 1907, a design attributed to Peter Hansen.

18   19

The wedding gift Hansen made for his bride, a substantial and straight-lined linen press ornamented with passages of his superb carving, was fitted with standard L. & J.G. Stickley copper hardware.[15] Peter and Ruth Anne Hansen were an aesthetically compatible couple, he primarily the designer and she the colorist. The houses where they lived and raised their family reflected their refined but non-doctrinaire Arts and Crafts taste: they decorated with a Voysey textile hung as a portiere; Fulper pottery; wall stencils of sailing ships and mottoes; Morris & Co. wallpapers and textiles; and L. & J.G. Stickley furniture mixed with American antiques.[16] In 1906 and early 1907, Peter Hansen, as a designer, and Ruth Anne Williams, as a "draughtsman," called on their training and their talents to contribute to the realization of Standard Stickley. Because of Gustav Stickley's practice of not giving public credit to his creative staff, it is impossible to know just what that contribution was. If their homes are any guide—especially the one Louise Shrimpton wrote about in *House and Garden* and *Country Life in America*—it was considerable.

18 Peter Hansen, 1906.

19 Ruth Anne Williams, ca. 1902.

20 The Hansens' living room fireplace. The L. & J.G. Stickley mantel clock, designed by Peter Hansen, is flanked by two lines from the poet Robert Browning: "God's in His Heaven / All's Right with the World" stenciled onto the wall.

21 An L. & J.G. Stickley Handcraft mantel clock, designed by Peter Hansen.

22 An L. & J.G. Stickley handcraft book table, designed by Peter Hansen.

During the era of Standard Stickley, the Craftsman Workshops was making a determined effort to expand the firm's retail distribution, an initiative that began with its 1904 trade advertising and publicity campaign. By January 1905 the campaign had had some success. That month *The Craftsman* published a full-page list of thirty retailers from Boston to San Francisco where the magazine was on sale. That these were actually the furniture dealers selling Craftsman products shows that Stickley's associates—the exclusive distributors he had begun lining up in late 1901—were falling into place.

Having established reliable, nationwide retail distribution, Stickley's firm next set out more aggressively to court the consumer. The first few years of Standard Stickley saw a flood of promotional publications issued by the firm.

Stickley issued "Chips from the Craftsman Workshops" in 1906 and then brought out a similarly titled sequel in 1907. These two small-format publications present a promotional message cast in autobiographical form. Though certainly ghostwritten for the busy Stickley, they recount his rural childhood, his experience in the 1880s and 1890s as a manufacturer of unremarkable but commercially successful furniture, and his awakening aesthetic conscience that led him to begin making Craftsman furniture. In these long, ruminative essays, Stickley traces the evolving Craftsman style and offers his progressive views—for instance, on the deleterious moral consequences of excessive mate-

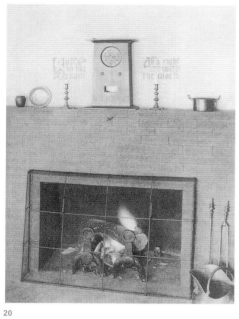

20

21

22

An Acorn

contains within it-
self the entire life
principle and germ
of the Giant Oak

JUST as truly this single
CRAFTSMAN chair em-
bodies the entire vital
principle of the whole range of CRAFTSMAN Products. The
piece here shown is first, last and all the time *a chair*, and
not an imitation of a throne, nor an exhibit of snakes and
dragons in a wild riot of misapplied wood-carving.

The fundamental purpose in building this chair was to
make a piece which should be essentially comfortable, durable, well proportioned and as soundly put together as the
best workmanship, tools and materials make possible.

What more should a chair be?   What more can it be and retain dignity and character?

THE CRAFTSMAN idea is the honest, straightforward attainment of the end
sought without any senseless beating around the bush, and this is true whether
in the making of furniture, the planning of a house, or the entire field of life
and work.

Does the thought interest you?

On request you may have entirely without cost a little book entitled "Chips"
in which there is a fund of information concerning the inception and development of CRAFTSMAN Furniture, Native Woods, Finishes, Why "Styles" come
and go, etc., mailed freely to you and any friends you name.

Gustav Stickley   *The Craftsman*
29 WEST 34th STREET,   NEW YORK CITY

rialism, and the need to conserve America's natural resources—that he expects his readers to heed. He is selling furniture here but he is also advocating an ethical mode of life. These booklets have few illustrations and many words; you do not flip casually through them. The texts are, in a literal sense, fictions; they are constructs that present Stickley's self-invented Craftsman persona. They are also seriously considered documents that, like Stickley furniture, demand close attention and an openness to the rigorous aspects of the Craftsman sensibility.

Moralizing promotional essays, once integral to Stickley's furniture catalogs, were thus segregated into separate booklets. The evident effort and expense required to produce them suggest the significance these homiletic pamphlets had for Stickley. But he was also a realist. He certainly understood that in cultivating a wider market he would inevitably be selling his furniture to people who simply liked its looks, or thought it serviceable, or affordable, or even "the latest thing," but who felt no particular need to embrace the Craftsman ethos. So his catalogs evolved into straightforward selling vehicles with clear product shots, furniture dimensions and prices, and abbreviated introductory texts. Probably because of tenuous business conditions—1907 was a year of precipitous downturn in American financial markets—Stickley stopped printing his long, thoughtful essays in booklet form. Of course he could still preach Craftsman doctrine by mounting the monthly platform of *The Craftsman* magazine. For all his seriousness of intent, however, Stickley was also trading on his celebrity in these publications. His portrait and facsimile signature were ever-present features of his booklets and catalogs, and his magazine regularly published major articles under his byline. His celebrity was an asset to be nurtured and enlisted in the Craftsman cause.

It was in 1907 that Stickley—undoubtedly to attract more advertisers— reported *Craftsman* magazine circulation figures for the first time: 16,000. Compared to, say, *Good Housekeeping*, a journal that at the time devoted many pages to handicrafts and reached more than 200,000 subscribers, the audience of *The Craftsman* seems very small. Yet the magazine was more influential than its narrow circulation suggests. Throughout the Standard Stickley years it was, in a way no other periodical ever matched, the essential, intertwining link among virtually all participants in the American Arts and Crafts movement. Artisans, artists, designers, architects, teachers, and others read *The Craftsman* and absorbed its aesthetic doctrine. They were loyal readers: it is not unusual to find copies today on which an earlier owner has written his or her name, in ink, on the front cover. These issues were kept in personal libraries and valued as if they were books. In addition to individuals, *Craftsman* subscribers included libraries, reading clubs, and other Arts and Crafts groups, and copies of the magazine distributed in this manner had multiple readers.[17]

Standard Stickley is not generally as well regarded today as early Stickley; it sometimes seems bland in comparison to the bolder and more varied pieces of 1900 through 1904. And, because more of it was made, it does not share with early Stickley the irresistible mystique of rarity. But there is a case to be made that Standard Stickley ranks among Gustav Stickley's significant achievements. It successfully embodied the Craftsman values of honest use of natural materials, integrity of construction, and, its greatest triumph, unity of

design. It was sane and sensible furniture: pared-down, functional, sturdy yet visually refined, and reasonably priced. In the words of an advertisement for a Morris chair in the March 1907 *Craftsman*: "The piece here shown is first, last and all the time a chair, and not an imitation of a throne, nor an exhibit of snakes and dragons in a wild riot of misapplied wood-carving." Standard Stickley, however, was more than the sum of its admirable attributes. It was also the visible and tangible sign of Stickley's moral earnestness, and through its forthright example he sought to make its users better people. As this advertisement goes on to say, honesty and straightforwardness were values that should guide not just "the making of furniture, the planning of a house," but also "the entire field of life and work."

Yet Standard Stickley was also a consumer product designed for routinized manufacture in quantity, and it was this furniture that brought Stickley and his firm a comfortable degree of prosperity. Standardization enabled Stickley to make good furniture and at the same time realize healthy profits. Through most of the Craftsman years his monthly salary was $416.67, making his annual base pay exactly $5,000. This was handsome but not unreasonable compensation, the equivalent today of almost $90,000. He was, however, wealthier than that amount suggests. In 1908 and 1909, for instance, he reduced his own salary by about half but added Eda to his payroll at $75.00 a week; that money went into the Stickley family's coffers. And, because he was effectively sole owner of the firm, he often drew cash from his business to cover miscellaneous personal and family expenses, including the small amounts of money he frequently gave to his wife, his sisters, and his children. The bonuses he earned from his business were on a much larger scale. Although the recorded numbers are not completely clear and hence difficult to interpret, by 1911 he was rewarding himself with extremely generous commissions. They were computed as a percentage of furniture sales, and averaged between $2,000 (i.e., about $35,700 today) and $4,000 ($71,400) each month.[18] Apparently, much of this money went toward underwriting *The Craftsman* magazine and funding the never-realized community that Stickley envisioned for Craftsman Farms.

In addition to the catalog furniture of the Standard Stickley era, the firm also made higher-priced custom order pieces for those seeking unique Craftsman work. As the monumental, Prairie School-influenced sideboard for his client R.M. Bond convincingly shows, Stickley was perfectly capable of constructing elaborate, formal furniture within the Craftsman idiom.[19] But it was the more prosaic production furniture that kept the Craftsman enterprise thriving, and during the Standard Stickley era the firm's furniture was to be found in American homes on an unparalleled scale. Thus Stickley was making sound, artistic furniture for "the middle-class individual," a dream he had pursued since the beginnings of his Arts and Crafts adventure.

With success came problems. Twice in 1905, in months coinciding with the release of "Catalogue D" and "Supplement to Catalogue D," Stickley was experiencing labor difficulties, a story told, with a hint of "we-told-you-so" glee, in *Furniture Journal*:

Although Gustav Stickley, in his excellent magazine, The Craftsman, *has voiced some of his socialistic theories, and is given to exalting the*

23 Advertisement for a Standard Stickley Morris chair, from *The Craftsman*, March 1907.

25

workman, he is subject to labor disturbances just like any other manufacturer, who has less altruistic ideas. His finishers have been out on strike recently. Last January Mr. Stickley gave his employees a banquet at which he said some nice things to them. The employees say that about a month later a cut in wages was made. The recent strike follows, it is claimed, a second cut.[20]

Having discovered that his firm was not immune from work stopping labor-management disputes, Stickley got his men back to the factory not by more blandishments but by establishing a generous new profit-sharing plan.[21]

Success also spurred competition. In April 1905 Stickley decided that he needed to protect his joiner's compass shopmark—and his "Craftsman" brand name—by making it his registered trademark.[22] Other manufacturers were exploiting the expanding demand for "Mission" furniture, and it was no secret that even at the lower range of the market this popular style could be very profitable for makers and retailers alike. An item in *Furniture Trade Review* pointed out that there could be a "large margin of profit on Mission goods that has not as a rule obtained on regular stock. A Mission desk, for instance, sold to the dealer for $8.00, was retailed in some cases for $16.00. This is a pretty good profit."[23] By 1908, one hundred and forty-eight American manufacturers were making "Mission" furniture, and, for many people, there was little to distinguish it from Stickley's scrupulously made Craftsman furniture.[24] His advertising grew increasingly strident about the firms that he accused—with more than a little justification—of copying his designs, but to little or no avail. His competitors were not to be the major cause of the bankruptcy that loomed, unseen and unexpected, in Stickley's future, but they would be a very real contributing factor.

24 The ideal Standard Stickley living room had a beamed ceiling, a brick or Grueby-tiled fireplace with a hammered copper hood, built-in cabinetry, paneled walls, and a decorative stenciled frieze. Its furniture, lighting, metalwork, and textiles were products of the Craftsman Workshops.

25 A custom-order sideboard with leaded glass cabinet doors built by the Craftsman Workshops built for a Florida client, R. M. Bond, from *The Craftsman*, October 1911.

During the summer and fall of 1902, Stickley developed his ideas about design reform, tentatively at first, yet growing progressively more confident throughout the following year. This redirected course prompted his decision to offer new sorts of Craftsman wares, and during this period the firm began producing light fixtures, decorative metalwork, and textiles. These objects shared the similar aesthetic purpose of unifying the interior ensemble. Opening a metal shop and a textile department, of course, was as much a commercial decision as an aesthetic one: "[W]hen furniture is ordered from Craftsman shops a color scheme including the fittings of the room, the fabrics, etc., will always be furnished on application."[1] Stickley was extending the Craftsman brand name into new product areas and making more goods to sell to his customers.

By the early months of 1901, Stickley furniture was being made with cast brass or iron drawer pulls and key escutcheons, but where that hardware came from remains a mystery. Nine years later, in the introduction to his 1910 furniture catalog, Stickley recalled that when he had begun making Arts and Crafts furniture he quickly realized that he needed "metal trim which would harmonize in character with the furniture, as none of the glittering, fragile metal then in vogue was possible in connection with the straight severe lines and plain surfaces. So I opened a metal work department in The Craftsman Workshops, and there we made plain, strong handles, pulls, hinges and escutcheons of iron, copper and brass." There is no evidence, however, that the firm had any special metalworking capabilities in 1901, the time period Stickley seems to

1 Detail of hammered strap-work on the #552 fall-front desk, oak, 1902.

be referring to here. While some space may have then been set aside in the Eastwood factory for shaping metal, it is more plausible that the earliest Stickley hardware was bought from an outside supplier. The firm did not establish its own metal shop until about May 1902, more than a year after hardware first appeared on the furniture. Stickley placed this metal shop not near the factory but in downtown Syracuse, in a gymnasium-sized one-story structure attached to the Craftsman Building. The former owner, the wealthy Edgar Crouse, had, years before, built it as an indoor exercise ring for his string of pampered horses.

Stickley had high ambitions for this shop. A notice in the May 1902 *Craftsman* announced the firm's plan "to develop the wrought iron industry," and begin making "electric light fittings, fire-sets, sconces, candlesticks, lanterns, locks and other household articles in metal."[2] Stickley marked the opening of the new shop by devoting most of this issue of the magazine to metalwork. Samuel Howe contributed two articles, one on enameling (a subject he knew well from his years with Tiffany) and one on a prominent collection of brass and copper vessels. Two other articles offered advice and inspiration to the would-be metalworker. Written by the artisans Amalie Busck and Mary Norton, and illustrated with examples of their handiwork, these articles guided readers through the basic methods and materials needed to practice this craft.[3] By publishing these primers on metal crafting processes, Stickley showed readers how to make things for themselves, while also guiding their appreciation of the Craftsman metalwork he would soon be offering for sale.

2 Cover of *The Craftsman,*
May 1904, illustrated with
this idealized drawing of a
Craftsman metalworker
constructing a lantern and
a lamp base.

3 Stickley donned a
shop apron for this publicity
photo taken in his metal
shop, from "What is
Wrought in the Craftsman
Workshops," 1904.

4

5

6

The opening of this metal shop coincided with two projects, one domestic and one commercial, that were dear to Stickley: the construction of the new interior of his family's Columbus Avenue home and the renovation of the Craftsman Building. The decorative metal objects used in those two structures were probably the first pieces to emerge from the firm's new shop. Photographs of this early Stickley metalwork (for instance, the lanterns and andirons visible in the Craftsman Building lecture hall illustrated on page 217) suggest that it had a vernacular, almost homemade, look to it. The designs seem to have been determined more by traditional metalworking techniques than by specific aesthetic principles. In the last half of 1902 the firm was experimenting with the design and construction of metalware, a process that paralleled its furniture experiments of a few years before.

The Craftsman metal shop was receiving frequent shipments of copper sheets by mid-1903.[4] It was also stocking up on supplies required for metalworking, for instance: borax, muriatic acid, benzine, gasoline, and many bales of the rags needed to clean and buff the work.[5] Other shipments, recorded as "castings," were also coming into the shop. This is evidence, according to the metal artisan Michael Adams, that the cast parts of Craftsman metalware—the bales on door and drawer hardware, for instance, and the standardized components of lanterns and chandeliers—were never made in house. During the fourteen years the metal shop was active, these castings were instead subcontracted to outside sources.[6]

Most Craftsman metalwork, however, was made by Stickley's workers. At first there were about seven of them, and their names, often only their last names, began to appear next to "Metal Account" headings in the company's ledgers during 1903: J. Douch, Hutzler, Merringer, Olinsky, F. Balch, who worked as a "molder," and G. Wykoffski, a blacksmith. The names of these workers suggest that they were foundrymen and blacksmiths drawn in part from Syracuse's immigrant population, and Craftsman promotional copy would later play up their European heritage and their well-honed Old World skills.

By June 1904, the number of men working in the metal shop had increased from about seven to a reported twelve, and by August a "Metal Sales" column had been added to the firm's ledger books and two employees were put in charge of selling these products. In November 1905, about two-and-a-half years after it was started, the metal shop's weekly payroll reached a substantial $133.87, an amount equal to nearly ten percent of Stickley's entire factory payroll. By September 1909 the Craftsman metal shop employed twenty-six workers.

4 The first head of Stickley's metal shop, Jerome Connor (on the left), photographed while still at the Roycroft, with an unidentified boy and man, ca. 1900.

5 The two wall sconces visible in the Stickley family's Columbus Avenue dining room suggest that early Stickley metalwork had an almost primitive appearance, from *The Craftsman*, December 1902.

6 Copper sconce by Amalie Busck, from *The Craftsman*, May 1902.

7   8

Stickley was making such rapid progress on so many fronts that it is not surprising to see his metal-working operation multiplying in size and output. His energy and zeal drove it forward. But he also progressed in this endeavor, as he did in all others, by hiring talented people with specialized skills.

One of the first was the Roycroft artisan, Jerome Connor (1874–1943), whom Stickley recruited after a visit to East Aurora, New York, in the spring of 1902. Connor apparently took charge of the firm's metal shop that summer, leaving western New York State and moving to Syracuse. He may or may not have been a blacksmith earlier in his life, but the sets of seahorse andirons that he made in the Roycroft metal shop—to W.W. Denslow's design—convincingly demonstrated his mastery at shaping metal objects. When Janet Ashbee stopped in East Aurora in December 1900, she judged Roycroft handiwork to be of generally uneven quality, but she was delighted by the "two great iron seahorses" she spotted in Hubbard's office fireplace.[7] Connor's talent and experience were crucial to Stickley as he got his United Crafts metal shop under way.

Besides adding Connor to his staff, Stickley continued—as he did at times with his furniture—to find design ideas in the work of a few admired contem-

poraries. His metalwork would not shed its vernacular qualities and take on its distinct identity until after he had seen the January 1903 exhibition of the Arts and Crafts Exhibition Society in London. During that visit Stickley seems to have paid as much attention to metalwork as he did to furniture. It was on this trip that he acquired four lanterns produced by the Faulkner Bronze Company, a Birmingham firm with a London showroom.[8] He then published photographs and measured drawings of these lanterns in the April 1903 *Craftsman*. They had cylindrical brass or wrought iron frames and iridescent glass inserts of yellow, blue, or sea green. All four lanterns were made with decorative strapwork fixed to their bodies by visible rivets; three had rounded or conical caps; and two had conventionalized motifs sawn out of their sides. The accompanying text in *The Craftsman* praised these light fixtures for their "agreeable combination of angles and curves necessary to the construction of the objects...the spacing of rivets...and the texture and treatment [i.e. patination] of the metal-work."

The elements of their design and construction praised in his magazine were to become familiar features of Craftsman lanterns executed in his own metal shop. In fact, an almost verbatim adaptation of one of the Faulkner Bronze Company light fixtures—with strapwork curving above its conical top—

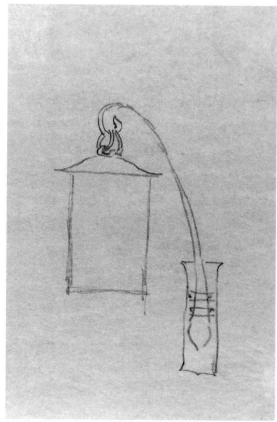

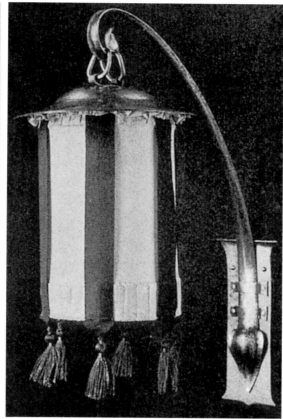

9

10

appeared in a drawing of the interior of Craftsman House #1 in the January 1904 issue of Stickley's magazine. A little over a year later, in March 1905, a Craftsman lantern of this design would be photographed for the firm's first metalwork catalog. Stickley had said nothing to identify their English maker when he published them in April 1903.[9]

Stickley did, however, acknowledge the source of the other metalwork he brought back from England; four examples of English metalwork in the May 1903 Craftsman were credited to the "Art Fittings Company of Birmingham." Art Fittings Limited, the actual name of the firm that Stickley bought this metalwork from, had offices and a showroom in London. Although Stickley said the firm was in Birmingham, there is no record of it in that city's directories of the era. It is therefore probable that Art Fittings Limited was not an art metalwork producer but was instead a distributor for a Birmingham manufacturer (or several manufacturers) that remains to be identified.[10]

Art Fittings Limited did not take part in the Arts and Crafts Exhibition Society exhibition in January 1903, and so Stickley must have made his purchases at the showroom. Possibly he first heard of the firm from his brother Albert, whose Grand Rapids furniture manufacturing company had established a fac-

tory and showroom in London in 1896.[11] Stickley apparently also noticed advertisements that Art Fittings Limited placed in The Studio. The firm's advertisement in the November 1902 issue, a month before Stickley left for Europe, illustrated a "seed pod" plaque and a rectangular salver. In London, he bought examples of both. Many of the Art Fittings Limited pieces acquired by Stickley were later reproduced in Craftsman copper, and these Craftsman wares were first cataloged by his firm in 1905.

LaMont Warner's files contain unpublished photographs of four examples of English metalwork, all of which share definite similarities of design and construction with Craftsman metalwork.[12] The flaring base, tapering profile and bands of rivet heads on one of these pieces, a coal scuttle, were reworked for the very similar Craftsman jardiniere first cataloged by Stickley in 1905. In addition to these four photographs, Warner also

7 Four Faulkner Bronze Company lanterns, acquired by Stickley in London in January 1903, from The Craftsman, April 1903.

8 This Craftsman lantern, first published in The Craftsman, January 1904, is clearly based on one of the Faulkner Bronze Company lanterns that Stickley bought, from "Catalogue D" (1905).

9 LaMont Warner's sketch of an unexecuted Craftsman lantern.

10 Warner traced his lantern sketch from this light fixture, designed by the English architect Claude New, from International Studio, February 1904.

11

12

13

14

filed a sketch of an electric wall sconce. This he had traced from a photograph of an English light fixture, designed by the architect Claude New, that had been published in *International Studio*. The Craftsman Workshops never put this exact sconce into production, but Warner's tracing is another reminder that Stickley and his designers often turned to English sources as they created Craftsman metalwork designs in 1903 and 1904.

By emulating the Birmingham metalwork that he had found in England, Stickley, practically overnight, reformulated Craftsman metalwork and infused it with greater sophistication than it had had before. In the process of translating his English models into the Craftsman idiom, however, he made significant changes. Craftsman metalwork was substantial and robust: its crisp hand hammering, rich patinas, and weighty, heavy-gauge copper were wholly unlike the Birmingham work on which many of its designs were based. Stickley's lack of inventiveness may be faulted here, but not the level of his craftsmanship.

In 1905, three years after the Craftsman metal shop had opened, Stickley's firm issued the catalog "Hand-Wrought Metal Work." Pictured in this first catalog was a comprehensive line of domestic objects: andirons; fire sets; table lamps, some with leaded glass shades; lanterns and chandeliers; jardinieres; wall plaques, as well as custom work available by special order. The

11 An advertisement for Art Fitting Limited, showing the firm's "seed pod" plaque and a rectangular salver, from *The Studio*, November 1902.

12 A Craftsman copper "seed pod" plaque, first cataloged by Stickley's firm in March 1905.

13 LaMont Warner kept this undated photograph of an English coal scuttle in his "Metalwork" file.

14 A Craftsman copper jardiniere, first cataloged in March 1905.

15 The second foreman of Stickley's metal shop, Valentine M. Kluge, shown next to a hammered copper Craftsman oil lamp, ca. 1905.

catalog's brief introduction painted a picturesque image of the Craftsman metal shop. Many of the artisans, it said, "can trace a long ancestry of toil; their forefathers having for generations exercised the same trade in…the old world." The names of Stickley's metalworkers, already mentioned, suggest that he did employ a partly immigrant work force; this introductory text may have been romanticized but it was grounded in reality. The catalog named only one worker, the head of the metal shop: "Max the Blacksmith." A masterful leader of near-Wagnerian proportions, he was depicted amid the smoke and rhythmic din of the metal shop, "[p]rojected against the firelight of the flaming forge, his sinewy frame satisfies with quick, decisive gesture, directing the processes of the men." Here the anonymous writer seems to have slipped into a fantasy of promotional rhetoric, but "Max the Blacksmith" did exist.

By 1904, Jerome Connor had left Stickley's firm, and "Max" replaced him as head of the Craftsman metal shop. Valentine Marks Kluge (1874–?), by profession a metalworker and machinist, was, like Peter Hansen, a German émigré trained in Europe. He joined Stickley's metal shop in 1903 and was its foreman in 1904 and 1905. His fellow workers dubbed him "Max," and an article about him in the *Syracuse Journal* claimed that "he has few equals in the country in brass, copper and iron work."[13] For all his skills, however, his tenure at the Craftsman Workshops was brief, and by 1906 he had left the firm and begun an art metal business of his own.

The next head of the Craftsman metal shop was nothing like the vigorous Max Kluge. He was a rather pleasant-looking young man, about twenty-five years old, who, despite his youth, had already acquired the skills of a master metalworker. He was also a competent manager, well suited to the increasingly business-like environment of Stickley's firm.[14] His name was Victor Toothaker.

16

1

18

19

Victor Toothaker (1882–1932) was chiefly a designer and maker of metal-work. He probably met Stickley at Paul Elder's San Francisco bookstore during Stickley's 1904 jaunt through northern California. There is no record of Toothaker's arrival at the Craftsman Workshops, but he may have left California after the devastating San Francisco earthquake of 1906. He became foreman after Kluge left, dividing his weeks between the metal shop, now moved from downtown Syracuse to a building behind the Eastwood factory, and an office in the factory itself. As foreman and chief designer of this department he was its highest paid member, earning a handsome salary of $25.00 a week. He also delineated Craftsman houses and illustrated *Craftsman* magazine covers, and Stickley favored his young employee by letting Toothaker sign this artwork; he chose to sign only his first name. But the Craftsman metalworking department remained his prime responsibility until 1911, when he left Stickley's firm and moved to East Aurora, New York, to become the manager of Elbert Hubbard's Roycroft copper shop.[15] The new Craftsman metal designs that appeared during Toothaker's tenure—years that coincided with the era of Standard Stickley—were certainly his.

Well aware of Morris's famous injunction, Stickley was careful to stress that Craftsman metalwork was both beautiful and useful. His catalogs made much of its sturdiness and utility, its refined plainness, and its pleasant compatibility with Craftsman furniture. But Stickley was always a colorist, and it was those "delightful gleams of color" radiating from the light-catching hammered surfaces of the metalwork that the firm's promotional writings habitually held up for admiration before the reader's gaze. Exactly what Stickley's metalworkers did to achieve those colors remains unclear. The descriptions of Craftsman metal finishing processes published in Craftsman catalogs were poetic but imprecise. Stickley said that his completed copper pieces were thoroughly cleaned with a strong solvent and then allowed to "age naturally." But quantity production could not have relied on such leisurely methods, and the patinas on Stickley's metalwork were certainly achieved by brief immersion in a coloring solution.[16] One may wish that Stickley had been more forthright about these processes, but patinas were important trade secrets, and he justifiably did not reveal them to the imitators and competitors crowding around him.[17]

Understanding the processes, however, may be less enlightening than considering the results. Craftsman patinas tend to combine two tones; they often have an overall dark brownish cast,

16 Craftsman hanging light fixture with checkerboard-pattern leaded glass and rows of square amber glass panels, designed by Victor Toothaker ca. 1910.

17 A leaded glass Craftsman lantern in the Glasgow Style manner, designed by Victor Toothaker ca. 1910.

18 A Craftsman table lamp with square amber glass panels matching those on the hanging fixture in [Figure 16] designed by Victor Toothaker ca. 1910. Toothaker's drawing of this lamp appears in *The Craftsman*, May 1910.

19 The third person to head Stickley's metal shop, Victor Toothaker, ca. early 1900s.

No. 262, Electric Portable

The Craftsman Workshops

Syracuse
New York

Under the direction of

Gustav Stickley

No. 293, Oil Lamp

Handwrought Metal Work

by master artisans, trained from childhood in all the processes of their trade

No. 294, Oil Lamp

Iron
Copper
Brass

Iron in armour-bright
finish

Copper in natural,
or vert antique finish,
produced
without aid of lacquers,
and growing finer
with age

No. 138, Fire Set

going almost to black in the recesses that are set off against slightly polished high spots.[18] These completely intentional contrasts accentuate the marks left by the planishing hammers that smoothed and strengthened the metal, and they visibly underline the Arts and Crafts interplay of construction and ornamentation as practiced at the Craftsman Workshops. These two-tone patinas are in comfortable accord with the double-hued qualities, the green-browns and gray-browns, of Craftsman wood finishes. And they complement, as well, the lustrous double colors that Stickley's needleworkers stitched into Craftsman textiles.

In the Craftsman office, on a late July day in 1903, Claude Bragdon composed one of his frequent letters to his mother. "I come to this quiet place to write letters at a beautiful Stickley desk," he told her. "Near me Miss Baxter sits working on a curtain. She has charge of that department."[19] This was Blanche Ross Baxter (1870–1967), a former teacher who came to the Craftsman Building in spring 1903 to manage Stickley's new fabric and needlework department.[20] Baxter's name has surfaced earlier in this narrative. With LaMont Warner, Irene Sargent, and others, she helped design the Syracuse installation of Stickley's 1903 Arts and Crafts exhibition, and it was she whom Stickley chose to oversee the stylish, much-admired Craftsman tea room where visitors could refresh themselves during the weeks the exhibition was open. In the fall of 1903, when Stickley's needlework department was just a few months old, Baxter traveled to Europe. Surely one of the reasons for her trip was to study textiles, just as Stickley had done in England and on the Continent earlier that year. When Stickley later moved his offices to New York City, Baxter was among the employees who followed him there.

The designs of Craftsman textiles originated in the firm's drafting studio: "In this place," according to a 1904 Craftsman booklet, "all designs and working drawings are made for the cabinet work executed at Eastwood, as well as for the metal and the needlework done in The Craftsman Building."[21] The textile designs were rendered in pencil on the same heavy brown paper used for the furniture drawings. Although not officially a member of the drafting studio, Baxter was nevertheless a designer of Craftsman textiles. Thus Blanche Baxter, a name unknown to American Arts and

20 Advertisement for "Standard Stickley" metalwork, from *The Craftsman*, October 1904.

21 Craftsman needle workers in the Craftsman Building, from "What is Wrought in the Craftsman Workshops," 1904. The seated woman in the center of the photograph is evidently Blanche Baxter.

22

23

Crafts history, was among the under-recognized group that provided designs for Gustav Stickley's Craftsman Workshops.

The textile department run by Baxter was at first quite small, no more than perhaps three or four women, all of whom lived in Syracuse. Almost nothing is known of them except their names—Ada Brainard, Winifred Fancher, and Blanche Gildersleeve—and it is not possible to match these names to any specific Craftsman textiles. Nor were these women Stickley's only needle-workers. To supplement the in-house group, he subcontracted textile making to local women who were dressmakers and seamstresses by profession; they worked in their homes and were paid by the piece. Alice Cornell made rugs for Stickley's firm. Ellen Matson made curtains. Lillian Littlehales made lampshades. Miss Colton made a bedspread and was paid $5.00. Blanche Baxter's older sister Emma made pillows and curtains.[22] Like Stickley's other artisans, these skillful needleworkers anonymously created a very high level of handiwork, and they were unheralded in their own time as they are in ours.

Although little is known of the needlewomen, the timeline of Stickley's adoption of textile work can be fairly precisely tracked. His attraction to this medium first surfaced while he was in England in January 1903, and when he returned home in February he brought back at least two examples of English Arts and Crafts needlework made by Ada Ellwood, the wife of J. S. Henry's furniture designer, G. M. Ellwood. While abroad Stickley also made arrangements to import a variety of British-made textiles from three well-regarded manufacturing firms. Alexander Morton and Company, of Darval, Scotland, provided him with woolen Donegal carpets. Another Scottish textile firm, Donald Brothers, of Dundee, also became a regular Stickley supplier at this time. Perhaps Stickley's most important source of imported textiles was G.P. & J. Baker, a London-based printed fabric manufacturer that made use of leading freelancers—among them Voysey and the Silver Studio—to supply its superb designs. G.P. & J. Baker was an exhibitor at the 1903 Arts and Crafts Exhibition Society exhibition, and it was almost certainly in that setting that Stickley first learned of the firm and saw examples of its work.[23]

At his own Arts and Crafts exhibition in March and April, Stickley's firm exhibited table runners in the Craftsman model dining room pictured in chapter four. Although identified as United Crafts products, they had actually been commissioned from Angelina Hurelle, a well-established, professional embroiderer with a studio in her Syracuse home. The opening of the firm's "Needlework and Embroidery" department was announced the following month, in the May 1903 issue of The Craftsman. In June 1903, textile articles began to appear regularly in The Craftsman.

Stickley's textile workers were plying their needles by June, and in July the first expenses for this new department—$30 for floss and $35 for linen thread—were entered into the company's ledgers.[24] That same month, photographs of Craftsman textiles made their first appearance in the magazine: a pair of curtains, a coverlet, and a decorative frieze. The ambitious frieze, worked on blue-gray linen, combined stenciled yellow ochre plant motifs and appliqués of matte red and sage green bordered with a plum-colored outline stitch. Although this frieze looked little like the Craftsman textiles that were to follow, it did anticipate them. Most of what would become standard elements were already evident: the irregularly textured, open weave fabrics; the conventionalized forms drawn from nature; and the techniques of appliqué, stenciling, and a limited repertoire of basic embroidery stitches. The textiles photographed for the July 1903 Craftsman were not offered for sale. Instead, the magazine suggested that they were suitable projects for home needlework-ers, and helpful, if sketchy, directions appeared with the photographs. Soon,

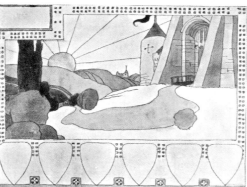

24

25

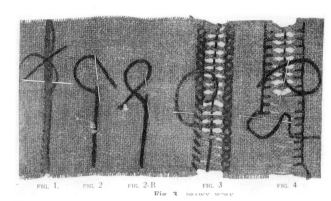

FIG. 1.   FIG. 2   FIG. 2-B   FIG. 3   FIG. 4

Fig 3 DRAWN WORK

28

however, the firm took the more practical step of offering textiles in kit form, with all the materials the amateur worker needed to complete the project herself. These kits were a new product for Stickley to sell, but they also offered a genuinely useful way to encourage readers to practice this craft.

July 1903 marked Harvey Ellis's debut in *The Craftsman* magazine, and his contributions to this issue included designs for two Craftsman "tapestries." Like the other textiles in this issue, Ellis's wall hangings combined the techniques of stenciling, appliqué and outline embroidery, but their somewhat naively drawn medieval imagery was purely Ellis's own. For the August *Craftsman*, Ellis drew his great textile tour de force, the elaborate, exuberant visual recounting of the folk-tale "Puss in Boots." In that same issue he made a foray in a completely different stylistic direction: assisted apparently by Claude Bragdon, he designed a group of portieres imbued with the linear sophistication of Mackintosh and his Glasgow Style contemporaries. One of the designs made use of a Japanese *mon*—looking somewhat like an American eagle here—which was such a frequent feature of Bragdon's architectural decoration. These portiere designs combined appliqué and embroidery on a coarse linen ground in what *The Craftsman*—using the term for the first time—described as "the manner known in England as 'peasant embroidery.'" Later in the year, Native American themes, worked in cross-stitch on Craftsman Canvas grounds, began to appear in the magazine. These textiles were based on motifs that Ellis was then introducing to the Craftsman Workshops.

The Ellis textiles published in *The Craftsman* magazine did not become standard production items. Ellis's place in the evolution of Craftsman textiles thus roughly parallels his importance to Craftsman furniture: he introduced refinements of form and color to both, and his influence affected the work of the firm for several years after his death. Ellis, though, did not just design individual objects; he created Craftsman interiors that imaginatively integrated furnishings and architecture, and there lay his even greater contribution.

Ellis arrived at the Craftsman Workshops in late May 1903, at exactly the same time that Stickley was forming his fabric and needlework department. From July, Ellis-designed inlays brought new, harmonious color to Craftsman furniture. Textiles served that same purpose in a Craftsman room. According to one of the firm's catalogs: "The fabrics chosen for window curtains, table scarfs, squares, centerpieces, pillow covers...form an important part of the decorative scheme. When the color, texture and designs of these harmonize with the character of the woodwork, walls and furniture the result is pleasing and restful. Therefore we give special

26 Previous: One panel of "Puss in Boots," as executed nearly one hundred years after Harvey Ellis designed it.

27 Original factory photograph of a #619 library table with appropriate accessories: a Craftsman table lamp and a Craftsman "Orange Design" table scarf, ca. 1909.

28 Because Stickley wanted customers to understand the methods used to produce his wares, he published this photograph of basic Craftsman stitches—couching, outline, hemstitch, cross stitch—as an illustration in the catalog "Craftsman Furnishing for the Home," 1912.

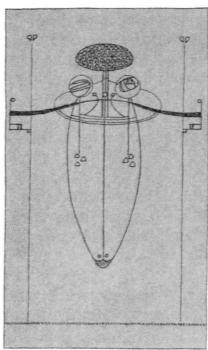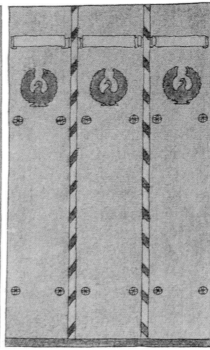

29

attention to fabrics and needlework so that there may be no discordant note in the interior."[25] It cannot be mere coincidence that these developments—the arrival of Harvey Ellis and the beginnings of Craftsman textiles—occurred at exactly the same time. That simultaneity is the clue to what was then on Stickley's mind: he was thinking about *color*—new uses of color and new color harmonies—to create the ideal Craftsman interior. Ellis, and in a narrower sphere Blanche Baxter, gave substance to his thoughts.

1903 and 1904 was an experimental period for Stickley's textile department. The materials and methods were settled on fairly quickly, but there was as yet little evidence of the "house style" that was later to emerge. Who designed these early Craftsman textiles? Besides Harvey Ellis and Blanche Baxter, the names of LaMont Warner and Louise Shrimpton are the ones that first come to mind. Another name that suggests itself is that of Samuel Howe. He is the most likely designer of the "peasant embroideries" that the firm produced in late 1903 and early 1904. By the end of 1904, as mentioned earlier, he had begun designing textiles for Leopold Stickley, and some of his work for the L. & J.G. Stickley Company suggested an Ellis-like borrowing from Native American

29 Two Craftsman portieres, the first, certainly by Ellis, is adapted from a Mackintosh motif created for The Rose Boudoir exhibited at Turin in 1902; the second, suggesting Bragdon's hand, incorporates a bird motif based loosely on a Japanese *mon*, from *The Craftsman*, August 1903.

30 A Gingko table scarf, designed by Louise Shrimpton.

motifs. Most of it, however, combined simple stitches and appliqué, and was presented to the public as "peasant embroidery," a term already well known to Gustav Stickley's customers.

In the second half of 1904 and into 1905, the textile designs that were to become the mainstays of the Craftsman Workshops began appearing in Stickley's magazine. Based on natural forms, usually flowers, vines, or trees, the designs were translated into geometricized shapes, and yet rendered with enough realism to make the original source of inspiration readily apparent. According to the firm's first needlework catalog, issued in March 1905, "The simplest stitches, in connection with the broad leaves and petal forms of the appliqué, are used to express the decorative motif, which more often than not is a pretty interpretation of some simple plant form, as the honeysuckle, the wild rose, or the cowslip."[26] Several of these Standard Stickley-era textiles can be attributed to their designers, Louise Shrimpton and Harriet Joor. The gingko, perhaps Stickley's best-known textile pattern, was created by Shrimpton in 1904.[27] And Rita Curry-Pittman, an authority on Newcomb College textiles, has discovered that Harriet Joor (1875–1965) designed the pinecone, dragonfly, china tree, and other familiar Craftsman textiles. Best known as a decorator of Newcomb pottery, Joor frequently published fiction and non-fiction in *The Craftsman*, and it was apparently through her contributions to his magazine that she came into Stickley's orbit as a freelance writer and as a freelance textile designer as well.[28]

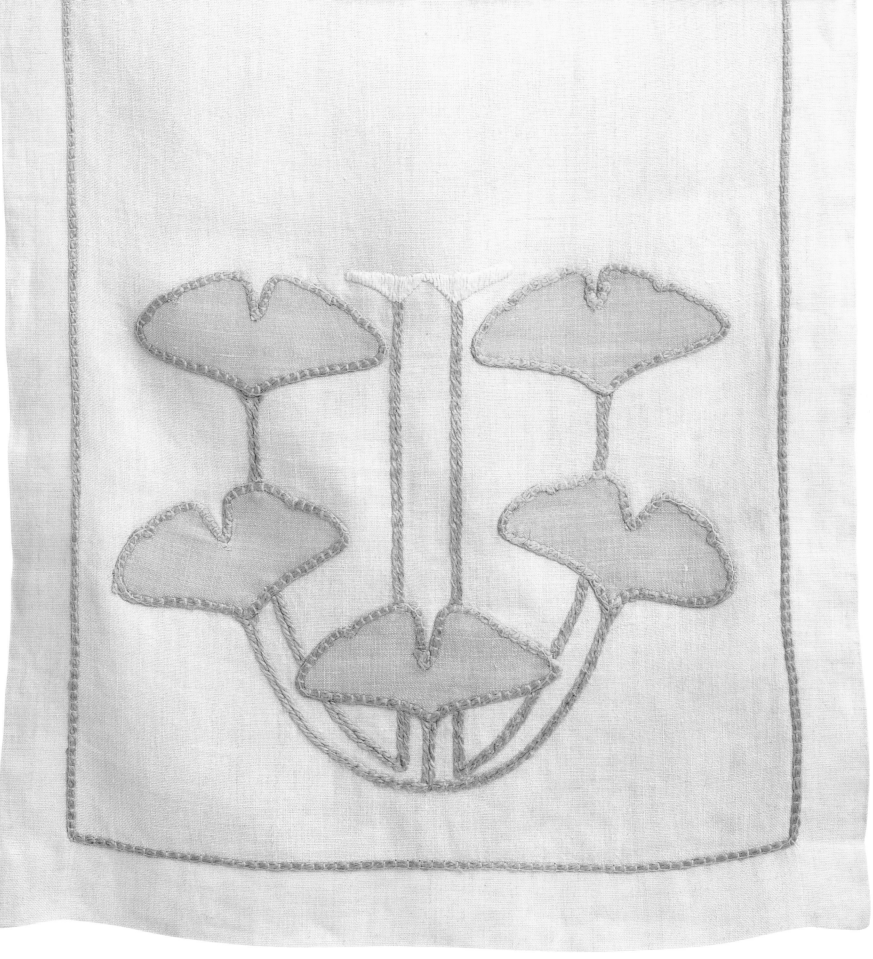

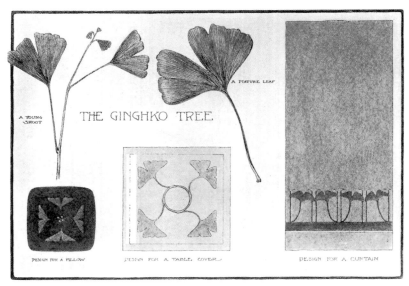

31

32

Using simple techniques executed with great skill, offering a limited number of regular patterns in pleasing colors, and making some use of sewing machines to supplement hand labor, the firm was able to offer distinctive, well-wrought textiles that its middle-class customers could afford.[29] This was exactly the formula that Stickley had already applied with such success to his furniture making. In the uniformity of their designs and the rationalized methods used in their making, Craftsman fabric designs after 1904 can be seen as the textile equivalent of Standard Stickley. And, as was true of Craftsman furniture and Craftsman metalwork, Craftsman textiles expressed Stickley's ever-present delight in double colors. They were often made of "bloom linen," a fabric in which the warp threads and the weft threads were different colors, and thus "show a charming play of surface color, changing in tone with every varying light."[30]

Because of the fragility of the plant fibers used in their making, and the susceptibility of dyes to sunlight, dust, and air, Craftsman textiles have not survived as well as Craftsman furniture and metalwork. Their relative scarcity suggests that few textiles were made, but the evidence shows otherwise. By 1909, six years after Stickley began it, the Craftsman fabric and needlework department had grown to twenty-three full-time employees, enough workers to produce textiles in considerable quantity. Yet this facet of Stickley's legacy remains little appreciated, and the women and men who created that legacy have been largely forgotten.

Although Craftsman metalwork and Craftsman textiles were beautifully designed and superbly crafted, it was not their individuality that the firm's promotional materials most strongly stressed. It was their ability to blend in. They were the most appropriate complements to Craftsman furniture, as Craftsman catalogs assured customers time and time again. According to one booklet, "All the designs we use for metal work are as strong and simple as the furniture itself." Another suggested that the "strong, simple designs and colorings" of the textiles "belong to the oaken furniture as naturally as the leaves on a tree belong to the trunk."[31] Metalwork and textiles vastly expanded the range of harmonious shapes, colors, and textures the firm had to offer, and Stickley's adoption of these media meant that the interior of the ideal Craftsman house—or indeed of any suitable house—could now be realized as a total work of Craftsman art.

31 "The Ginghko Tree," drawn by Louise Shrimpton, from *The Craftsman*, July 1904.

32 A China Tree table scarf, designed by Harriet Joor.

33 Craftsman furniture, textiles, lighting, metalwork, and woodwork created the Craftsman interior as a total work of art, from *The Craftsman*, October 1905.

It was perhaps inevitable that Stickley would find reasons to leave Syracuse and move to Manhattan. As he increasingly shifted his attention toward *The Craftsman* magazine, it was simply a matter of good sense for him to set up his office in an urban center of publishing and draw on its much wider pool of writers, editors, illustrators, and designers. New York City was also a thriving hub of furniture manufacturing and wholesaling, and Stickley must have felt the need to establish himself amid his industry colleagues, suppliers, and the reporters from the trade journals based in lower Manhattan. Competitive imperatives in the retail marketplace drove this move as well. In 1905, the Tobey Furniture Company, the L. & J.G. Stickley Company, and Elbert Hubbard's Roycroft Shops had opened retail stores in New York. Stickley certainly saw that they had arrived there ahead of him. The metropolitan area was a great and growing marketplace that he, like his competitors, was intent on directly reaching.

There were other motives as well. Stickley had grown restive in the provincial atmosphere of Syracuse. Feeling hemmed in by what he had come to see as the limited horizons of his upstate New York community, he was drawn to the city for the possibilities of professional advancement that it held out to him. As long as he stayed in Syracuse, no matter how much national success he enjoyed, Stickley and his firm would remain an essentially regional phenomenon. If he wanted to pursue his ambitions on a national stage, he would have to do it from New York City. His reasons were also partly personal. One of his grandsons later said that Manhattan appealed to Stickley because "the standards of New York society were a little freer than Syracuse."[1] Stickley thus came to the city to test himself in its competitive arena and to enjoy its many pleasures, just like millions of others before and since.

The move had been germinating in the back of his mind for a long time. The large department store that Stickley had wanted to open in Binghamton in the 1880s was, as noted earlier, an overly ambitious concept, and he did not pursue it. As a writer in *Furniture Journal* later commented, "Of course if he had he would have gone broke on the scheme, for Binghamton was not large enough for it."[2] New York City, so Stickley must have reasoned, *would* be large enough and was therefore the right place to revive this dream of a new retail enterprise.

By late 1901, Stickley had sold his Arts and Crafts furniture in New York City through James McCreery & Co., a large, long established Manhattan retailer. In the spring of 1905, however, Charles Coutant, McCreery's store manager and one of Stickley's friends, left that firm for a competitor, A.A. Vantine & Co., and Stickley shifted his allegiance.[3] It was with Coutant and Vantine that Stickley made his first, concerted drive to establish a substantial retail beachhead in the rich New York market. The venture promptly failed. News of this undertaking first appeared in the 10 April 1905 issue of *Furniture Trade Review*, which carried an item announcing that "A. A. Vantine & Co. have been preparing to open an 'arts and crafts' shop on Fifth Avenue....[T]he stock will be composed entirely of the furniture products of Gustav Stickley, of Syracuse." This new shop, carrying Craftsman furniture, metalwork, and textiles, opened in early May and folded less than a month later: "The venture of A.A. Vantine & Co. with Mission furniture was short-lived....[T]he entire stock has been purchased by Abraham & Strauss and offered to the people of Brooklyn through a large announcement in the dailies...at sixty cents on the dollar. This furniture is all the product of Gustav Stickley."[4]

1 Detail of a Wilkinson-designed #510 bookcase, oak, 1901.

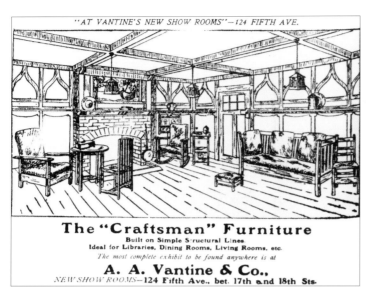

2

3

The reason why this venture fell apart so quickly is not known, but it is possible to guess. A.A. Vantine's emporium was famous for selling very elaborate decorative objects—the "elegant trifles" that it imported from the Orient. Craftsman furniture must have seemed unduly stark in such an environment and it clearly had no appeal to regular Vantine customers. Whatever caused this abrupt failure, for Stickley it must have been a bruising experience. At exactly the same time that he was conscientiously building his national network of associates, he was given another sharp reminder of the risks of ceding control of his distribution. He now found himself with no retail presence whatsoever in New York City. When he ventured back into this market six months later, he did so entirely on his own and under the Craftsman aegis.

On 3 December 1905, his firm wrote a $300 check for rent on its New York City "showrooms," and an announcement in that month's issue of *The Craftsman* told readers of the opening—at 29 West Thirty-fourth Street—of the first Craftsman retail store. By choosing this part of the city Stickley was on familiar territory: the Waldorf-Astoria was on the Fifth Avenue end of this block, and McCreery's would shortly open a second New York store across the street from the Waldorf.

In *The Craftsman* magazine, Stickley presented his new store not as a mere retail outlet but as a slightly exclusive club for like-minded souls: "We are glad to announce to our friends that The Craftsman is establishing a Branch Exposition Department in New York....This will enable us to show The Craftsman idea of rooms...where the surroundings will be comfortable and beautiful in their practical simplicity. An entire floor will be devoted to the Exposition and for the reception of all who are interested in the Craftsman

Movement."[5] The trade press view was, as ever, more direct. In its estimation, this was simply a furniture store arranged as a group of model rooms, a clever method to stimulate sales: "[T]here will be a continuous demonstration of the use of 'Craftsman' furniture, not by the carrying of stock, but by the seeming furnishing of a number of rooms, which will convey the idea much more readily to visitors."[6] Model rooms were not new to Stickley: he had installed one in McCreery's Twenty-third Street store in Manhattan in 1901; he had featured Craftsman model rooms at his 1903 Arts and Crafts exhibition; and in 1904 he created a model dining room for Marshall Field.

This approach to retailing was actually a recasting of what had become a central Craftsman aesthetic belief—the room as a unified work of art—into an effective form of merchandising. In his ambition to succeed as a retailer in New York City, Stickley was, in fact, increasingly shifting his emphasis to marketing the Craftsman "brand." This was probably a necessary step, and it was certainly very smart. Despite the compromises that had led to Standard Stickley, the furniture remained unlike what most shoppers were accustomed to, and it was not always easy to like at first sight. It was too austere, too visually uncompromising (and it did not blend comfortably with other styles), and yet Stickley was earnestly endeavoring to make good, honest furniture and sell it, if not to the masses, at least to a wide, middle-class market.

Thus he arranged his store to look more like a living room than a furniture shop, and described his sales staff as a "corps of assistants," whose designated role was not merely to sell merchandise, but to "make suggestions for decorative combinations, color schemes and interesting furnishings." He knew he had to teach his customers to see the beauty of his furniture. To bring in potential buyers

4

Stickley sent out warmly worded messages inviting his "friends" to visit: "These rooms make a comfortable resting place for our New York callers, and Craftsman subscribers are most welcome visitors."[7]

Stickley became a long-distance commuter on the New York Central & Hudson River Railroad. An item in *American Cabinet Maker and Upholsterer* said that "Mr. Stickley will spend part of his time at the New York office, and when in Syracuse, will have his desk at the factory in Eastwood."[8] Hereafter he was to have less direct involvement with his furniture-making operation, and would spend less time with his family. Dividing his weeks between Syracuse and New York City and traveling long hours on trains must have proved a stressful regimen, and so he rented an apartment on West Ninety-seventh Street to be closer to his main place of business. How often he went home during these years is not known, but he was there for the holidays.[9] Barbara Stickley, by then in her early twenties and a student at Smith College, left school and shared this apartment with her father, working each day in his office. While working in New York she frequently saw another of her father's employees, his circulation manager, Ben Wiles, a young man, who, like herself, had been raised in an upstate New York town. They would marry at Craftsman Farms in 1911.

There was, apparently, another reason behind Barbara Stickley's move to Manhattan. According to Wiles family lore, she had been dispatched by her mother to "chaperone" her father,

2 A. A. Vantine advertisement for its new Craftsman furniture department, from *The New York Times*, 14 May 1905.

3 Stickley's Craftsman retail store at 29 West Thirty-fourth Street, New York, from *The Craftsman*, October 1913.

4 The Craftsman retail store at 41 West Thirty-fourth Street, New York, from *The Craftsman*, April 1913.

who had established an intimate relationship with another woman. The identity of this woman remains a mystery, but the story of Stickley's involvement with her was eventually known not just to Eda Stickley, but to his children and some of his grandchildren. Eda, who remained with their five other children in Syracuse until the family moved to Craftsman Farms, missed her husband and unhappily endured his long absences.[10]

By 1908, Stickley moved his architectural department and the offices of *The Craftsman* magazine to a nearby building at 41 West Thirty-fourth Street. He needed this extra space to house his burgeoning enterprise. His customers were welcome there, too. In this building they could look at portfolios of Craftsman houses and inspect dollhouse-sized models of Craftsman bungalows and cottages. They could also view displays of many of the products advertised in the magazine. This was good merchandising, a potentially valuable service to readers, but it was also a means of making *The Craftsman* magazine more attractive to advertisers. The display areas of this building allowed advertisers to put their products in front of interested, potential customers. *The Craftsman* thus positioned itself as a trustworthy and knowledgeable link between consumers and the manufacturers who advertised in the magazine. In his associates' stores Stickley had already intertwined *Craftsman* magazine readership and Craftsman furniture sales, but this integration of advertising and product merchandising reached an even more sophisticated level of marketing.

Perhaps because Stickley's firm had standardized its production methods and was increasingly engaged in up-to-date consumer marketing, there was a slight sense of disquiet growing among some members of the Arts and Crafts constituency. For instance, in a 1907 *Good Housekeeping* article discussing vari-

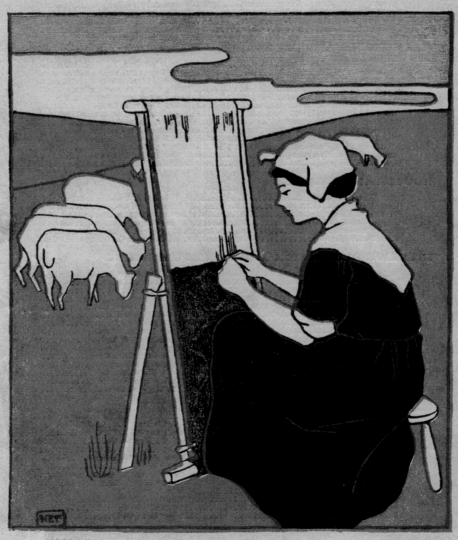

VOL. XIV, NO. 1   APRIL, 1908   25 CENTS

THE CRAFTSMAN

SMALL FARMING AND PROFITABLE HANDICRAFTS
IDA TARBELL, A PIONEER IN TRUST INVESTIGATIONS
LORADO TAFT AND THE SCHOOL OF WESTERN SCULPTORS

TWENTY-NINE-WEST-THIRTY-FOURTH-STREET-NEW-YORK

ous American craft workers and craft-based businesses, the journalist Alvan Sanborn remarked that the "Rookwood pottery has lost none of its artistic importance in becoming a commercial enterprise and the same may be affirmed, though somewhat less emphatically, of the...hand-made furniture shops in Syracuse, New York."[11] Despite such faint, occasional criticisms, the heart of Stickley's enterprise remained faithfully within the Arts and Crafts fold. This was especially true of *The Craftsman* magazine.

In 1908, the magazine continued to keep its editorial focus on art, architecture, design, and country living, and, if anything, the space it devoted to handicrafts increased over that of recent years. It offered readers detailed, practical instruction in metalworking, cabinetmaking, stenciling, textile dyeing, rug making, and needleworking. Ernest Batchelder's illustrated, multi-part series "Design in Theory and Practice" appeared at this time, as did the ceramist C.F. Binns's analytical and prescriptive article on "The Arts and Crafts Movement in America," his prize-winning entry in an essay contest sponsored by the magazine. And a new theme, environmental preservation—framed in Rooseveltian terms as protection of "national assets"—became an important subject to the magazine that year.

By this time, *The Craftsman* had a new editor, Mary Fanton Roberts (ca.1864–1956), who had joined the staff in 1905 and would remain in her role from then on. Although she came to the magazine with a fairly slender resume as a writer, she was nevertheless an experienced magazine journalist who had good connections among a wide group of potential contributors outside of Stickley's orbit. Like other creative collaborators Roberts came into her own at the Craftsman Workshops, certainly learning from her boss (Stickley was nominally the editor of *The Craftsman*), but she also made his magazine more accessible to general readers and she expanded its scope to encompass current painting, photography, theater, and dance.[12]

Many of the writers, editors, and illustrators Roberts attracted to the magazine were women. *The Craftsman* had tended to see women in their traditional roles as wives and mothers, and to the extent that it had an editorial stance on "women's issues," it generally confined itself to suggesting ways to make housework more pleasant and efficient.[13] During Roberts's tenure, however, the Craftsman Workshops grew somewhat more enlightened. In March 1904, for instance, *The Craftsman* had published drawings of three modest cottages said to be suitable for single women.[14] The article mentioned in passing that any of the cottages might make a good first home for a young married couple, but it stressed that finding a pleasant place to live on a small income was "largely a woman's problem" that these cottages were meant to solve. Despite the writer's attempts to present this subject in the most positive possible light, the image this article created of women living alone was fairly gloomy: these cottages would appeal to a "middle-aged woman stranded in some forlorn hall-bedroom, or in...the home of others." Because this hypothetical woman had so little money she would understand that to "come within her very small means, the 'humble habitation' must be located where land is of low value." No suggestion was made that this woman might decide to enhance her "small means" by earning money. Five years later, in Stickley's 1909 compilation of house plans, *Craftsman Homes*, these cottages were published once again along with some of the text from the original *Craftsman* article. Although still directed

toward women of limited means, they were now said to be "inexpensive but charming cottages" designed for "women who either work at home or possibly in a shop or office." The cottages could be built "in some suburb not too far away from the place of employment." Such thoughts were not uncommon in popular magazines of the day, but for *The Craftsman*—a magazine that employed professional women who lived in the city or commuted from neighboring suburbs—they signaled a slight but significant shift in emphasis that recognized a new reality.

Craftsman readership rose to its high point of 22,500 in 1910. This was well below the level of the era's mass-circulation periodicals—*Good Housekeeping*, for instance, now had 300,000 subscribers—but its distribution was equivalent to other national magazines that allotted generous editorial space to Arts and Crafts topics. In 1910, to name the three journals that were perhaps closest in content to *The Craftsman*, *International Studio* had 12,000 readers, *House Beautiful* 25,000 readers, and *House and Garden* 34,000.[15] Seen in the context of such highly regarded peers, *Craftsman* circulation was eminently respectable.

1908 was another period of intense activity for Stickley. In the spring of that year, for instance, he traveled again in Europe; this was his fourth—and his last—trip abroad for which documentary evidence still exists. The magazine revived the Craftsman Home Builders' Club, which had been dormant for the past two years. This time, however, there was an astonishing difference: now the club would publish Craftsman houses that existed not just on paper but that were actually being constructed. In December Stickley announced his latest venture, the Craftsman Home Building Company. The initial house in the new series, erected in Beechhurst, Long Island, for a client named W.H. Phillips, was offered as "the first that we are building as well as designing, and so this is the first time that we can say that we are testing out by actual experience, under our own supervision, every detail of plan, construction and finish which we recommend."[16]

A new magazine for farmers and would-be farmers, *The Yeoman*, was announced by Stickley this year. It had an ambitious editorial program. Conceived as a vehicle providing useful instruction to anyone making a living growing crops and pursuing profitable handicrafts, it was to be an advocacy journal encouraging the establishment of small, family farms while also promoting land reclamation and the conservation of natural resources. Its "how-to" features would be filled with specific, practical guidance on the day-to-day problems faced by farmers, and Stickley tried to induce every *Craftsman* subscriber to subscribe to *The Yeoman* as well.[17] According to the November issue of *The Craftsman*, "the initial number of The Yeoman is well under way," and Stickley's ledgers show that his firm was indeed spending money to start up this new publication. Yet this well-intentioned educational foray never made it into print.

In 1908, Stickley also formed The Craftsman Company of New York City, a privately held corporation that operated his Manhattan retail store.[18] A further sign of his growing confidence in the health of his business was his decision to open a second Craftsman retail store on Boylston Street in Boston. Late in the year, he announced his plans for Craftsman Farms, and began buying parcels

5 *The Craftsman* magazine covers were often illustrated with idealized pastoral scenes during the years that Stickley's firm was headquartered in Manhattan.

6

of arable land in Morris Plains, New Jersey, thirty-four miles west of his New York City base. Here he intended to build a new home for his family, while also developing the site as a school, craft colony, and farm operated on the latest agricultural principles. And, just a few months later, in 1909, still another venture, the Craftsman Publishing Company, came into being.

A case can be made that all of these offshoots grew organically from the main body of the Craftsman enterprise; Stickley certainly thought they did. It is perhaps closer to the truth to say that they were symptoms of flawed logic. With *The Yeoman*, for instance, Stickley proposed to supply "practical… detailed…definite instruction and information" to farmers, market gardeners, and home growers. With the Craftsman Home Building Company he proposed to enter the residential construction business. The problem, of course, was that he lacked the requisite expertise; in these fields the Craftsman was essentially a layman. Stickley apparently thought that he could hire a staff of experts to make these ventures successful. That was what had always worked for him in the furniture business. But furniture making was a discipline he had mastered absolutely and knew how to manage. These other, more recent ventures diffused his attention and moved him into areas in which, despite his good intentions, he and his firm had little of value to offer. Optimistically begun during his years of greatest financial success, these were missteps that would sap his financial resources and ultimately contribute to the failure of his Craftsman enterprise.

Taking one step at a time, Stickley's entry into New York had at first been guided by his characteristic caution. But by 1912, with the circulation of *The Craftsman* magazine at a healthy level, and with his Craftsman products selling nationally via mail order and through his associates' stores, Stickley felt ready for further expansion. Perhaps the stark Vantine failure of 1905 had been forgotten, or dismissed as an anomaly. Stickley opened another Craftsman retail store, his third, at 1512 H Street in Washington, D.C. Then he prepared to take over a new twelve-story office tower designed the year before by the firm of Mulliken and Mueller, Architects.[19] It rose at 6 East Thirty-ninth Street in Manhattan, and, as the only tenant, he gave it the name he wanted: the Craftsman Building. Here, under one roof, he consolidated several floors of retail space, business offices, public lounges, and a restaurant. It was the culmination of dreams he had had about retailing since his unrealized Binghamton department store plan, and throughout the remainder of his life he was to persist in the belief that creating the New York City Craftsman Building was one of his greatest accomplishments.[20] It was not; it was tragic folly.

His attention increasingly fragmented by the many branches of his business, Stickley had stretched himself even thinner by over-committing his firm's resources to this costly tower of offices and retail space. In 1913, the fifty-five-year-old Stickley signed a twenty-one year lease that obligated him, over that period, to pay a breathtaking $1,300,000 in rent. Driven apparently by his rising ambitions, he had expanded into an entire skyscraper, and then at great expense constructed its interior spaces in the Craftsman mode. He continued to produce his well-made Arts and Crafts wares, but he had chosen to market them in a manner far removed from Arts and Crafts tradition. Compounded by unlucky timing, this building would be his undoing.

The Craftsman Building may have been a magnificent mistake, but considering Stickley's early life it is an understandable one. He had grown up on his parents' hardscrabble farm, and then, after his father abandoned the family, he spent his teenage years learning the furniture trade; he helped support his mother, sisters, and brothers by doing hard, physical labor on the floor of his uncles' Pennsylvania chair factory. At the same time, stirred perhaps by the books he read, he began to realize that there was a world of wider possibilities beyond the factory walls. Still, he toiled for three or four decades in the noise and grime of a succession of furniture factories, and his ledgers and business papers that survive today give off a palpable whiff of sawdust, machine oil, grit, and smoke. Much of his working life had been spent in harsh, industrial conditions, and the dream of inhabiting—and being in control of—a clean, quiet space in a tall Manhattan office tower had to have been irresistible. The Craftsman Building, like the remodeled interior of his house in Syracuse, was a stage setting where Stickley could assume the roles he had long striven to play: successful manufacturer, department store retailer, restaurateur, publisher, opinion molder, taste maker. With the opening of this new building he had become the great impresario of the American Arts and Crafts.

An article with Stickley's by-line in the October 1913 *Craftsman* said, "this building is now the Craftsman home." He seems to have forgotten that a "Craftsman Home" had for nearly a decade meant a modest, detached, suburban or rural residence. Now, oddly flipping his terminology, "Craftsman Home" had come to signify an urban stack of offices and retail space. The article continued:

> Here are the showrooms for furniture, metal work and fabrics made in my cabinet and metal workshops at Eastwood, New York. Here is The Craftsman Magazine with its several departments. Here are the drafting rooms of the Craftsman architects; the bureaus of Craftsman Service—architectural, gardening, agricultural and real estate; the home-builders' library; the lecture hall, the club rooms for Craftsman subscribers, and the homelike Craftsman Restaurant. More important than all, perhaps, here is the big Craftsman Permanent Home-builders' Exposition, occupying five floors and including everything that the homemaker might need to see, and know….Such an exposition as this must surely prove invaluable to the American homemaker.[21]

Stickley's "Exposition," like the smaller one he had held on Thirty-fourth Street, was also meant to benefit manufacturers, many of whom were already advertising in his magazine. It offered them an opportunity to sublease exhibit space to display their goods in a spacious, centralized Manhattan setting conceived as a single source of products and information for anyone building or furnishing a home. Everything on view in the Exposition would be implicitly granted a kind of Craftsman "seal of approval." These were seemingly appealing incentives to hold out to manufacturers. Stickley apparently envisioned that the Exposition would bring a two-fold financial benefit to himself: it must have brought some added advertising revenues to *The Craftsman* magazine and, beyond that, the manufacturers who occupied display space were helping to defray part of the $60,000 annual rent of the Craftsman Building. Unfortunately, he was never able to attract as many manufacturers as he had hoped, and some percentage of these spaces remained empty.[22]

6 Stickley's Boston retail store, at 470 Boylston Street, undated photograph.

7

Though much too lavishly realized, the New York City Craftsman Building was, at least conceptually, a brilliant stroke of marketing. Here Stickley had devised an integrated way to sell his products—and those of participating manufacturers—to an engaged buying public that he kept motivated with that monthly mix of promotional messages and Arts and Crafts orthodoxy, *The Craftsman* magazine. Visitors to the Craftsman Building could begin by taking an elevator to the eighth floor, walk through the exhibits and end up back at street level, something like the modern-day museum-goers at the Fifth Avenue Guggenheim or shoppers in some of today's department stores. They would first examine Building Materials. Home Decoration and exhibits of model rooms were on seven, Home Equipment on six, Garden and Grounds on five, and Rugs and Interior Decorating on Four. The building's visitors could then descend to the third floor for Craftsman textiles, Draperies and House Furnishings, to the second floor for General Furniture Display, and then finally arrive back at the first floor. There Craftsman furniture was displayed along with Craftsman metalwork and Grueby, Fulper, Hampshire, and Ruskin pottery.[23] After taking in the lessons the Exposition had to offer, and having been shown along each step of the way by helpful Craftsman "guides," potential home builders would then "be able to call in one of our architects and talk over the whole matter, going into every detail of the planning and construction as thoroughly as possible."[24] At the pleasant, convenient New York City Craftsman Building consumers could find whatever they needed for their homes, even plan a new home, and they could be assured that

everything they bought would be beautiful, practical, tasteful, affordable. This, at least, was the theory. In reality, the furniture displays were surprisingly pedestrian and hardly different from what one would find in any typical American furniture store of the day. The glimpses of the building's interior published in *The Craftsman* magazine suggest that Stickley had much more square footage than he could possibly fill. Even in these publicity shots his wares seem not very appealing; they are lost in the vast and cavernous spaces.

Stickley's 1903 Arts and Crafts exhibition at the Syracuse Craftsman Building had been designed as an edifying assemblage of hand-wrought objects. Although, as was typically true of such exhibitions, most of the objects on display were for sale, the real point of this event was the encouragement of handicrafts and the improvement of public taste. The Craftsman Homebuilders' Permanent Exposition, in the New York Craftsman Building, was quite a different matter. It did have an educational gloss, but it was a frankly commercial undertaking meant to stimulate retail sales of manufactured goods intended for use in the home. Handcrafted wares were little in evidence.

By 1913, Stickley was referring less frequently to the Arts and Crafts movement, and had begun emphasizing instead what he called the "Craftsman Movement," a phrase he had first used when he moved to New York eight years before. The seemingly inevitable branching out of his firm had led it, in Stickley's pronouncements, to a higher realm that transcended commercial

identity. As he said in a *Craftsman* magazine article, it had evolved into "a movement, and not merely an individual enterprise." Under the heading of the "Craftsman Movement," a coinage obviously resonant of "the Arts and Crafts movement" (and also perhaps the "Morris Movement," a term then in use at Morris & Co.), he gathered together his firm's fundamental concerns:

> *Today the Craftsman Movement stands not only for simple, well made furniture…it stands also for a distinct type of American architecture….It stands, too, for the companionship of gardens, the wholesomeness of country and suburban living and the health and efficiency which these imply. It aims to be instrumental in the restoration of the people to the land and the land to the people. It is always for progress, for scientific farming, for closer cooperation between the producer and consumer, and less waste in both agricultural and industrial fields. It stands for the right of the children to health and happiness, through an education that will develop hands as well as heads….Civic improvement is close to its heart, political, as well as social and industrial progress; it desires to strengthen honest craftsmanship in every branch of human activity, and strives for a form of art which shall express the spirit of the American people.*[25]

The thinking that underlay the Craftsman Movement was enlightened, progressive, admirable, and article after article in *The Craftsman* magazine advanced this commendable set of ideas. Now, in the fall of 1913, Stickley told his readers that the opening of the Craftsman Building was not only the next stage in the Movement's progress, it was also "a fitting culmination for all Craftsman activities." But this longed-for "culmination" was veering down an increasingly commercial path.

The Craftsman Building, according to a leaflet distributed by the firm, was "The Homelover's Headquarters, in the Shopping Centre of America." Stickley published a street map pointing out other nearby attractions: Lord & Taylor, Bonwit Teller, B. Altman, Tiffany & Company, the Waldorf-Astoria, the Metropolitan Opera, all no more than a pleasant stroll from Grand Central Terminal or the Pennsylvania Rail Road station. His customers were to be pampered. Concierge service was available to the buildings' visitors, and shoppers were urged to stop in to relax, meet friends, and refresh themselves with afternoon tea. A maid was stationed in the women's Club Room. This space, a lounge with Craftsman writing tables and comfortable chairs, was predominantly decorated in an un-Craftsman-like heliotrope, and its delicately scaled furniture and accessories were tinted soft shades of green and pale rose.

The men's Club Room, also on the eleventh floor, was more traditional: it was all dark oak and

7 The cavernous Craftsman furniture display room on the first floor of the New York City Craftsman Building, from *The Craftsman*, December 1913.

8 Models of Craftsman houses on display in the Craftsman Building, undated photograph. The model to the right is an early version of the log house built at Craftsman Farms.

CRAFTSMAN ADVERTISING DEPARTMENT

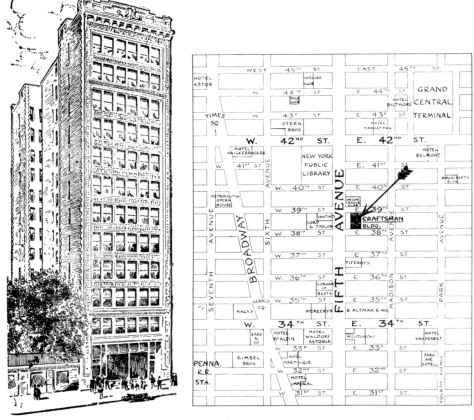

When You Come To New York—

be sure to visit the Craftsman Building no matter how limited your time may be. Make it a point to come to the Building at the very first opportunity; if you put off your visit to the last minute, you are certain to regret it—there are so many things of interest here which you will wish you had more time to examine. The Craftsman Building is really a treasure-house for the homelover. The four floors devoted to furniture and furnishings are worth coming many miles to see, while for anyone about to build or remodel or re-decorate, the exhibits in the Homebuilders' Exposition are of incalculable value as a means of saving time, money and trouble. Homebuilders who are wise in looking after their own best interests should plan to spend several days in studying the Exposition.

The Craftsman Building is conveniently situated in the best known, most accessible part of New York, within a few blocks of the Waldorf, Vanderbilt, Biltmore, Belmont, McAlpin, Knickerbocker, and other leading hotels, near the principal clubs and theatres, and in the midst of the famous Fifth Avenue shopping section which the visitor is sure to frequent. Craftsman readers are cordially urged to take advantage of this convenient location by making the Craftsman Building their headquarters while in New York, using the delightful club rooms and rest rooms freely, both for their own comfort and as a rendez-vous for meeting friends, etc. The Craftsman Restaurant on the top floor, of which you have heard so much, will prove for you, as it has for so many others, one of the most delightful eating-places you have ever visited.

And by all means, when you do come, let us know that you are a Craftsman reader, and give us the opportunity to welcome you to your "own club-house."

Gustav Stickley

10

11

hammered copper, and redolent of rich Craftsman leather. It had a handsome Craftsman fireplace—patented by Stickley in 1912—constructed of irregularly textured, vari-colored tapestry brick.[26] As added inducements to attract shoppers to the Craftsman Building, Stickley adorned the library and lecture hall areas of this floor with "copper and brass, pottery, crystal, rich brocades and sheerest of gauzes." A woman sat at a hand loom demonstrating weaving, and another woman, a Native American, made baskets of sweet grass and reed. The Craftsman Building offered nothing less than "a new way to shop in America."[27] It was not merely a store, it was "the Craftsman Bazaar." Stickley the merchant worked hard to create a retail ambiance of great charm.

The eleventh floor also had a children's playroom. In 1914 Stickley hired Helen Speer, a designer and retailer of toys and children's furniture, to establish and oversee this playroom and to offer customers her professional services: "Mrs. Speer is always ready to design new furnishings and toys for those who desire them, or to help plan the arrangement, furnishing, color scheme or decorations for nursery or playroom."[28] Speer had probably come to Stickley's attention when she created a similar children's room in the Vanderbilt Hotel, not far from the Craftsman Building at Thirty-fourth Street and Park Avenue. Her furniture was sturdy, geometric, and usually painted with washable ivory white enamel accented with blue and gray geometric shapes. Stickley must have recognized and admired the Josef Hoffmann and Koloman Moser influence evident in Speer's furniture for children. Her approach to furniture design mirrored his: she emphasized good proportions and freedom from period styles, and she was guided by the overarching idea that "[t]he influence of good design is of high value during the child's formative period."[29] *The Craftsman* had been making similar statements for over a decade, and Speer's work

blended easily into the Craftsman Building and made it an even more appealing place to shop. In the playroom she designed, as one *Craftsman* writer promised, "children play in the sand [and] rock upon see-saws, while the mothers shop, exactly as they do in bazaars across the water."[30]

On the top floor of the building the Craftsman Restaurant was open for lunch, tea, and dinner. A string ensemble played unobtrusive music, and occasionally there were dances in the evening. As he did throughout the building, Stickley spent freely on the appointments of his restaurant, and practically everything in it, or so it seems, was identified by its brand name.[31] All of the silver was specially commissioned from the International Silver Company and the Oneida Community, Ltd., and stamped with the Craftsman joiner's compass logo. The china used for lunch and dinner service was a white ware made by the Onondaga Pottery Company of Syracuse and decorated with a Craftsman pinecone design. Each piece of the cream-colored Lenox porcelain used for afternoon tea was marked on its face with "the Craftsman emblem." The restaurant offered a menu of simple, healthful fare, that included, among other dishes, Craftsman salad, Craftsman fruit cocktail, Craftsman crab meat, Craftsman beef steak, Craftsman planked sirloin, and even, for fifteen cents, a bottle of milk from Craftsman Farms. The fruits, vegetables, and spring water served in the restaurant came from Craftsman Farms, and they were delivered to the city via the firm's fleet of four motorized "omnibusses" made by the Autocar Company of Ardmore, Pennsylvania.

9 The Craftsman Building and a street map of the surrounding area. The Stickley firm called it "The Homelover's Headquarters, in the Shopping Centre of America," from *The Craftsman*, April 1915.

10 Men's club room on the eleventh floor of the Craftsman Building, from *The Craftsman*, April 1914.

11 Children's furniture designed by Helen Speer, on the eleventh floor of the Craftsman Building, from *The Craftsman*, November 1914.

12

13

Like the men's Club Room, the restaurant, too, had an open fireplace, this one faced with brown and mauve Grueby tiles. Stickley's metalworkers made a hammered copper hood for it, embossed with words paraphrased from the Old Testament, "Where young men see visions and old men dream dreams."[32] This biblical paraphrase has a curious autobiographical appropriateness for Stickley: at fifty-five he admitted in *The Craftsman* magazine that he was becoming an "old man," and yet, as he was proving daily in the Craftsman Building, he retained his questing spirit and youthfully—if not always sensibly—pursued his splendid visions and dreams. As his grandson, Gustav Stickley III recalled, "He was a perfectionist.... It had to be right, and he would spare no expense to make it right, which is why he went bankrupt. He was not a good businessman in the sense of making money."[33]

In addition to the Craftsman Building's various customer services and its welcoming atmosphere, the firm also attracted visitors by exploiting the appeal of Stickley's celebrity: "I want all my friends who come to visit the new building to feel that I shall be personally at their service....More than once people have come from a long distance to visit my workshops...and I have discovered afterward that they felt they should not take my time and have imagined I was too busy....I do not want this to ever happen in the new building."[34] A legendary charmer, Stickley must have deftly put his customers at ease. But Stickley's celebrity could not overcome the flawed logic that had drawn him into the Craftsman Building. It was, first of all, too costly for his firm. And, secondly, despite his imaginative efforts to attract customers, he nevertheless made the mistake of demanding too much of them. It is hard to imagine that a casual department store shopper browsing, say, for window curtains or a footstool, would want to be confronted by several floors of shingles, nails, and cinder blocks. Perhaps some people bought building materials in the Craftsman Permanent Homebuilders' Exposition, but not nearly enough.

However much time Stickley may have spent greeting customers, his days in New York City were increasingly occupied by matters of business and finance. On 1 October 1912, he consolidated the Gustav Stickley Company of Syracuse (his factory) and his retail stores in New York, Boston, and Washington, D.C., and formed a new stock-issuing entity called Gustav Stickley The Craftsman Incorporated.[35] The Craftsman Publishing Company was a separate corporation, but Gustav Stickley The Craftsman Incorporated owned all the shares of its stock. By mid-1914, about six months after taking over the Craftsman Building, Stickley's enterprise needed additional capital. To attract $150,000 from new investors, it made a public offering of 1,500 shares of Craftsman preferred stock that July, valuing the stock at a hundred dollars a share and promising to pay an annual dividend of seven percent. This was an unusual move for Stickley, who had heretofore retained tight control over the stock of his corporate entities. Except for token grants of stock to Eda, his older children, and to those few key employees who were invited to join his board of directors, he had kept the rest of the shares in his own name.[36]

Now, however, the Craftsman Workshops was losing money. It failed to make a profit in 1912 and 1913, and, in 1914, because operating the expensively outfitted Craftsman Building was so costly, the firm was suffering even heavier losses. Looking to raise cash quickly, Stickley had earlier that year taken the unprecedented step of putting his furniture on special sale and advertising it in New York newspapers. His firm's weekly payroll alone has to have been considerable. He had about two hundred men working in his Eastwood factory, and in New York he maintained a "corps

12 The bright, sunlit Craftsman Restaurant, on the top floor of the Craftsman Building, from *The Craftsman*, January 1914.

13 Lenox porcelain, each piece marked with the joiner's compass, used for afternoon tea at the Craftsman Restaurant, from *The Craftsman*, January 1914.

14 Luncheon menu, offering many Craftsman dishes, from "The Craftsman Restaurant," 1914.

Luncheon

FRUIT COCKTAILS.

Craftsman 40   Grapefruit 30
Pineapple 30   Grapefruit, Supreme 50

OYSTERS, CLAMS AND SCALLOPS.

Cape Cod on Shell........ 25   Lynnhavens on Shell...... 30
Stewed in Milk, 30; Cream 45   Fried with Tartare or To-
Stewed, Craftsman 50   mato Sauce 40
Pan Roast, Boston........ 60   Little Neck Clams on Shell 25
Roasted in Shell with Bacon 45   Little Neck Clams Steamed 50
Scallops and Bacon........ 40   Roasted in Shell with Bacon 35
                    Pilaff of Scallops 40

RELISHES.

Celery 20.   Stuffed Celery 30.   Stuffed Mangoes 15.
Queen Olives 15.   Ripe California Olives 20.   Radishes 15.
Pin Money Pickles 10.   New Dill Pickles 10.
Salted Almonds 20.   Indian Mango Chutney 20.   Sardines 25.
Anchovies on Toast 40.   Caviar on Toast 40.
Sardines on Toast 30.   Romanoff Beluga Caviar 1.25.

SOUPS.

Clam Broth, Cup 20.   Consomme, Cup 20.
Chicken Broth, Cup 25.   Chicken Consomme, Craftsman 40.
Chicken with Okra 30.   Tomato Bouillon 25.
Cream of Tomato 25.   Sorrel 30.   Puree of Green Peas 25.
Chicken with Home-made Noodles 30.

FISH, LOBSTER AND CRABS.

Broiled Live Lobster 1.00.   Lobster Cardinal 75.
Lobster, Newburg (Chafing Dish) 1.25. Crab Meat, Craftsman 60.
Crab Flakes, any Style (in Chafing Dish) 1.00.
Finnan Haddie Broiled with Butter Sauce 35.
Finnan Haddie, Newburg 75.   Kingfish Broiled 40.
Sea Bass Broiled 40.   Smelts 30, with Tartare Sauce 40.

STEAKS, CHOPS, ETC.

Beefsteak, Craftsman 60.   Small Sirloin or Tenderloin 90.
Sirloin or Tenderloin Steak, Double 1.40.   Extra Sirloin 2.50.
Planked Sirloin, Craftsman 2.50   English Mutton Chop (1) 70.
Plain Mutton Chop (2) 50.   Lamb Chops (1) 35, (2) 60.
Broiled Sweetbreads 75.   Mixed Grill 60.

BROILED.

Spring Chicken ...... 80-1.50   Duckling 1.00-2.00
Squab Chicken .... 1.25   Guinea Hen 1.00-2.00

ROAST.

Squab 1.00.   Spring Chicken 1.50.   Duckling 2.00.
Guinea Hen 2.00.   Ribs of Beef 50.   Turkey Sliced 75.

COLD MEATS.

Roast Beef 50   Turkey 75
Beechnut Ham 35   Chicken ½ 80
Virginia Ham 50   Sliced Capon 75
Tongue 30   Guinea Hen ½ 1.00
Assorted Cuts 75   Boned Chicken 50
                  Lobster ½ 60

POTATOES.

Boiled, Baked or Mashed 10.   French Fried 15.
Lyonnaise 20.   Hashed Brown 20.   Hashed in Cream 20.
Hashed in Cream with Cheese 25.   Sweet Potatoes Baked 15.
Fried or Grilled 20.   Kentucky 20.

SALADS.

Craftsman 30.   Chicken 50.   Lobster 60.
Stuffed Apple 40.   Lettuce Hearts, with French Dressing 25.
With Roquefort Cheese Dressing 35.   Tomato 25.   Arco 35.
Kuroki 35.

CHEESE.

Camembert 20.   Port du Salut 20.   Roquefort 20.
Cream 15.   Gorgonzola 30.   Stilton 25.   American 15.

FRUIT.

Basket of Assorted Fruits in Season, per person 25.
Grapefruit 25.   Orange 15.   Apple 10.   Banana 10.   Pear 15.
Cal. Preserved Figs with Cream 25.   Brandied Peaches, each 25.
Grapefruit and Orange Marmalade 20.   Bar-le-Duc Jelly 35.

TEA, COFFEE, ETC.

Ceylon, Oolong. English Breakfast, Orange Pekoe or Green
Tea, Small Pot 10, Large Pot 20.   Coffee 15, Large Pot 25.
After Dinner 10.   Cocoa 20.   Horlick's Malted Milk 15.
Craftsman Farms Milk, Bottle 15.   Buttermilk, Bottle 10.

of architects" as well as the editorial, circulation, and advertising departments of *The Craftsman* magazine; the size of these staffs is not known. In addition to those employees, Stickley had a workshop on East Thirty-seventh Street where his willow furniture was made, and a hundred and twenty-three people on salary in the Craftsman Building, thirty-seven of whom worked solely for that most quixotic of all his ventures, the Craftsman Restaurant. Most of the Craftsman Building staff was assigned to the retail department, but there was also a cook (apparently for Stickley and his guests), a painter, a gardener, three chauffeurs, three chauffeur's assistants, and a man named John A.C. Groner, whose title was "President's assistant."[37]

On 24 July 1914, Stickley signed an agreement with a Chicago stock promoter, Joseph H. Dodson—who also made birdhouses and advertised them in *The Craftsman* magazine—to manage his public offering of Craftsman preferred stock. For both Stickley and Dodson the whole experience was a frustrating affair. Dodson had trouble finding willing investors. Stickley, seeing that his stock had few takers, decided that Dodson wasn't really trying. On 28 July, just four days after hiring Dodson, Stickley directed one of his managers, Hyman Askowith, to send off a letter demanding action. "One of Mr. Stickley's peculiarities," an exasperated Askowith wrote to Dodson, "is that he demands a lot from a man in very short order."[38] Dodson's effort to sell stock in Stickley's faltering enterprise never made much headway, and it must have foundered altogether after 1 August, the day that the European powers went to war. Even though it was initially a noncombatant, the United States immediately felt the effects of this fast-spreading war. A wave of panic selling hit American stock markets. In an effort to keep that selling in check, the New York Stock Exchange, after closing on Friday, 31 July, was to remain closed until 12 December.[39] By that date Stickley could no longer have had any hopes of attracting investors who might be willing to buy his stock. Further compounding his difficulties, retail prices were already rising by 2 August, and with the beginnings of war-time inflation Americans quickly found themselves with less discretionary cash in their pockets.[40]

Stickley's stock offering may have been a failure, but he printed 5,000 copies of a prospectus that, today, yields fascinating insights into his business operations.[41] This prospectus is a promotional document with two main objectives: to convince potential investors that the firm has enough income to pay the promised semiannual dividend and to assure them that it has sufficient financial strength to keep the stock secure.[42] Thus, every facet of the firm appears here only as a precious and profitable asset. Although the prospectus offers little specific financial information, it details Stickley's Craftsman ventures, laying out their respective financial positions and depicting the considerable scale of his enterprise. It stresses the effectiveness of the firm's integrated marketing, and shows "how closely interrelated are the various branches of the Craftsman business." The wholly owned Eastwood factory site is assigned a value of $180,000—exactly $150,000 more than the assessed value of the property ten years before. The prospectus shows how much Stickley's channels of distribution had changed over the past decade: "While Craftsman Furniture is sold in large quantities direct to the consumer, the wholesale trade of the Company constitutes the largest item of its business. It is handled as an exclusive line by the biggest merchandising

15 Stickley's tragic urban folly, the Craftsman Building, from *The Craftsman*, December 1914.

firms [i.e., the associates] in all the principal cities of the United States, and also sold in various foreign countries." *The Craftsman* magazine, the most widely read and influential journal of the American Arts and Crafts movement, makes an appearance in the prospectus as well: "It constitutes in reality an asset of the... Company. The magazine is included in the Company's financial resources. Its actual value today may be considered as approximately $300,000—which is the amount that has been invested in its development.... [A]s a medium of publicity and prestige [it] is of great value to the Company." Even the Stickley family home comes under the Craftsman corporate umbrella. Craftsman Farms is described as "A Stock, Dairy and Fruit Farm near New York City, with an approximate value of $200,000." It is said to be "a very important asset of the Company."

The prospectus does not reveal how much Craftsman furniture Stickley was making in his factory, but the quantities—and the earnings they generated—were clearly considerable: "During a period of six years ending October 1913, the net earnings of the business from the manufacturing and sale of Craftsman Furniture and Furnishings averaged $84,000 per annum." (October 1913 was the month Stickley opened the Craftsman Building.) Since the firm had in fact lost money in 1912 and 1913, the preceding four or five years must have been extremely profitable. During that time, Stickley's Craftsman Workshops was flush with money, and he had used perhaps as much as $500,000 of that cash to spend heavily on two undertakings—both partly commercial—that were equal expressions of his high-minded idealism: *The Craftsman* magazine, and his demonstration farm and planned craft community at Craftsman Farms. It is impossible to justify his extraordinary expenditures as reasonable costs of doing business. They were not "investments," as the prospectus claimed; they were, sadly, losses. They are also reminders of Stickley's lack of interest in mere financial success; he needed to become a public force for good, to make and sell "honest" objects, to be an authentic apostle of the American Arts and Crafts movement. He had achieved that status, but it was not enough. The poor Midwestern farm boy, now grown to comfortable middle age, was caught in the grip of urban yearnings, and in addition to the money he lavished on his magazine and his farm, he exchanged even more of his hard-earned capital pursuing the seductive tug of high-priced New York City real estate. Ensconced in his office on the tenth floor of the Craftsman Building, Stickley had "thoroughly overextended himself."[43]

Did Stickley never consider the irony of the Craftsman Building? In that tall, modern office tower, he tried and failed to join together two irreconcilable ways of life: the essentially rural, handicraft-based ethos of the Arts and Crafts movement and an urban, consumer-oriented, retailing and manufacturing corporation. He had achieved that fusion of contradictory impulses within himself, and, to a considerable extent, he had constructed his Craftsman enterprise to encompass those same polar opposites. But if he pondered this clash of values, there is no evidence that such ambiguities ever distracted him from striving after his ambitions. Stickley had a penchant for compartmentalization. The citified, mercantile aspects of his character thrived in New York. West of the Hudson River, in the farming country of central New Jersey, a set of separate, parallel, and equally powerful impulses—his love of the countryside, his joy in life spent outdoors, his deep, enduring need for domesticity—flowered at Craftsman Farms.

When You Come To New York—

be sure to visit the Craftsman Building no matter how limited your time may be. Make it a point to come to the Building at the very first opportunity; if you put off your visit to the last minute, you are certain to regret it—there are so many things of interest here which you will wish you had more time to examine. The Craftsman Building is really a treasure-house for the homelover. The four floors devoted to furniture and furnishings are worth coming many miles to see, while for anyone about to build or remodel or re-decorate, the exhibits in the Homebuilders' Exposition are of incalculable value as a means of saving time, money and trouble. Homebuilders who are wise in looking after their own best interests should plan to spend several days in studying the Exposition.

The Craftsman Building is conveniently situated in the best known, most accessible part of New York, within a few blocks of the Waldorf, Vanderbilt, Biltmore, Belmont, McAlpin, Knickerbocker, and other leading hotels, near the principal clubs and theatres, and in the midst of the famous Fifth Avenue shopping section which the visitor is sure to frequent. Craftsman readers are cordially urged to take advantage of this convenient location by making the Craftsman Building their headquarters while in New York, using the delightful club rooms and rest rooms freely, both for their own comfort and as a rendez-vous for meeting friends, etc. The Craftsman Restaurant on the top floor, of which you have heard so much, will prove for you, as it has for so many others, one of the most delightful eating-places you have ever visited.

And by all means, when you do come, let us know that you are a Craftsman reader, and give us the opportunity to welcome you to your "own club-house."

Gustav Stickley

"If only one could get a little space of ground, and establish a little colony of one's friends and get things into bright working order—and enlarge one's field of working gradually."[1] So John Ruskin, in a letter written to a young friend in 1868, voiced the yearning for community and rural simplicity that pervaded the Arts and Crafts movement. Similarly, William Morris and Edward Burne-Jones proposed a "monastic brotherhood" while still students at Oxford, and later, in the early 1860s, they aspired to a communal life of art and handicraft in the Arcadian setting of Morris's Red House. A generation later, followers of Ruskin and Morris on both sides of the Atlantic would succeed in establishing country communities with widely varying quotients of craft, commerce, agri-cultural competence, social and political adventurousness, and sentimental rusticity. For many Arts and Crafts practitioners at the turn of the twentieth century, living and working in idyllic, retired enclaves, and leaving behind the ills and pressures of an increasingly urbanized and industrialized society—going "back to the land"—was a very compelling idea.[2]

Gustav Stickley, too, felt the pull of the pastoral. The photograph of his factory published in *The Craftsman* in 1902 had portrayed it as a country workshop framed by trees and surrounded by broad fields. During his West Coast travels of 1904, he and George Wharton James had made optimistic plans for a colony of small-scale farmers, artisans, and handicraft students, but nothing came of that brief, perhaps vacation-induced, West Coast fantasy. In the spring of 1907, however, Stickley, in a letter he wrote from his Manhattan office, told Henry Turner Bailey that "[w]e are thinking of settling on a farm here near New York."[3] The following summer he began buying land in Morris Plains, New Jersey. He had come to know this area of country estates and rural retreats because his friend, the cartoonist Homer Davenport, owned a gentleman's farm there, and Gustav and Eda often went to visit. They "just fell in love with Morris Plains," recalled their daughter Marion, but its affordable farmland and its commuter rail line were certainly the kinds of practical factors that induced Stickley to buy property.[4] Now he prepared to transplant his unreal-

ized California dream to a landscape of comparable natural beauty—though a less hospitable climate—three thousand miles to the east.

Not everyone in Stickley's family shared his enthusiasm for New Jersey farm life. His eldest daughter, Barbara, was happy living in New York City and wanted to stay there. Mildred, Hazel, Marion, and Ruth were equally reluctant; they had many friends at home in Syracuse, and didn't want to leave.[5] What Gustav, Jr. thought about the prospective move is unrecorded, but from what is known of his life at the Farms he must have sided with his sisters in resisting their father's plans. Stickley, however, was not to be dissuaded. He had decided to build a rustic family compound, and, by promising his daughters that their friends would always be welcome guests (a promise he kept), he won them round to his point of view.

Stickley assembled the real estate where he was to build Craftsman Farms like pieces of a jigsaw puzzle, buying land over time from several different owners and gradually fitting it together. He made his first three purchases, totaling about fifty acres, in June 1908. Most of the land that became Craftsman Farms, however, was bought in the three-year period of 1909—1911, with the largest single purchase, about five hundred acres for which Stickley paid $5,600, completed in February 1910. Additional real estate transactions were still taking place as late as 1914, and Craftsman Farms eventually encompassed about six hundred and fifty acres of fields, hills, and woodlands.[6]

Stickley had become a successful and much wealthier man during the decade of 1900 to 1910, and he apparently spent about $200,000 developing Craftsman Farms. In marked contrast, he sold his Syracuse house in 1910 for only $8,500—furniture included.[7] His New Jersey land purchases reflected the greatly changed financial circumstances of the upwardly mobile Stickley. The head of a thriving enterprise, he had become accustomed to giving orders, and in his business dealings with others he could at times be brusque.

1 Detail of the strap-hinged #967 sideboard, oak, ca. 1902.

With a staggering lack of tact, he told the owner of an orchard plot he was trying to buy that "poor people have no right to own property." This family later remembered him as a man with "wonderful dreams" who could also be "rather ruthless."[8] These comments convincingly capture both sides of Stickley's character, and are quite at odds with the benignity of his carefully cultivated Craftsman persona.

It is unpleasant to think of Stickley's thoughtless behavior toward those farm dwellers whose lives he claimed he wanted to emulate. His years in the furniture business had evidently taught him that he was an exceptionally capable man, likely to be right in his judgments. He had also learned that on occasion it was necessary to be tough-minded and direct. He handled his land purchases at Craftsman Farms as his experiences of life and work had taught him, at times insensitive but always determined to fulfill its best possibilities and his own. Certainly he saw himself as the savior of properties that had been poorly managed and allowed to fall into disrepair. Recalling a day spent exploring the New Jersey countryside in search of likely real estate, Stickley spoke of stopping at "a shabby little farm cottage" where the stone walls marking the boundary lines had long since tumbled down. He looked in dismay at the fallow earth, and, he said, vowed to "come back to reclaim the land, pouring balm on its wounded sides, bringing sweet water down the hillsides to freshen it…covering the low hills with purple bloom and beautifying the sunny ridges with odorous fruit."[9] This statement is self-dramatizing and overwrought, as purple as the blooms it imagines on the hills; but it must be read as a prose style of another era. And if it masks it a hard reality—Stickley's acquisitiveness—it also contains a truth. Although his magazine sometimes overstated Stickley's achievements at Craftsman Farms, he did revitalize this land. A *Craftsman* article of 1910 portrayed him showing a visitor around the grounds, pointing out his recently completed roads, cottages, gardens, and orchards, and then exclaiming with obvious pleasure, "There was nothing here but abandoned farms when we began a year ago."[10]

Land reclamation, the transformation of barren country into fertile and profitable acreage through irrigation and improved agricultural practices, had been one of the leading themes of Stickley's planned California community, and it would be again at Craftsman Farms. In the first decade of the twentieth century, with the encouragement of President Theodore Roosevelt, conservation and land reclamation had become issues of national concern. A Reclamation Fund, established by Congress in 1902, provided money for irrigation projects for arid Western land, and, according to Roosevelt, this initiative would lead to "the securing of stable, self-supporting communities," populated by a "self-respecting, industrious yeomanry" that would work productively on the reclaimed land.[11] In 1908, the year Stickley began buying New Jersey land, Roosevelt assembled "idealistic, well-educated, middle-class professors, social critics, and government officials" for the first Country Life Conference.[12] With Roosevelt's energetic support, this meeting led eventually to the creation of the Country Life Movement. The participants in this "Movement"

adopted the back to the land ethos because, as they believed, simple, healthful country living held for many the promise of meaningful occupation, financial independence, and release from the urban crowding. Thus Stickley, a Roosevelt admirer, was reflecting enlightened thinking of his era when he envisioned a similar program that was to be put into practice at Craftsman Farms.

From its very beginnings, as with most of Stickley's undertakings, there was a duality to his view of Craftsman Farms. Seen from a purely commercial standpoint, it was an adjunct to his firm meant eventually to yield prestige and bring in healthy profits. Stickley initially announced his intention to build at least two factories on the site, one of them a furniture factory, and he planned to move freight in and out by connecting them with a spur to the nearby railroad line.[13] These manufacturing facilities, however, were never built, and by living at Craftsman Farms and working in New York City, Stickley—the furniture maker—put ever greater distance between himself and the part of the enterprise that he understood best: his factory in Eastwood, New York. Though financially a branch of Stickley's firm, the Farms had for him a second, non-mercantile meaning. It remained physically and symbolically apart, standing as an antidote to the stresses of commercial, urban life, a haven created "in quiet defiance of the discordant roar of the city."[14] At first Stickley referred to the Farms as a "Craftsman Village," in one sense reminiscent of the Guild of Handicraft's Cotswold workshops, and in another, more intimate sense, a nostalgic evocation of the Midwestern pioneer settlement of his youth. Describing an early morning walk with a visitor across the Farms' wooded acres, Stickley wrote in *The Craftsman* that "I regard as treasured possessions the recollections of my boyhood. Life was full of hardship and toil…but it was also full of exhilaration and interest….The smell of a forest today brings back to me my whole childhood."[15] This Proustian glance backward at years gone by also anticipates Stickley's near future: he almost seems to be contemplating the Chromewald—that is, "forest-color"—furniture that his firm would begin manufacturing in 1916.

Like Stickley's proposed western settlement, Craftsman Farms was meant to encompass a development of modest homes with garden plots and a colony of artisans who would practice their crafts in its beautiful, natural setting. Stickley also planned a Craftsman Farms school where students would be taught practical handicrafts while also learning the most up-to-date methods of farming. They would master these skills by doing hard, physical work that included constructing the cottages where they were to live: "As to the actual building of the houses" promised a *Craftsman* writer, "the students will be allowed to work side by side with experienced carpenters, stone masons, wood finishers, cabinetmakers, blacksmiths and coppersmiths."[16] They would have the further benefit of attending lectures on literature, music, and art, and Stickley himself would initiate them into the mysteries of woodcraft. And, like those Oxford students Ruskin had recruited decades earlier to do good works among the rural poor, they were also to be taught the useful art of making roads. Although Stickley's school program was hearty, pragmatic, and all-American, there was much of Ruskin about it. For instance, one of its guiding principles was Stickley's stated belief that "the laborer must use his brain and soul and use them well; the brain-worker must cultivate both interest and practical experience in manual endeavor. Only in this way shall we get the all-round

3

man."[17] Such thoughts are the Americanized descendants of Ruskin's famous injunction in "The Nature of Gothic" that "the workman ought often to be thinking, and the thinker often to be working, and both should be gentlemen, in the best sense."

Stickley's pedagogic views were in large measure adapted from ideas advanced by the American educator John Dewey (1859–1952) in his brief but influential treatise *The School and Society* (1899). *Craftsman* articles on the subject of education often reiterated concepts gleaned from Dewey's writings: a preference for practical experience over a too-great reliance on "book learning"; an emphasis on teaching handicraft skills to children; the belief that much of education must take place out-of-doors in contact with the natural world; and the sense that the household and the neighborhood were central to building character and inculcating habits of order, industry, and responsibility.[18] The school Stickley had in mind would lay great stress on vigorous physical activity and self-reliance. This emphasis on "manliness" grew in part out of his own youthful experience. As one *Craftsman* writer reflected, "the freedom of thought and

strength of individual conviction that characterized [Stickley's] remarkable and useful career…were due to that tremendous struggle against primitive conditions that marked the life of the pioneer settler forty years ago in what was then 'the West.'"[19] Yet Stickley was not merely responding to his own biography or to recent, progressive ideas about education; he was also aligning himself with some popular and commonly held ideas of his time.

In the late nineteenth and early twentieth centuries, the American West had taken shape in the public imagination as a place where neurasthenic Eastern youths could—by confronting harsh frontier realities—become tough, muscular, independent men. The three great exemplars of this tradition, as the historian G. Edward White has written, were the artist Frederic Remington, the writer (and Roosevelt friend) Owen Wister, and Theodore Roosevelt. All three were born in the East but then tempered during young manhood by sojourns in the rugged West, and each reached the height of his popularity in the first decade of the twentieth century, the years when Stickley began formulating his school plans.[20] Their almost exact contemporary, he certainly knew the well-

4

publicized stories of their undaunted Western exploits.[21] References to Remington and Roosevelt are scattered throughout *The Craftsman* magazine. Exhibitions of Remington's painting and sculpture were favorably noticed in the reviews section of *The Craftsman,* and in 1909 the magazine published a glowing profile of this most "virile" American artist.[22] Roosevelt's exhortative utterances were occasionally excerpted in the magazine—twice in 1910 during the time the Stickleys were settling in at Craftsman Farms—and in its editorial stance *The Craftsman* was a reliable supporter of his presidential policies. Savoring the memory of the challenges he had faced in his years as a range-riding cattle rancher and hunter, Roosevelt was to write in his *Autobiography* (1913): "We felt the beat of hardy life in our veins, and ours was the glory of work and the joy of living."[23] This eagerness for thrilling hardship was exactly what Stickley hoped to instill in the boys of his school.

Stickley's school plans continually shifted, as did his ideas on what to charge for tuition; some students, however, would be admitted free: "The boys that we have in mind for this school in citizenship are the less fortunate youths of the land, those who have not had the right kind of help from parents or friends."[24] Yet his altruism was necessarily tempered with pragmatism. Most of the boys would pay steep tuition fees so that the school could be self-sustaining. In pursuit of practical life experience, they would also provide Stickley with free labor for his farm: they were to hoe and dig, plow his fields, chop wood for his fireplaces, and build the cottages he planned to tuck into the wooded hillside of his estate. Stickley's school prospectus—his earnest "learn-by-doing" blueprint—recalls something of the whitewashing of Tom Sawyer's famous fence. As an additional source of revenue, and to teach his students that work had financial consequences, the garden produce they were to grow at the Farms would be sold locally and, it was hoped, bring in profits. As a writer in *The Craftsman* optimistically said, "We see no reason why a large sum cannot be earned each year by the school."[25]

Four years after announcing his school, still having attracted no students, Stickley conceded that he must have been doing something wrong. Yet his difficulty could not have simply been that his educational concepts were too

5

demanding or too innovative. In fact, long before Stickley conceived his Craftsman Farms school, there were successful, well-established English and American precedents. In the latter decades of the nineteenth century, for instance, boarding schools in the eastern United States were stressing preparation for "the 'active work of life' and spoke of boys 'standing on their own feet,' developing 'manly' attitudes, and learning to fend for themselves in the 'rough and tumble' game of life."[26] Perhaps the closest parallel to what Stickley had in mind was Interlaken, a school for boys in LaPorte, Indiana, which came to his attention when its superintendent, Raymond Riordon (1877–1940), submitted an unsolicited manuscript about Interlaken to *The Craftsman*. The magazine published it in May 1912.[27]

Riordon's essay—promoting his school and its methods—argued that true education came only partly from reading books, and that the most important lessons had to be learned "through labor—through work with the hands." Interlaken's goal, resonant of Ruskin's ideal "gentleman" and of Dewey's views as well, was to inculcate in its students both the "will to do" and the "power to think." Because it seemed so directly to validate his own personal and professional experiences, and stressed independence, diligence, and clear thinking as the necessary bases of a productive life, Stickley found the Interlaken program irresistible. It fitted his ideas exactly. Deciding that Riordon could solve his enrolment problem and realize his educational vision, he announced in the October 1912 issue of *The Craftsman* that this young and apparently successful educator had been brought in to oversee the school at Craftsman Farms.

One of Riordon's first assignments was to write a second promotional article for *The Craftsman*, this time on the Farms' school, sounding the by-now familiar themes and saying approvingly that Stickley "wants boys to grow up with the chance to labor, think and see life as he did in his youth. He wants them to have the advantage of hard work."[28] No stranger to Craftsman ideals, Riordon lived in Indiana in a Craftsman house modified for him by the Chicago architect George Washington Maher. He also had ties to Elbert Hubbard, and had formulated a program for him in 1911 that was nearly identical to the one he created for Stickley a year later. The Roycroft School of Life for Boys, in East Aurora, New York, did attract some students, but it never became a viable educational entity and Hubbard quietly closed it in February 1914.[29]

Stickley's ideas about his school were generous, public-spirited, inspired by extraordinary depths of kindness and a desire to do good, but in the end, unrealistic. He said he could accommodate fifty students but none arrived; even his staunchest partisans were evidently reluctant to hand over their sons' education to a school run by a furniture manufacturer. In 1913, in response to a fundraising campaign at the YMCA in nearby Morristown, Stickley donated $2,000 worth of Craftsman furniture for the use of its members.[30] He had been unable to muster a school of his own, but he could support institutions established for the benefit of the adolescent boys and young men he had once hoped to attract as students. And, with Stickley's initial though unspecified support,

4 The north end of the log house, looking toward Craftsman Farms pastures and the low hills beyond.

5 The Stickleys set out an informal assortment of decorative and functional family possessions on their dining room sideboard.

6
7

Riordon founded a boys' school in Highland, New York, in 1914. It followed the Interlaken model, and he ran this school successfully for the rest of his life.[31] By the fall of 1914, his foray into education thwarted, Stickley established the Craftsman School Bureau, a clearing house and advisory service for students and parents, providing information on private schools, and located in the men's Club Room in the Craftsman Building.

Craftsman Farms, as first conceived, was to be partly financed by a Stickley real estate venture. His idea was to set aside ten acres of the property to divide into half-acre plots and sell the land to families wishing to live a self-sufficient life in an area of rural beauty. He would then build a modest but artistic Craftsman house or bungalow for each family—which they would buy from him—and he expected that the shared concerns of the families living in these houses would inevitably lead them to form a cooperative community.

6 The living room in the log house and its tokens of comfortable family life: a library table with books and magazines, a piano, and, to the right, a big, open bookcase filled with books, ca. 1911.

7 The girls' bedroom on the second floor of the log house, ca. 1911.

8 The north end of the dining room: The ladderback chairs and footstools are Standard Stickley items; the round dining table, adorned with a Grueby bowl, and the corner cupboards are special order pieces.

As Stickley envisioned it, the men of this community would take the train each day to work in the city and come home in the evening to enjoy their families and restore themselves amid the peaceful greenery of the countryside; women and children would stay home and tend the gardens. This was not unlike the way that Stickley himself lived at Craftsman Farms. There was idealism in this real estate plan; it suggested Stickley's genuine quest to find a good way to live his life and to share that mode of living with others. In his prescient though not unprecedented vision of suburban living, he had become an early apostle of what David Shi has defined as "commuter pas-

toralism."[32] Stickley foresaw a tightly-knit neighborly community composed of small, unpretentious houses, built of local stone and wood, and in harmony with the natural environment. Even though he did not invent this idea, and achieved it only to a very limited degree, he became one of its vocal national advocates.[33] Because he had some taste for personal luxury he was perhaps not the perfect messenger, but his "small is beautiful" message was vital nonetheless. Stickley's nearly fifteen-year-long advocacy of houses built on a human scale—in tune with nature and with one another—places him in a long and honorable American tradition.

Of course, his plan to establish a residential community was also a means to bringing in needed capital. Even with the substantial monthly commissions he was earning from his firm, his personal wealth was not great enough to endow this undertaking on the scope that he envisioned. In the hope of finding funds to help pay for Craftsman Farms, Stickley, of necessity the inventive merchant, decided that with his real estate development program he would, in effect, buy land wholesale and sell it retail. If that notion sounds familiar it is because it is just what he had hoped to do in southern California in 1904.[34] And this plan had further echoes in his scheme of sub-leasing exposition floor space in the New York City Craftsman building to help subsidize the rent and generate income.

The house in which Stickley lived with his family at Craftsman Farms was the structure originally intended to serve as the club house for his ideal community.[35] This was the log house, a roomy, T-shaped structure of about 5,000 square feet with a first floor made of peeled and stained chestnut logs taken from the surrounding woods, and a second floor that was balloon-framed and sheathed in cedar shingles. Constructed by the Craftsman Home Building Company, it was begun in 1910 and completed in 1911, while the Stickleys were living in a cottage at the Farms. Giving readers a tour of the log house in a

8

Craftsman magazine article, the writer Natalie Curtis evoked its connections to tribal halls of medieval Germany, the heroic operas of Richard Wagner, and the Icelandic verse sagas of William Morris. In Curtis's view, the visible structure of the log house followed the traditions of Japanese timber construction, and she further saw the log house as a contemporary embodiment of that most mythic American archetype, the log cabin of the pioneers.[36] Yet the more apparent inspiration—the grand, log-built Adirondacks camps that the Stickleys had seen each year on their vacations—was curiously unmentioned by Curtis and in all other writings about Craftsman Farms. There was perhaps an even plainer motive: Stickley's daughter Barbara later said that building a log cabin had always been one of her father's dreams.[37]

Some of the furniture at the Farms was made of chestnut specifically for the log house, some came from the former Craftsman Building in Syracuse, and some was Standard Stickley available through Craftsman catalogs. Contemporary photographs of the living and dining rooms suggest that in furnishing his house, Stickley valued comfort, informality, sturdiness (and, no

doubt, cost-cutting where possible) over sheer style; this was a family home, not an arrangement of Craftsman model rooms. Still, he made these interiors as beautiful as he could. Following ideas he recommended to his customers, Stickley softened the effect of the heavy oak and chestnut pieces by interspersing lighter willow chairs and settles. Like the furniture, the downstairs walls and ceiling beams were predominantly brown, and the interior wood trim and the staircase were stained leaf green. The curtains, table runners, portieres, Craftsman and Donegal rugs, and other textiles, were burnt orange, green, pale gray, or yellow-green, and gleams of complementary colors were found in objects made of hammered copper, brass, and iron, and glazed ceramics.[38] This combination of harmonious colors and textures, wrote Curtis, "reminds one of the forest."

Family silver and china serving platters were set out in the dining room. They were perhaps visually discordant notes in this otherwise staunchly Arts and Crafts interior, but in his own home sentiment and convenience obviously mattered more to Stickley than stylistic purity. In describing these interiors in

The Craftsman, Curtis spoke of "the harmony of the carefully-designed furnishings with the more primitive dignity of the log construction," but she put greater emphasis on their charm, comfort, and "wide hospitable spaces." Even though Stickley's photographer must have rearranged and straightened things before photographing these rooms, they nevertheless had a relaxed, unpretentious, and lived-in appearance. The books and magazines in evidence in the living room, for instance, certainly served as photographic props; set out in casual stacks on the tops of library tables, however, they were also unassuming tokens of everyday life being lived at Craftsman Farms. Although they were handsome and generally harmonious, there was little evidence in these rooms of the artfully orchestrated "room as a work of art." That aspect of domestic architecture had absorbed Stickley during the Ellis era, but it was Stickley's more virtuosic contemporaries—among them Wright, the Greenes, Voysey, Baillie Scott, Mackintosh—who in their own domestic commissions had willed such cool and exquisite interiors into existence. Stickley's own house was noticeably a family home.

The bedrooms on the second floor of the log house contrasted with the more masculine, essentially brown and green, rooms downstairs. Gustav and Eda's master bedroom was done mainly in a sunny yellow (a reflection of Eda's taste?), and had a matte yellow Grueby tile fireplace. The small, rather cramped, bedroom of Gustav, Jr. is known to have had among its furnishings a pair of Craftsman beds with paneled head- and footboards. The girls' bedroom, shared by Mildred, Hazel, Marion, and Ruth, was blue and gray. Its walls were covered with a gray Japanese grasscloth, the fireplace was faced with blue Grueby tiles, and the furniture was gray oak inlaid with copper and precious woods tinted yellow-green, and, surprising for Stickley, a vivid gray-blue. A large, luxurious Oriental carpet covered most of the bedroom floor. In the words of Natalie Curtis, this room had "both delicacy and strength, and is thus appropriate to the ideal of the modern woman."

Stickley's expectations for Craftsman Farms were at best only partially met. The compound did not become a rural community, a garden suburb, an artisan colony, or a school; and it was apparently such a cash drain that it was never the corporate asset he had hoped for. It was, however, a fertile and well-stocked working farm and a home his family liked. It also had public relations value. Between 1908 and 1913, The Craftsman published at least eighteen articles focused on Stickley's vision of Craftsman Farms, and in several of them he was seen to be living simply, in a comfortable, unpretentious house. The Farms held up a model lifestyle for Stickley's readers/customers to emulate: within this rural setting of the kind idealized by the Arts and Crafts movement, it was perhaps the ultimate expression of his "Craftsman" persona. Yet over the previous decade the nature of that persona had shifted. In 1901, Stickley appeared in his publications in the guise of "Master of the Crafts," the reformist leader of a guild-like band of skilled and dedicated artisans thriving in a rural workshop. Now he had become "Master of Craftsman Farms," living, figuratively, off the land and fancifully imagining self-sufficiency: "As I walk over the fields and hills in the morning, I find that my home has grown up from my dream...[and] so rich is the development about me that the acres of Craftsman Farms supply its needs with much to spare from the dairy, chicken house and garden. Indeed if we were living in Medieval

times and a nearby New Jersey baron should decide to annex us, we could stand a siege for many a month living in peace and plenty."[39]

Stickley had first conceived of Craftsman Farms as a kind of summing up of all his Arts and Crafts aspirations, a little green Utopia. It became instead the beautiful, rustic country home and farm of a successful businessman, and it profoundly merged with his sense of self. By 1909, even before the log house was begun, Stickley had taken to referring to himself as a "farmer."[40] The Farms possessed productive gardens, peach, apple, plum, and cherry orchards with three thousand trees, and twelve acres of vineyards; Stickley said that he had one-hundred-and-fifty acres under cultivation. He also kept horses, a herd of Holstein cattle and had a fully populated chicken house that was two hundred feet long. A farm of this size required a regular crew of hired hands to keep it running. Stickley also employed a succession of Japanese and English gardeners and several domestic servants who did the family's cooking and cleaning. The house was amply staffed: "In our home," said Marion, "we had a man just to take care of the fireplaces."[41] Stickley was at last leading "the simple life," though on a fairly lavish scale; he preached the virtues of plainness while living in his "Craftsman manor house" and pursuing an active brand of leisure that required a measure of wealth.[42] "The simple life," as Stickley once observed, "is not necessarily the humble life."[43]

There may have been contradictions inherent in the way he lived—contradictions he seems never to have noticed—but there were admirable qualities as well. Stickley could have built a conventional country estate and retreated behind its gates, his privacy and comfort assured by his money. That would have been more sensible. Instead, he tried to create the kind of life for himself and his family that his magazine commended to its readers. This experiment in community ultimately foundered, and if its reality remained remote from Stickley's dream of what Craftsman Farms could be, it was still a sincere endeavor and, as things have turned out, one of his invaluable gifts to posterity.

At Craftsman Farms Gustav and Eda Stickley were once again sharing a home full time, though only a few brief, random glimpses survive to record their family's established routines. Stickley, as Marion remembered, rose each day at six, well before it was time to catch the train for his morning commute, and got his farm workers started on their chores.[44] Eda and her daughters who were still at home spent some of their daytime hours sewing and doing needlework, and in the summer the girls and their brother played tennis with friends. The children probably rode the Farms' horses. Marion, in her late teens, learned to drive one of her father's "omnibusses" on the Farms' roads, and Stickley, indulgent with his daughters, bought her a car of her own. In the evenings after dinner, Stickley, as had been his habit as long as his children could remember, sat and read. He favored biographies and art books; the boy who had been denied much formal education grew up to be the classic autodidact poring over books, unremitting in his pursuit of self-improvement and knowledge.[45]

The family followed a busy social schedule, though Stickley seems not to have often entertained friends. His visitors were mostly people associated with his work; writers from The Craftsman magazine regularly visited Craftsman Farms. His

9 In the living room at Craftsman Farms, Stickley used both oak and willow Craftsman furniture, exactly as he advised his customers to do in their own homes.

10   11

daughters gave large parties and dances, holding the first one in July 1911, shortly after the family moved into the log house. Stickley encouraged the girls' socializing. He had his factory make a batch of tenon-and-keyed Craftsman sawhorses so that extra, temporary dining tables could easily be set up for the guests. There were parties at the house "all the time," recalled Marion. "My father wanted us to have fun."[46] The Craftsman willow furniture in the living room was, in addition to its aesthetic qualities, easy to move aside to make space for dancing. Gustav and Eda were considerate parents: while their daughters and friends danced downstairs, they would stay upstairs in their room, contented by the fireplace.[47]

There were family weddings and vacations. In January 1913, with Barbara married to Ben Wiles and Ruth still in school, Eda took Mildred, Hazel, and Marion on a cruise to Bermuda—a vacation that took place just a few months before Stickley announced the opening of the New York City Craftsman Building. One of the few known photographs of Eda, stately in a well-tailored suit, her face veiled against the Bermuda sun, survives from this winter trip. In September 1915, six months after the bankruptcy of her father's firm, Mildred was married in the flower garden at Craftsman Farms. And, in June 1916, Marion's wedding took place on the long front porch of

the log house. At all these festive events the house was filled with banks of fresh-cut flowers, the grounds were lit by garlands of Japanese lanterns, and a dance orchestra played late into the night. All three married daughters moved into cottages on the property; Stickley, as he had dreamed of doing, had created a bucolic family compound, and was happy to have his extended family close to home.

Life was in many ways an idyll for the Stickleys at Craftsman Farms; Stickley called it his "Garden of Eden." But it was an imperfect paradise. Even though "Gustav was always good to Eda," he was almost wholly absorbed by his work, and she sometimes felt isolated and lonely at the Farms, probably even more so than in Syracuse.[48] Entertaining Stickley's business associates had to have been stressful for this shy, retiring woman.[49] The unhappiest person at Craftsman Farms, however, was Gustav Stickley, Jr. "[My father] grew up on the farm," said Gustav Stickley III. "He hated it. I guess my grandfather…was a very demanding individual."[50] Even before moving to New Jersey, Gustav, Jr. had been packed off to a military academy near Syracuse in Manlius, New York; several times he ran away from school. At Craftsman Farms he was expected, as were his sisters, to do his share of chores, but he could never do them to his father's satisfaction. As liberal as Stickley was with his daughters he was strict with his son and

unwilling—or perhaps unable—to show his boy affection. Alienated from his stern father, Gustav, Jr. turned to the one other family member who, like him, was slightly out of her element in the determinedly hardy environment of Craftsman Farms: his mother, who "doted on him."[51]

Reading the descriptions of the grueling educational regimen Stickley outlined for his school at the Farms, it is impossible not to see it as an externalization of his conflict with his son. Gustav, Jr. was about fourteen when the school was first announced, a source of frustration to his father, and exactly the age of the students Stickley sought. Stickley clearly wanted his son—the child of a comfortably well-off East Coast family—to experience something of what he now saw as the character-enhancing frontier conditions of his own early life. The Craftsman magazine had once approvingly quoted some thoughts of Theodore Roosevelt that Stickley must have found particularly relevant to life as he had come to see it:

10 Eda Stickley in Bermuda, January 1913.
11 Gustav Stickley, Jr., ca. 1910.
12 Some of the Stickley family at Craftsman Farms, left to right, Gustav, Jr., Mildred, unidentified woman, Marion, Marion's husband Carl Preim, and Gustav; the young girls are Stickley's granddaughters, Edith and Barbara Wiles, ca. 1917.

I ask only that what every self-respecting American man demands from himself, and from his sons, shall be demanded of the American nation as a whole....You work yourselves, and you bring up

your sons to work. If you are rich, and worth your salt, you will teach your sons that though they may have leisure, it is not to be spent in idleness....We admire the man...who has the virile qualities necessary to win in the stern strife of actual life."[52]

While his school was still in its early planning stages, Stickley said in a *Craftsman* magazine article that the whole undertaking would prove worthwhile "even if it educate no other boy than my own to what I believe a man should be."[53] Gustav, Jr. had other ideas. He eventually fled Craftsman Farms, joined the Navy and served on the troopship *Leviathan* during World War One. After the war he stayed briefly with his father in Syracuse, and then took a traveling job with the Happiness Candy Company, and spent the next several years on the road.[54]

At Craftsman Farms we see something of Stickley's strengths and shortcomings as husband, father, countryman, and neighbor. We also sense his delight in his daughters, his joy in creating the only home he would ever build, and his deep satisfaction in working out of doors, directing his farm hands, and bringing fallow land back to life. Following his bankruptcy, Stickley lost Craftsman Farms, and his once close-knit family scattered. But, for the moment, he was playing a role he delighted in: he was the Master of Craftsman Farms, tilling the soil, in charge, and fully alive. "My father," said Marion, "loved our farm."

In September 1914, *Craftsman* readers must have been surprised to come upon an advertisement for a "New Craftsman Dining-Room Suite," a grouping of fumed oak Stickley furniture that included a vaguely Hepplewhite-like sideboard. This sideboard had machine-stamped "brass trim" in place of the customary hand-hammered copper hardware of Standard Stickley, the back of the china cabinet was lined with velvet, in "any color desired," and both pieces were ornamented with contrasting bands of inlaid wood. This bland assemblage was promoted as "a new and interesting departure in Craftsman Furniture." Another advertisement in this issue offered "Five Pieces from Our Chinese Chippendale Set," made of "hand-rubbed and hand-carved" mahogany. More of the firm's recent furniture, adapted from period styles, appeared the following month. In the unsigned article "An American Style in Furnishing," these recent designs were said to represent a logical and desirable evolution of Craftsman design. "Mr. Stickley's latest models," claimed the article's anonymous author, "retain the old ideal of simplicity, with an added sumptuousness." Thus began the outpouring of eclectic and unconvincing revivalist furniture that Stickley would publish in his magazine for the remainder of its existence. Because it had been more than a year since his firm had been profitable, he must have felt that he had no choice but to reduce his reliance on the forthright Arts and Crafts wares he was known for and introduce new and different designs that he hoped would appeal to the widest possible market.

Descriptions of this new work in *The Craftsman* magazine emphasized its ability to harmonize with any domestic interior, with any style of furniture. Largely abandoning the muted tones of the embroidered and appliquéd Craftsman textiles of earlier years, Stickley photographed this furniture against backgrounds of figured linens and boldly colored flowered chintzes in

tune with "the prevailing vogue for bright pattern." He and his designers (whose names remain untraced) had to come up with something new to revitalize the firm, and they had little time to do it. Suggesting the great time pressures they were facing, the caption under one of the new period-style pieces shown in *The Craftsman* in December 1915 admitted, "The drawer and door pulls have not yet been put on."[1]

Making an effort now to follow trends instead of set them, the firm experimented with painted furniture. In 1916, in addition to the vibrantly patterned fabrics and decorative accessories he was now recommending, Stickley introduced a line of furniture with vivid hues applied to the surface of the wood. He named it "Chromewald." Its distinctiveness came from what was said to be its elaborate finishing process: the wood was sanded smooth, polished with a pigmented oil, and then fumed a deep brown. As a final and unique step, the surface was given a coat of gray or blue or brown paint that was hand-rubbed to reveal the lush brown wood tones underneath.[2] Writing about Chromewald in *The Craftsman*, Mary Fanton Roberts described it as having "a velvety finish that was like looking through a mirror at the wood, and every inch of the surface seemed to vary in tone." Chromewald's great claim was that it harmonized beautifully with all colors, and readers were assured that it was modish and thoroughly up to date, and also charming, old-fashioned, and quaint.[3] As his enterprise inexorably neared its end, a constant stream of such promotional messages flowed freely through the pages of *The Craftsman* magazine. The past fifteen years of Arts and Crafts furniture production had been trumped by designs that were merely ordinary, and the eras of early Stickley and Standard Stickley receded into memory.

1 Detail of a 1916 Chromewald chest, with its distinctive surface of hand-rubbed blue paint.

2

3

Stickley did everything he could to make Chromewald a success. In the summer of 1916 he introduced it to retailers at the Grand Rapids Furniture Exposition; he had shunned this trade show every year since the New Furniture launch in 1900, but now, with his new wares, he urgently needed greater distribution than he had ever had before. Eager to please the merchants and buyers attending the show (their numbers thinned because of the war), he stocked his display space with cigars to hand out as promotional favors. But the most remarkable part of the campaign to sell Chromewald was "One Man's Story," an article by Mary Fanton Roberts published in the May 1916 issue of *The Craftsman*. The man, though not named, was of course Gustav Stickley, and there was real ambivalence in the way Roberts described him. Her text was blatantly promotional. Depicting herself standing next to a Chromewald couch, she said:

> So clear, so beautifully finished was the surface of the wood that it harmonized exquisitely with every color.... As one studied the proportion of the couch, the tone of the wood, the depth of it, and the richness, its constant variation in every change of light, it seemed almost to have the quality of a Stradivarius violin....One's first impression of such a wood finish is that it must be a very fragile thing....But this is not true of the new Chromewald furniture. It is, so far as we reckon time in speaking of furniture, imperishable; it will not check, crack, split or warp. The color will not wear off.[4]

Yet there was equally a genuine sadness in this article, a sadness that Roberts, who had worked closely with Stickley for more than a decade, must have felt nearly as deeply as he did. Some of her promotional passages had an unmistakably bittersweet quality. She described Stickley, in his quest to create Chromewald, as a man "living with his woods and his colors as a musician lives with his instrument, dreaming far into the future." And she concluded her musings with the thought that Stickley "had somehow endowed [Chromewald] with the memories of the woodland days." Here again is that poignant remembrance of "forest color," the avatar of Stickley's Midwestern childhood. When Roberts's article appeared, more than a year had passed since the firm had gone into bankruptcy. While never referring directly to that calamitous financial event, she nevertheless used astonishingly candid language to depict Stickley's emotional state. He felt "broken" and "bewildered." He was overcome by "sorrow," "seeming failure," "isolation," even "despair." Though purportedly written to stir enthusiasm for Chromewald, "One Man's Story" was an odd,

2 Advertisement for the "New Craftsman Dining-Room Suite," from *The Craftsman*, September 1914.

3 Chromewald library table and willow chair against a chintz background, from *The Craftsman*, May 1916.

4 A 1916 Chromewald chest of drawers, with turned legs reminiscent of the turnings seen on furniture made by The Gustave Stickley Company in 1898 and 1899. This piece has descended in the family of Barbara Stickley Wiles.

4

5

6

affecting, and in places painfully frank essay laced with intimations that Chromewald was fated to be Stickley's final gesture. It had the quality of an elegy, a last, heartfelt goodbye to a fallen giant, although Stickley would tenaciously battle on for nearly another year.

Stickley's woes were partly caused by changes in the American cultural landscape, and mass-circulation periodicals of this era, such as *Good Housekeeping*, provide a telling index of shifting popular taste. In 1905, for instance, the magazine began a handicraft department. It continued to publish frequent feature articles on Arts and Crafts subjects into the early years of the next decade. In 1912, however, the magazine published a monthly series on interior decorating by Elsie de Wolfe (1865–1950), and by this time *Good Housekeeping*, like most popular periodicals, had essentially stopped running articles about the Arts and Crafts. The visibly hand-wrought qualities of Craftsman wares were beginning to look dated in a world increasingly drawn, on one hand, to antique quaintness and Colonial charm, and, on the other, to bright color and cosmopolitan sophistication. These antithetical trends were evident not just in the popular media of the day but in the pages of *The*

Craftsman as well. An article in the April 1913 issue praised, without reservation, the unCraftsman-like clapboard-sided, white painted "modern Colonial house" that it said many American architects were then beginning to build. In another article, in May 1913, Roberts wrote exuberantly about the just-ended Armory Show, describing "the wave of excitement upon which the Cubist and Futurist painters floated into New York....Matisse and Cézanne were household words. We learned how to pronounce Gaugin correctly and ceased to shy at Rédon's colors." Two years later, in *The Craftsman* for December 1915, Roberts told her readers that the bold, vivid sets and costumes that Léon Bakst had created for the Ballets Russes had influenced "the color sense of the entire world."[5] Although her enthusiasm led her to into hyperbole, Roberts was certainly right about the obvious fact of changing American tastes. Stickley was compelled to fashion a response to this drastically changed environment.

This response was a lame one. Under more favorable circumstances, and given more time, Stickley's historicizing furniture styles might have had some success. But by renouncing the furniture that had expressed his Craftsman principles of refined simplicity and structural honesty, and turning instead to furniture that he made because he hoped it was what people wanted to buy, he sacrificed those distinctive qualities that—while not then widely understood or appreciated—had long set his products apart. Fighting for economic survival, Stickley had transformed himself once again. This time, however, though it was far from what he intended, he became a furniture manufacturer like a hundred others, and his pedestrian reproduction wares of 1915–1916 looked very much like furniture made by other unimaginative American manufacturers at that time. About forty pieces of Stickley's Chromewald were said to have been made, and little was sold. The remainder he gave to his children.[6]

The problems caused by slowing sales of Craftsman furniture and Stickley's inability to find a successful alternative were made fatal by the firm's imprudent business decisions, and on 23 March 1915, Gustav Stickley The Craftsman Incorporated was forced to declare bankruptcy.[7] Stickley's over-optimism had led him to spend too freely on The Craftsman magazine and on Craftsman Farms and, in his most misguided step of all, on the vast and costly New York City Craftsman Building.[8] An IRS inspector, poring over the books of the defunct firm in 1919 and looking to extract more taxes, wrote to his supervisor that "A superficial examination of the books for the period from June 1, 1914 to March 31, 1915 show [sic] that heavy losses were incurred through the operation of the New York store and the loss is apparently so large that ... I don't believe that enough additional tax could be found to off-set this loss....The returns on file show the company ... sustained a loss in each year since 1912. They had to borrow money in order to [cover operating expenses and repay loans]."[9]

Stickley's financial vulnerability was compounded by the world events that were about to divert people's attention from the everyday domestic pleasures of furnishing their homes. Ten months after he confidently opened the Craftsman Building, Europe went to war. Stickley's initial optimism about his new building, although easy to fault in hindsight, was not unfounded. His expectation of ongoing healthy trade conditions, in fact, simply reflected what was then the conventional wisdom of the American furniture industry.

The state of trade can be tracked through periodic reports in Furniture Trade Review. Ninety years later, knowing the mortal damage about to be inflicted on Stickley's firm, these brief editorial notes make chilling reading. On 10 November 1913, the exact moment that the new Craftsman Building was beginning to welcome customers, the editor of Furniture Trade Review, William Berri, published an enthusiastic lead item headed "A BRIGHT OUTLOOK" and commented: "It seems to be the consensus ... that in the furniture industry, as well as others, there is a clear field ahead for a confident expansion of business. Not that there is anything in the nature of an unhealthy boom in sight, but a safe and stable business that is the foundation of a sure prosperity." By 10 May 1914, Berri was qualifying his earlier certainty: "[T]here has been some perceptible slackening of business....a shortage in the movement of goods compared with previous seasons." By 10 August he could only throw up

5 Keeping pace with changing tastes, the colors on The Craftsman covers became brighter and more vivid in the last two years the magazine was published.

6 The revival-style furniture made by Stickley's firm in 1915 and 1916 was little different from wares then being offered by other manufacturers, as evidenced, for instance, by this dining set made by the Imperial Furniture Company and advertised in Furniture Trade Review, 10 June 1915.

his hands. "With the loosing of the dogs of war ... one man's guess is as good as another's regarding the effect upon the trade of the United States." Although he tried each month to remain upbeat, Berri had to concede on 10 November 1914 that "the aggregate furniture output of the country for the entire fall is of course diminished, compared with last year." Stickley was not immune to the effects of cataclysmic world events that he, like others in his industry, had failed to foresee. Had he not been so heavily burdened with overhead and debt in 1913 and 1914, he might have ridden out the weakened retail market of the war years. That was not to be.

The newspaper reports on the bankruptcy clarify the impact of bad decision-making, unlucky timing, and, in 1913—the year Stickley moved into the Craftsman Building—a sharp rise in short-term interest rates that abruptly raised his cost of borrowing.[10] This was the lethal combination that forced the failure of Stickley's firm. According to one newspaper account, "The leasing of the twelve-story building on thirty-ninth street exclusively for Craftsman uses is responsible for the receivership proceedings.... When the corporation signed the twenty year lease about a year ago there was not enough surplus on hand to carry the expenditure, it is said, but ... the venture would have turned out all right if it had not been for the tightening of the money market during the war."[11] The brief New York Times article about the bankruptcy unwittingly underlined the extent to which Stickley's aesthetic, even after fifteen years of Craftsman proselytizing, remained little understood. "[T]he assets consist mostly of furniture of a peculiar style that ... if sold at auction ... would go at great sacrifice."[12]

Manufacturing ceased during the three months following the bankruptcy, and the court-appointed receiver representing the firm's many creditors, a man named William Henkel, began selling store fixtures and available merchandise to raise cash. Henkel offered to pay the creditors one-third of the amounts due to them, but most rejected the offer and then, as a group, they took the additional step of issuing a formal statement expressing their lack of confidence in the firm's ability to survive.[13] The Craftsman Restaurant, which had most likely been a money-losing venture all along, was closed, although unaccountably it reopened the following October. A few months later, however, it closed for good and its fixtures were quickly liquidated. In further need of cutting its overhead, the firm closed its Boston and Washington stores and canceled their leases.

His retail and wholesale business in tatters, Stickley continued to publish The Craftsman magazine. By March 1915 the Craftsman Publishing Company was losing money and it was $25,000 in debt to the Pacific Bank of New York and owed an additional $10,000 to the parent organization, Gustav Stickley The Craftsman Incorporated. For all its financial troubles, however, The Craftsman had become the part of his enterprise that meant most to Stickley, and in the twenty issues published after the bankruptcy the magazine continued to offer its readers substantive Arts and Crafts articles that have proved to have lasting importance, including contributions by the architects Irving Gill and Bertram Goodhue and articles on Marblehead Pottery and the ceramist Henry Chapman Mercer. It is true that the magazine had become an increasingly shrill publicity outlet promoting the firm's new furniture styles, but it is hard to imagine that most Craftsman readers would have been anything but bemused by Stickley's latest wares.

Lacking the cash to subsidize his magazine any longer, and in no position to obtain credit, Stickley covered the cost of monthly publication—starting with the May 1915 issue—by assigning the magazine's advertising revenue directly to its printer, Ernest F. Eilert of the Blumenberg Press. Six months later Eilert joined the Craftsman Publishing Company's board of directors, and, having made his printer his partner, it was apparently Stickley's pay-as-you-go approach to publishing that kept the magazine afloat another year. Another new board member arrived during the magazine's waning days; this was Bessie Coons Rogers, a Stickley employee who, in 1912, had married Stickley's long-time friend and business associate, the widowed G. Tracy Rogers. She had joined, presumably, to speak for her husband's interests. Most advertisers had left the flagging magazine by the time the November and December 1916 issues appeared, however, and publication ceased at year's end. On 20 November 1916, Gustav Stickley resigned as president and director of the Craftsman Publishing Company. In January 1917, *The Craftsman* was absorbed into another periodical, the *Art World*, and in May of that year several *Craftsman* editors launched a magazine called *The Touchstone*, but Stickley's involvement with publishing had come to an end.

Craftsman Farms was also in jeopardy. A summary of the assets and liabilities of Stickley's firm, dated 18 March 1915 and apparently drawn up by an accountant retained by his creditors, includes the accountant's comment that "I have not put in the farm as an asset for the reason that there is a first mortgage of $50,000 due to the bank on it and I doubt at a forced sale there would be any equity coming to us from that."[14] Shortly after the bankruptcy, Stickley raised $50,000—somewhat recklessly it would seem—by taking out a second mortgage in that amount on Craftsman Farms from the Pacific Bank of New York. He also borrowed $50,000 from G. Tracy Rogers in July of that year, pledging his real estate holdings and his life insurance as security. In the fall he went back to Rogers and borrowed $19,000 more, and eventually his indebtedness to Rogers grew to nearly $100,000. The company struggled mightily to keep itself afloat.

Despite these huge infusions of cash, things quickly unraveled. In May 1916, Stickley announced that his retail store now occupied only the second and third floors of the Craftsman Building.[15] The following month he mailed Craftsman stockholders the corporation's semiannual report; he needed to print only fifty copies. This one-page letter calmly made the extraordinary announcement that the firm was giving up retailing to "devote all of our attention in the future to the wholesale business."[16] Left unsaid was the obviously painful fact that the retail venture in the New York City Craftsman Building had been a colossal waste of money.

Also left unsaid was the fact that the decisions to make these cutbacks had not come from Stickley. They had been urged on him by G. Tracy Rogers. Gustav Stickley The Craftsman Incorporated was now operating largely on Rogers's capital, and to protect his interests Rogers injected himself into the management of the enterprise. Although Stickley retained the title of president, and continued to play the role of the firm's public face, Rogers was now on the payroll and earning a larger salary than Stickley. As the corporation's secretary, an attorney named Howard E. Brown, wrote to a stockholder in October 1915,

7 By late 1915, G. Tracy Rogers had taken control of Stickley's enterprise.

"Mr. Stickley is at present permitted to draw only just enough salary from the Company to live on in the most economical way … Mr. Rogers and the bank virtually control the policy of the Company."[17] Stickley, in other words, was no longer in charge. Some of the firm's uncharacteristic initiatives in the final year and a half of its existence—for instance, its enthusiasm for the prosaic Chromewald furniture—can perhaps best be explained by the presence of the forceful and very determined G. Tracy Rogers, keeping an eye on his money.

As 1916 ended and 1917 began, it was increasingly unlikely that the firm could be returned to profitability and that Stickley would ever regain control. Yet he tried. Although living at Craftsman Farms and working daily in Manhattan, he seems to have traveled by train to Syracuse every week to supervise activities at his factory. When he wasn't at the factory he was in his New York office firing off impatient telegrams to his Eastwood lieutenants: "Express at once samples of Chromewald as per letter," demanded one message. Another asked, "When will you ship single bed Wanamaker. Also Wilmot order. Wire immediately."[18] According to Howard E. Brown, Stickley was hard at work sixteen hours a day and "[t]he nervous strain is about all that he can possibly stand."[19]

Stickley's determination and energy and, it must be said, his desperation, are evident throughout the final months of his failing firm, and so is his personal integrity. His business enterprise bereft of cash, he did what he could to reward his few stockholders with their expected income, and in January 1917 he sent out small dividend checks drawn from his personal bank account.[20] The month before, however, there had been a reorganization that he had had no choice but to accept, and in December 1916 he and his brothers Leopold and J. George (and a few months later Albert), formed Stickley Associated Cabinetmakers, an amalgamation of L. & J.G. Stickley, Inc., Stickley Brothers Company of Grand Rapids, and Gustav Stickley The Craftsman Incorporated that lasted until 1919. Leopold Stickley was president of this firm, Gustav Stickley vice-president.[21] Leaving their children for the present at Craftsman Farms, Gustav and Eda Stickley headed back to Syracuse, and in late February or early March of 1917 they moved into the Wolcott, a local boarding house. According to tradition, Gustav and Eda had separated by this time, but that is not true; in this period of crisis they stayed together.[22]

Stickley now divided his time between what had once been his factory in Eastwood and the L. & J.G. Stickley factory in Fayetteville. His duties for this new firm also brought him at times to its general offices and wholesale showroom on the third floor of 6 East Thirty-ninth Street, the former Craftsman Building. At the same time he worked briefly for the Simmons Company of Kenosha, Wisconsin, a firm that billed itself as "The World's Largest Makers of Metal Beds and Springs." Although he was still trying to sell Craftsman and Chromewald furniture, in March 1917 Stickley—perhaps having learned a thing or two from Simmons—filed a patent application for his recent invention, a couch that could be readily converted to a single or double bed, and a year or so later he and Leopold formed the Stickley Extension Bed Company, Inc., of Syracuse, New York, to manufacture and market their "couch bed."[23] In April 1917, America entered World War One, and that must have effectively ended all of Stickley's hopes of reviving his moribund Craftsman enterprise. The following year, the firm's remaining common stock was divided equally among three partners: one-third to Gustav Stickley, one-third to Leopold Stickley, and one-third to G. Tracy Rogers.[24]

7

The realities of Stickley's personal life during the year or two after the bankruptcy remain unclear. His high-profile failure certainly shattered his spirit. Stickley's strength finally faltered, and the will power he had always been able to summon "was just not there....figuratively speaking and almost literally speaking he just walked away."[25] According to tradition, Stickley had a nervous breakdown—an acute immobilizing depression—and was briefly hospitalized.[26] This episode apparently occurred in 1917, shortly after the dissolution of the Craftsman enterprise, because surviving minutes of Stickley Associated Cabinetmakers' board meetings show that Stickley was usually absent, and that his long-time aide, Frederick Arwine, generally attended these meetings as his proxy. Stickley's despondency in the period following the bankruptcy is palpable in a letter he sent from the Stickley Associated Cabinetmakers offices on 19 October 1917. Addressed to Howard E. Brown, it said, in its entirety: "I will be here tomorrow all day and would like to see you some time. Preferably in the morning, but it won't matter much. I can be here any time to suit your convenience."[27] Along with his business failure and his own temporary emotional breakdown, there was the added anguish of Eda's illness. In 1917, at the age of fifty-seven, she suffered a paralyzing stroke.

Craftsman Farms was sold in August 1917 to George and Sylvia Farny. The sales price was reported to be $100,000, but the actual amount was closer to $60,000, and included the furniture and farm equipment. The bank holding the first mortgage on the Farms threatened foreclosure, and to avoid the financial losses that foreclosure would inevitably bring, the property was offered for sale through several brokers. There was only one offer—from the Farnys—and it was immediately accepted. The decisions about the disposition of Craftsman Farms were made not by Stickley but by G. Tracy Rogers.[28]

In 1918, Stickley moved out of the boarding house and was renting the upper floor of a modest two-family house at 832 Sumner Avenue, in Syracuse, and three of his children, Hazel, Ruth, and Gustav, Jr., now returned from the Navy, were living with him. Barbara and her family were living nearby in a tiny house at 1010 Westcott Street, and Mildred and her husband and daughter had rented half of a two-family house at 137 Roosevelt Avenue. Only Marion stayed in New Jersey, moving with her husband to the town of East Orange. Eda lived the final two years of her life being cared for in Mildred's home, and she is remembered by two of her granddaughters only as a mute presence, immobile in a large wicker chair, her feet propped on a stool, a shawl wrapped tightly around her shoulders.[29] The Syracuse addresses where Stickley and his children lived in these years are all within a few blocks of one another, separated by no more than a short walk, and their closeness bears witness to the fact that the member of this family, while now occupying separate houses, were in truth still together. In the two or three years following Gustav's bankruptcy and Eda's stroke, both were in "great distress," and "needed care."[30] The eldest daughters, Barbara and Mildred, became the family's responsible adults, nursing their mother, bolstering their disconsolate father, and caring for their younger siblings.

8 Advertisement for Stickley's toy company, Lustre Wood Products, from the trade journal *Toys and Novelties*, August 1920.

9 Stickley and his daughter Marion, ca. early 1930s.

As the Arts and Crafts scholar Coy L. Ludwig has discovered, Stickley and Ben Wiles went into the toy business in June 1919. They and two partners incorporated their new firm, Lustre Wood Products Company, and declared their intention to manufacture and market "toys, novelties, wood products, furniture."[31] Stickley was named president. For at least two years, in 1920 and 1921, Lustre Wood Products Company set up a display at Toy Fair, the major industry trade show then held at the Hotel Imperial in New York City, and Stickley helped man the booth. The firm offered its "Priscilla" doll cradle ("decorated with attractive pictures of the story of Priscilla as told by Longfellow"), the "Bluebird" child's table and bench, the "Skooner," and other wooden toys and children's furniture. All of these pieces were offered in the firm's "beautiful 'chrome lustre' finish," an apparent reincarnation of Chromewald, available in three colors: "Old Ivory," "Sky Blue," and "Goldenrod." How Stickley felt about finding himself in the toy business is not known, but it was a reasonable step for him to take. He had certainly learned something about that business when Helen Speer had designed children's furniture for him at the Craftsman Building in 1915. Beyond that, he had expertise in woodworking, wood finishing, and furniture design and marketing, and he had contacts among suppliers to whom he could subcontract the production of these goods. He was in his early sixties, he wanted to keep active and he needed to earn an income, and his admirable son-in-law Ben Wiles helped set him up in business. There is no record of Lustre Wood Products after 1921, but by that time Stickley had moved on to other things. He was thinking once again about one of the lasting passions of his life. He decided to invent a new kind of furniture finish.

It is generally known that Stickley lived the last quarter-century of his life with his daughter Barbara and her family in the Columbus Avenue house in Syracuse that he had remodeled years before. She and Ben bought it—with most of its Craftsman furniture still in place—in 1919. After Eda's death Stickley moved in, taking over a third floor bedroom and claiming it as his own. He did not, however, live only in that house. He spent about half of his time with Barbara in Syracuse and perhaps an equal amount with Mildred, who moved to Rochester in 1925.[32] Occasionally Stickley would spend three or four weeks with Gustav, Jr. and his wife Gladys; they, too, were now in Rochester, having moved there at Stickley's request in about 1926. He told his son that he had perfected a formula for a revolutionary wood finish that he was planning to sell to furniture manufacturers, and he intended to set up a company to market this finish. He wanted Gustav, Jr. to come in with him, but in the end Stickley decided that the finish wasn't ready and needed further work. His plans for this commercial undertaking were shelved, his son began looking for a paying job, and Stickley went back to experimenting.[33]

Throughout the late 1920s and into the 1930s Stickley remained obsessed by furniture finishes. He experimented continually, usually in his room in the Wiles's home, and a grandson, Ben Wiles, Jr., remembered that although Stickley dressed neatly and invariably wore a tidy black bow tie, "his work clothes would be stained with layers of discarded furniture finish formulas, and sometimes [he used] a rope for a belt to preserve his belt for more important times. But even in his work clothes his presence commanded respect."[34]

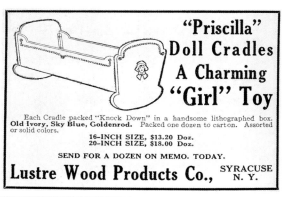

8

9

10

A granddaughter, Edith Wiles Bradford, recalled that Stickley seemed to spend all of his time either concocting furniture finishes or talking about furniture finishes. "His mind was going all the time," she said, "but the family knew he was dreaming."[35]

Between June 1930 and June 1933, Stickley wrote several times to Mildred—who was then, like many others in Depression-era America, going through hard financial times—and to her teenage daughter Ruth.[36] These few letters seem to be the only personal correspondence of Stickley's that has survived. When he wrote them he was in his early seventies, still clinging to the unrealistic dream that he could earn a living with his new furniture finishes. These letters are stark evidence of his penury in his later years, but they also show—whatever his earlier failings may have been—that he was a good father and grandfather. These letters are radiant, although Stickley's ability to spell and to form grammatically coherent sentences was always a little tentative. They reveal essential truths about Stickley's character: his love of family; his determination to reassure his daughter and lift her spirits; his tenacity with his furniture finish experiments,

10 Stickley with his daughter Mildred, her daughter Ruth (standing beside him), and five of his Wiles grandchildren, in Skaneateles, New York, ca. 1923.

11 A simple, Shaker-like chair, made by Stickley for one of his grandchildren in the late 1930s.

12 Gustav and Eda Stickley's grave markers in the Morningside Cemetery in Syracuse.

even in the face of repeated disappointments; and his never-ending need to dream big dreams. These are excerpts:

June 16, 1930

To Mildred and Ruth: "Your special [delivery letter] was certainly a most pleasant surprise, & added much to the enjoyment of the day. I am especially grateful for the enclosed as I needed it very badly....We are only here [Skaneateles, New York, at the Wiles's lakeside cottage] for the day, but are cumming out for good the last of this week....As for myself I have now arrived at a point where the finish is perfectly satisfactory & ...everything is very promising & I ought to soon begin to show results."

August 2, 1930

To Mildred and Ruth: "Dupont Co...sent an expert to look into [my finish]...he cam to the cottage & stayed until two in the morning. After that I meet him in Syracuse & he finished some sample pannells himself....It shure all looks good to me as I am shure I can satisfy them....It shurely is good of you to write me so often."

November 2, 1930

To Mildred: "It is always a great source of disappointment to me when I think of the years I have spent in trying to perfect my finish & as time goes on I think

11

12

more & more that it was a mistake. But however that may be it cant be helped now, & and I am more than thankful to be able to tell you that at last there are definite signs of success in the near future. I am back with the Simonds Co again & am having splendid results [the firm founded in 1902 by his former partner, the late Elgin Simonds, was still in business]. I have just sold them my first order for 300 pounds & they gave me a ck in advance so now I have a little money in my pocket & that is something to be thankful for isn't it."

Despite his chronic lack of money and his inability to start any kind of viable business, Stickley achieved a kind of contentment during the 1920s and 1930s. A summer snapshot, taken in Skaneateles in about 1923, shows him with some of his family. Stickley has put on weight and a comfortable paunch pushes out the front of his buttoned cardigan. His mustache has reappeared, fuller now, and he seems serene and benign, yet his face betrays perhaps a hint of resignation. These grandchildren would grow up to have mixed feelings about their once-famous grandfather. Some felt lingering resentment that he had paid so little attention to Eda and their children during the heady years of Craftsman success; others held on to memories of him as a kind and delightful childhood companion, a good listener and fascinating talker, always dignified, impressive, charismatic. In time they came to see him as a great man, if an imperfect one, an imaginative but impractical dreamer.

In the late 1930s, as Stickley entered his eighties, he was often to be found at the factory of the Mottville Chair Company, near Skaneateles, talking with the owner, A.J. Allen, about the inevitable topic—furniture finishes. The two men were avidly experimenting, trying to create new milk-based finishes using soured milk.[37] Stickley's enduring obsession with wood finishes—his love of *color*—continued unabated into old age, even though by that time he had no realistic hope of deriving financial benefit from anything he might develop. He designed and made his last furniture at the Mottville factory, simple, straightforward, Shaker-like chairs, with rush seats, and turned legs and finials. These few chairs, given to members of his family, were similar to

chairs he had made in Binghamton in the 1880s on a primitive lathe, and exhibited the simplicity and sound hand craftsmanship that he had preached throughout his Craftsman career.

In the early 1940s, Stickley learned how to drive a car. And, after a period of estrangement in the 1930s, he and his brother Leopold became friendly once again, and Gustav began traveling frequently to his brother's Fayetteville house. But despite an active old age he could not fight time forever. On 17 April 1942, following a day of strenuous effort carrying books up and down the stairs at the Wiles's Columbus Avenue house, Stickley fell ill. Hospitalized, he developed pneumonia and three days later, on 20 April, he died shortly after one o'clock in the afternoon. A memorial service was held on 22 April.[38] The only mourners were family members and one or two friends of Ben and Barbara Wiles. No fiercely loyal contingent of old factory hands showed up that day to honor their fallen leader; that well-worn story is simply myth.[39] The day was gray and dreary: cold, cloudy, with snow flurries and periods of intermittent rain. After the funeral, Stickley's remains were taken to Morningside Cemetery and his children and some of his grandchildren stood quietly by the gravesite. He was buried next to Eda.

His daughter Barbara, whose husband had largely supported her father for the past twenty-five years, paid for the funeral with five hundred dollars of her own money. She remained ambivalent about her father, never quite forgiving the drawn-out absences from the family during the Craftsman years, but on his death certificate the unsentimental Barbara loyally wrote that his usual occupation was "President" and that his business was "manufacturing of furniture." Stickley hadn't manufactured furniture or held a regular job in decades, and he had ceased to be a public force of any kind since the closing of his Craftsman enterprise in 1916. At the time of his death he was loved by his children and grandchildren, but he was impoverished and his life had been marred by failure. The obituaries were modest for a man who had once been so eminent.[40] By 1942, Gustav Stickley, The Craftsman, had long been forgotten.

1

On 29 November 1999, at Christie's New York, a private collector paid $596,500 for the sideboard from Stickley's Syracuse home. This was the highest price ever paid at auction for a piece of twentieth-century American furniture. More recently, on 29 September 2002, the on-line auction service eBay offered a Craftsman fireset—iron tongs, shovel, poker, and a stand to hold them—that drew forty-two bids before it was sold for nearly $13,000. The fact worth noticing here is not so much the object's price but the torrent of bids from competitors vying to buy it. The high price of the sideboard and the fevered bidding for the fireset are signs of the thriving collectors' market for products made by the Craftsman Workshops. Stickley would perhaps be astonished by the amounts of money now paid for the furniture, metalwork, and textiles that he once offered to his primarily middle-class customers.

Although Stickley's work is much coveted today, I think a better measure of his worth is his significance not to our time but to his own. His stature during the years the Craftsman Workshops flourished was evident in many ways; it may be gauged, for instance, by references to him that appeared in the era's press. In a January 1904 article from *Architectural Review*, the living room of a substantial Neo-Georgian house was described as "almost entirely furnished with Gustav Stickley's arts and crafts furniture."[1] An article from the June 1906 *Good Housekeeping* pictured a modest new home that was "one of the Craftsman houses designed by Gustav Stickley."[2] Neither magazine needed to explain who Stickley was. The architects who read this limited-circulation professional journal and the women who read this popular "shelter" magazine already knew. Interiors of houses furnished with Craftsman wares were often published in periodicals of the day. For example, the handsome living room featured in the February 1910 *House and Garden* was shown to readers as a model they would do well to emulate. Stickley exerted a profound influence on his contemporaries—the architects, designers, artisans, and homeowners who embraced the Arts and Crafts and heeded the lessons he sought to teach.

I have tried to create a balanced view of Gustav Stickley, and I have not spared him. This book has not minimized his entrepreneurial strivings or ignored the profit-pursuing imperatives that, as the years went by, increasingly drove his firm. Nor has it deflected attention away from the dreaming, quixotic side of his nature that muddled his business judgment and ultimately led to catastrophe. This book has been candid as well about the

The living room in Mr Hillman's home, which, by the way, is one of the Craftsman houses designed by Gustav Stickley

2

3

Craftsman Workshops' occasional appropriation of British designs. And it has put aside the romantic fiction that Stickley was a solitary designer, showing him instead to have been more of a "design director" who led a shifting group of talented collaborators. Set against those truths are Stickley's idealism, energy, ability to inspire others, and his instinctive mastery of color, form, and proportion.

Gustav Stickley's enterprise published the essential journal of the American Arts and Crafts movement, *The Craftsman* magazine. And, for a little more than a decade, his enterprise created furniture, metalwork, and textiles that were distinctive, meticulously made, and affordable to many. Whatever contradictions we may find in him now, a hundred years ago this gifted, imaginative man was a unique creative force in America. "The opportunities for escaping our commonplace furnishings are few," said a writer in *Art Interchange*, "and craftsmen of Mr. Stickley's artistic power and individuality are altogether too few among us."[3]

1 Living room at "Three Rivers Farm," from *Architectural Review*, January 1904.

2 Living room at the Hillman house, from *Good Housekeeping*, June 1906.

3 "Upwey" living room, from *House and Garden*, February 1910.

Past writings about Gustav Stickley have tended to focus only on Stickley himself and have therefore omitted a crucial part of his story. One aim of this book has been to correct the still-prevalent misperception of Stickley as a furniture designer whose inventions were solely his own. In fact, as evidence presented throughout the book has shown, it was his everyday practice to surround himself with talented but usually anonymous "creative collaborators" who worked alongside him. Gustav Stickley was the overarching figure who conceived and shaped the enterprise, but his reliance upon teamwork was much greater than he acknowledged to the public.

The purpose of this appendix is to create a fuller picture of Stickley by recording the lives and work of the men and women who were his creative collaborators. Three important collaborators—Harvey Ellis, Mary Fanton Roberts, and Irene Sargent—will not be found in this Appendix because information about them is readily available in other works.[1]

BLANCHE BAXTER (1870–1967)

Shortly after joining the Craftsman Workshops in 1903, Blanche Baxter helped design the installation of Stickley's Arts and Crafts exhibition in the Craftsman Building, and she managed the Tea Room set up during the two-week run of that show. Baxter became manager of the firm's textile and needlework department when it opened in May 1903, undertaking some of the needlework herself and overseeing the other workers. Perhaps most important, she was a designer who created patterns for this department, and Stickley paid her small sums for her designs.[2]

Blanche Ross Baxter was born in Hornell, New York, and moved with her parents to Syracuse by 1887. In the late 1890s, as evidence of her artistic interests, she had joined an organization called the Vernon Art Club, and in 1901 she became a teacher at the Dakin Brothers Business College in Syracuse; her background in art and business would have made her attractive to Stickley's

firm. Baxter probably met Stickley at the Park Presbyterian Church in Syracuse, where both families were members.

She traveled to Europe several times, and on one trip, in 1907, she crossed paths with a former colleague, LaMont Warner, who wrote to his wife saying, "This morning I went to the Am. Ex. Co.... I was about to go out when up walks Blanche Baxter. I ran across [her] in the Louvre this PM. Blanche did not seem 'togged' as much as usual."[3]

As is evident from Warner's letter, Baxter shared with other needleworkers a delight in wearing clothes that showed off her handiwork; she liked to be handsomely "togged." Even though the Craftsman needlework department remained in Syracuse, Baxter moved to Manhattan when Stickley established his office there, and she stayed with the firm in some capacity at least until 1912. She lived in New York City until shortly before her death in 1967.

CLAUDE BRAGDON (1866–1946)

Established with his own upstate New York architectural firm by the late 1890s, Bragdon was in occasional contact with Stickley's firm. He visited the Eastwood factory in December 1900 with his friend Henry Wilkinson to see the "New Furniture" that Wilkinson had designed. He married Wilkinson's sister Charlotte in 1902. In July and August 1903 he spent several days in Syracuse working in the Craftsman Building, writing two *Craftsman* articles and, apparently, collaborating with Harvey Ellis on some of the furniture and textiles published in the magazine that summer. In later life Bragdon was a stage designer in New York City, a memoirist, and an author of books on the esoteric Spiritualism he had come to embrace.[4]

Claude Fayette Bragdon was born in Oberlin, Ohio, and grew up in a succession of towns in Ohio and upstate New York.[5] By 1884 the Bragdon family had settled in Rochester, and within two years the talented and ambitious

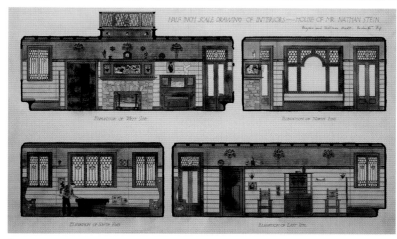

young Claude had landed a job as a draftsman and begun his architectural career. In fairly short order he became head draftsman in the office of H. & C.S. Ellis, at a time when Charles Ellis, in Harvey Ellis's absence, was the firm's sole principal. As Bragdon later wrote, "The office had been full of Harvey's drawings, which moved me to admiration, emulation, and despair, for he was one of the finest pen-and-ink draughtsmen this country had ever produced."[6] While in Charles Ellis's employ, Bragdon doggedly honed his design skills while publicizing his name by entering the frequent competitions sponsored by architectural associations and the architectural press. Eager for a more challenging professional arena and a more cosmopolitan milieu, he traveled to New York City and made the rounds of architectural firms in the hope of finding a job. After several demoralizing days of rejection, he was hired as a draftsman by the architect Bruce Price.

He worked for Price only briefly, however, and in the early 1890s he went back to upstate New York, joining Green and Wicks, "the leading architectural firm in Buffalo," he later wrote. After two years there he returned to Rochester and it was in the mid-1890s that he met Charles Ellis's older brother Harvey.

Harvey Ellis was the infinitely gifted mentor; Bragdon, fourteen years his junior, was the student. In time they became good friends and professional colleagues, and Bragdon later acknowledged his debt to his teacher: "[I]t was to him that I and others turned for the solace of good talk, brilliant wit, wise counsel, and for inspiration and instruction in the arts of which he was so admirable a master."[7] In 1895, his artistic sensibilities enlarged by his friendship with Ellis, Bragdon departed for a year in Europe, where he continued diligently to school himself in his profession. Back in Rochester the following year, he established the firm of Bragdon and Hillman, an architectural partnership with James Constable Hillman (1863–1932) that lasted eight years.

In 1897, Ellis and Bragdon published admiring, good-natured appreciations of one another for the *Brochure Series of Architectural Illustration*.[8] Bragdon, however, whose piece appeared first, tempered his praise by damning some of Ellis's buildings. He called them "failures, though interesting failures. They are too fanciful, too exuberant." A tinge of rivalry colored his assessment of his friend. Despite Bragdon's long hours of diligent labor and his regimen of self-improvement, he overflowed with "despair" because he knew it would never be possible for him to match the supple line that seemed to flow so easily from the tip of Ellis's pen. Nonetheless, he was to become an accomplished architect and renderer. Perhaps his most notable structures were the Nathan Stein house in Rochester (1899) and the great New York Central Station in Rochester (1913), with its arcaded facade and its vast, Grueby-tiled interior.

Bragdon's domestic architecture and the furniture he designed for some of his clients reveal his familiarity with *International Studio* and English architectural journals. A Bragdon cabinet visible in his elevation drawing of the east wall of the Stein house was modeled on a cabinet that Baillie Scott had created as part of his Darmstadt commission for the Grand Duke of Hesse.[9]

The three-part window with an arched central transom in Bragdon's elevation of the north end of the interior of his house for Nathan Stein also had an English source. It was his rendition of the "Ipswich" window typical of the English architect Richard Norman Shaw, and versions of it appeared frequently in the domestic architecture of both Bragdon and Ellis.[10] Yet Bragdon looked toward Japan as well. He evidently kept in his office a copy of Thomas Cutler's 1880 book, *A Grammar of Japanese Ornament and Design*.[11] Bragdon's eye was attracted by the Japanese family crest, or *mon*, and one of Cutler's plates illustrated thirty examples of these "badges of nobility and gentry." Bragdon used several of these *mon* designs as decorative elements in the Stein living room.

1 Claude Bragdon drawing of the Nathan Stein interior, 1899.

2 *Mon* birds from *Grammar of Japanese Ornament and Design*.

3

4

JEROME CONNOR (1874–1943)

Jerome Connor was born in Ireland and came to the United States with his parents in 1888, settling in Massachusetts. After the death of his father two years later, he went to New York City and supported himself as a sign painter, machinist, and stonecutter; he also turned to prizefighting to supplement his income. By 1899 Connor had joined Elbert Hubbard's Roycroft Shops, an organization with a penchant for finding and shaping natural, undeveloped talent. Connor quickly matured into a fine graphic artist, metalworker, and sculptor. Stickley recruited him in the spring of 1902, and by July of that year Connor and his wife, Ann Donohoe Connor, a Roycroft bookbinder, left western New York State and moved a hundred and fifty miles east to Syracuse. Connor's drawings and charcoal sketches were soon being offered for sale at the Craftsman Building—just as they had been at the Roycroft—and he was helping to establish Stickley's new metal shop. Max Kluge succeeded Connor in the Craftsman metal shop in 1904, and Connor moved on to a new career as a creator of monumental public sculpture, which was to occupy him for the rest of his life.[12]

PETER HANSEN (1880–1947)

Hansen's first few years in the United States were largely unrecorded, but he apparently worked in Manhattan for both Stickley and the Hayden Furniture Company during 1906 and 1907. He left the Craftsman Workshops and moved to Fayetteville, New York by March 1907 to become chief furniture designer for Leopold Stickley.[13] Hansen married Ruth Anne Williams in 1907 and remained with the L. & J.G. Stickley Company into the 1940s.

The son of a farmer and a "country woman," Peter Heinrich Hansen was born in the town of Rödemis, Schleswig-Holstein, in the northern reaches of Germany. He received formal training as a cabinetmaker in Flensburg.[14] After leaving school he worked in the north German city of Kiel at Kunsttischerei Nebendal, a cabinet shop that specialized in making, or possibly restoring,

"artistic" tables. Hansen then moved from Keil to Potsdam, and was still in Germany in early 1905, but a few months later he fled his native land in protest against its expanding militarism.[15] Hansen arrived in New York City on a German liner, the *Graf Waldersee*, on 2 November 1905 and first lived on West Thirtieth Street, not far from Stickley's office on West Thirty-fourth.

SAMUEL HOWE (1854–1928)

From 1902 until 1906 Howe contributed twelve signed articles to *The Craftsman*, some illustrated with his own drawings, and served as a judge for two of the design contests sponsored by the magazine. Perhaps his visibility in *The Craftsman* brought him to the attention of Leopold Stickley, for whom he designed textiles and delineated model rooms in 1904 and 1905.

Born in England in 1854 and trained as an architect, Howe and his wife Phoebe immigrated to the United States in 1883 and settled in New York City. In the 1880s and 1890s, he practiced architecture, worked as an interior decorator, published articles on architectural subjects, and wrote one book, titled *Indoors,* in 1894. During this time he was also employed by Louis Comfort Tiffany, for whom he designed stained glass windows.

From 1905 to 1915, Howe worked as an illustrator for *House and Garden* and *Vogue*, and was a frequent contributor to *International Studio, House Beautiful, Country Life in America, American Architect and Building News*, and other periodicals. In addition to his architectural work of these years, he was also a decorative painter and architectural delineator, and a regular participant in the annual exhibitions of the Architectural League of New York. In 1906 and 1907 he exhibited paintings of the house and

3 Ad for Valentine M. Kluge Co. from the 1907 Syracuse city directory.

4 Model room designed by Louise Shrimpton, ca. 1906–7.

5 Louise Shrimpton chair design featured in *Palette and Bench,* September 1910

6 Cover of September 1910 *Craftsman* illustrated by Victor Toothaker.

7 Dining room attributed to LaMont Warner, 1901.

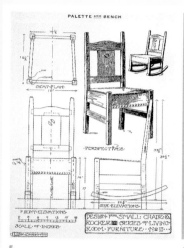

5

6

7

gardens at Laurelton Hall, Louis Tiffany's Long Island home. By 1927 Howe was working for the Mosaic Tile Company of Zanesville, Ohio, although he maintained his New York City architectural office and lived with his wife in Camden, New Jersey.[16]

GEORGE H. JONES   (1865–1927)

Jones and Stickley probably met in 1896: The firm of Stickley & Simonds was then making "marquetry chairs," and Jones, already preeminent in his field, would have been the most likely supplier. For 1903, during the period that Harvey Ellis was at the Craftsman Workshops, Stickley's ledger books record that the firm was sending design sketches to Jones in New York, and Jones, in turn, was regularly shipping packages of completed inlay and marquetry to the Eastwood factory. There is ample evidence that Jones also created some of Stickley's inlay designs. Although the pace of shipments from Jones to Stickley slowed after Ellis's death, they continued on a fairly regular basis for another decade.[17]

George Henry Jones was born in New York City, the son of an English father and a German mother. Trained in the crafts of inlay and marquetry, he opened his first workshop at Eighth Street and Broadway in 1893, in what was then the thriving furniture-producing quarter of lower Manhattan. Jones also created designs for the furniture manufacturers and architects who were his customers. In 1896, he moved his growing business further uptown to a larger workspace on the corner of Twenty-third Street and Second Avenue and *Furniture World* reported that "His present establishment is the largest marquetry shop in the country."

That year he began doing business as "Jones, the Marqueterie Man," recognizing, like his later patron Gustav Stickley, the value of creating a memorable brand name. He also shared with Stickley the belief that a craft worker should make intelligent use of power-driven machines. Like Stickley's, his workshop was equipped with "all the latest improved machinery used in manufacturing marqueterie," much of which he had designed and patented himself.

VALENTINE M. KLUGE   (1874 – ?)

Valentine Marks Kluge, by profession a machinist, was born in Germany. Trained as a metalworker, he "developed great skill in artistic work" before immigrating to the United States in 1898.[18] By 1900 he and his wife Bertha were living in Brooklyn, New York. Kluge moved to Syracuse and joined Stickley's metal shop by 1903. He was the shop's foreman in 1904 and 1905, and became an American citizen in October 1904. By 1906 he was on his own, and the following year he was the vice-president of the V.M. Kluge Company, a recently formed Syracuse firm that advertised itself as "Designers and Manufacturers of Art Metal Work/chandeliers, lanterns, lamps, trays, etc."[19] Kluge's firm, which was apparently in existence for only three years, thus made exactly the same kinds of domestic objects that the Craftsman metal shop produced. There is evidence that in some instances the firm signed its work, but it is also likely that the V.M. Kluge Company was the maker of some of the unsigned Arts and Crafts metalwork now attributed to Stickley or one of the better-known Syracuse metalworking firms.[20] Kluge left Syracuse and returned to New York City in 1908, and his later career remains untraced.

LOUISE SHRIMPTON   (1870–1954)

Louise Shrimpton joined Stickley's firm about 1902.[21] Neither her name nor her initials ever appeared in *The Craftsman*, but Shrimpton worked for Stickley as an illustrator and delineator for his magazine; her role as the anonymous illustrator of the "Home Training in Cabinet Work" series is discussed in chapter 6. Most important, she worked alongside Harvey Ellis and LaMont Warner as a designer of Craftsman furniture and textiles.[22]

8

9

Louise Allen Shrimpton was born in Syracuse and lived there most of her life. She was a student at the School of the Museum of Fine Arts in Boston, where in 1893 she completed a four-year course of studio art in the department of drawing and painting. She also studied design, receiving instruction in "proportion, the elements of architectural and decorative form...line drawing, the use of color and perspective."[23] Ernest Fenellosa, the Museum's prominent curator of Japanese art, gave well-attended lectures at the school, as did Charles Eliot Norton, Harvard's first art history professor, a founder-member of the Boston Society of Arts and Crafts, and a close friend of Ruskin. Shrimpton thus became familiar with the decorative arts in the Museum's collection, with Japanese art, and with Arts and Crafts ideas, and this background would prove crucial in her later career. She returned to Syracuse in 1899, seeking assignments in commercial art.

Shrimpton left the Craftsman Workshops about 1906, and by 1907 she was delineating model rooms for the L. & J.G. Stickley Company. Unsurprisingly, her L. & J.G. Stickley interiors carried evident reminders of her years at the Craftsman Workshops. The fireplace hood and andirons in one of these model rooms, for instance, were Craftsman designs, and the border of the carpet was a pattern cribbed from Harvey Ellis. (The Ellis carpet is illustrated on page 92.) Shrimpton would later acknowledge his designs in an essay she wrote more than a decade after his death.[24] Although they represented only a brief interlude in her career, these handsome L. & J.G. Stickley renderings were perhaps Shrimpton's finest published work, and there can be no doubt as to their attribution because she signed them with her "LAS" monogram.

Shrimpton next embarked on a career as a magazine writer and illustrator. For nearly a decade, her by-line appeared in many nationally distributed periodicals, including *House Beautiful*, *House and Garden*, *Country Life in America*, and *Good Housekeeping*. She also wrote and illustrated two woodworking series, one for *Good Housekeeping* (1908) and another for the art journal *Palette and Bench* (1910).[25] They followed the same basic formula established earlier in *The Craftsman* magazine's "Home Training" series, the difference being that here Shrimpton signed her own work.

Describing a design she created for *Good Housekeeping*, Shrimpton wrote: "Perfect fitness to use for which the piece is intended, together with good proportions and pleasing line and color, are the essentials in wood working as in all other crafts.... Frankness and simplicity...are needful. Beauty of finish is the best ornament."[26] These are the words of American Arts and Crafts orthodoxy, plainly expressed, and the passage reads like one of Stickley's homilies from *The Craftsman*. Although most of her magazine pieces centered on home and domesticity, and residential architecture, viewed from an Arts and Crafts perspective, she also wrote articles explaining how to make portieres, how to decorate walls using stencils, and how to embroider table runners and curtains. Shrimpton became a uniquely effective popularizer of the Arts and Craft ethos, carrying the lessons she had absorbed at the Craftsman Workshops to a wide national audience.[27]

VICTOR TOOTHAKER (1882–1932)

In addition to illustrating covers for *The Craftsman* magazine, Victor Toothaker devoted his time in the office to designing Craftsman metalwork, and, evidence suggests, to designing some Standard Stickley furniture as well. Stickley's payroll records from 1907 show that Toothaker divided his weeks between the metal shop and an office in the factory itself. But managing the Craftsman metal shop remained his prime responsibility.

Victor Toothaker was born in Pueblo, Colorado, and was trained in metal craft at an early age by his blacksmith father. By about 1903 or 1904, he was working in copper, brass, and iron, making candlesticks, table lamps, light fixtures, andirons, and other handicrafts that were sold by the Arts and Crafts bookseller Paul Elder in his San Francisco store. According to "An Arts and Crafts Book Shop in Greater San Francisco," a catalog Elder issued in December 1906, the brass and copper light fixtures in this building were "fashioned by the ingenious Toothaker."[28]

He left the Stickley firm in 1911 when he married Anne Knights of East Aurora, New York, and became a designer for the Roycroft copper shop and

10

11

also its manager. By 1914, while still working in East Aurora, he was also drawing model rooms for the Grand Rapids furniture firm run by Gustav Stickley's brother Albert; they appear that year in Stickley Brothers' advertisements for its "Quaint Furniture" in *Good Furniture* magazine. Toothaker left the Roycroft about 1915. For the next four years he designed wrought iron lamps and light fixtures, first for his own firm, the Toothaker Shops, in East Aurora, and then, after 1919, for the Charles V. Daiger Company of Boston, although he lived during those years in Detroit and Cleveland. He rejoined the Roycroft briefly in 1931 when he and his wife returned to East Aurora. Toothaker died the following year at the age of fifty, and Karl Kipp and Elbert Hubbard II conducted his funeral service.[29]

LAMONT A. WARNER (1876–1970)

By September 1900, a few months after the Grand Rapids launch of Stickley's New Furniture, a new designer joined the firm. This was LaMont Warner, whose first assignment during those autumn months would have been to produce designs and working drawings for furniture in the robust structural style that Stickley would introduce early the following year.[30]

LaMont Warner was a Craftsman designer from late 1900 until late 1906, that is, throughout nearly all of the precedent-setting era of early Stickley furniture. Were it not for Stickley's practice of masking his employees' identities behind the Craftsman corporate facade, Warner would be recognized today as one of the significant furniture designers of the American Arts and Crafts movement.

Warner was identified as an employee in the Stickley firm's ledgers, and Syracuse city directories of the era show that he was working in the Craftsman Building. His "LAW" monogram occasionally appeared in *The Craftsman*; for instance, on his drawings of a Standard Stickley dining room in May 1904, and a set of inlaid bedroom furniture in June 1904 (see illustration, page 100).

LaMont Adelbert Warner was born in Stamford, New York, and was an 1898 graduate of Pratt Institute, where he majored in design under Arthur Wesley Dow and had his first exposure to Japanese decorative arts.[31] After graduation, Warner's first jobs were with Manhattan decorating firms. Then he was hired by Stickley and moved to Syracuse. He stayed with Stickley until he left to accept a teaching post in the art department, headed by Dow, at Columbia University's Teachers College.[32]

Warner's design files still exist, and they reveal his close study of British Arts and Crafts. One of his file folders, for example, is labeled "Modern English," and is filled with pictures of furniture and interiors cut out of *International Studio*, including several published images of Baillie Scott's 1897-98 Darmstadt commission.[33] He also owned *Modern British Domestic Architecture and Decoration*, a lavishly illustrated special issue published by *The Studio* in the summer of 1901.[34] From this one publication Warner gleaned pertinent examples of the work of three British designers—Baillie Scott, C.F.A. Voysey, and Mackintosh—who exerted a formative influence on the Craftsman Workshops.

In the summers of 1907 and 1909, when he was an assistant professor at Teachers College, Warner traveled to Europe. Although he was no longer a member of Stickley's firm, Warner's letters home to his wife Emma occasionally shed light on matters relevant to the work he had done there. One letter offers a surprising glimpse of the Arts and Crafts garments apparently favored at the Craftsman Workshops: after landing in Antwerp in May 1907, Warner wrote, "The workmen on the dock…wear the linen or denim smock frocks like the ones we had at Stickley's."[35] After visiting a museum in Brussels, Warner wrote to Emma saying, "The things I admire most are the pieces of Gothic furniture of the sixteenth century. I can see how I can use a great many of the ideas in new pieces for Stickley. I mean however to think out the whole scheme—then talk it over and if he falls in—all right. If he does not then I will present the scheme

8 Baillie Scott dining room, 1901.

9 Voysey dining room at "The Orchard," 1901.

10 C.R. and Margaret Mackintosh dining set, 1901

11 Henry Wilkinson designed #165 settle, 1901.

12

13

to someone else. Perhaps Gus would like the ideas."[36] This letter reveals that Warner was now submitting designs—on a freelance basis—to a rival firm. The Stickley mentioned here was not Gustav but Leopold.

On both of these trips Warner enjoyed going to places tourists liked to visit— the Tower Bridge in London, for instance, and Stonehenge—but he was studying British decorative art as well. One day in 1907, for instance, he stopped at the Brook Street retail shop of C.R. Ashbee's Guild of Handicraft.[37] Shortly after arriving in London for the second time, in June 1909, he made a daylong pilgrimage to the Victoria and Albert Museum.[38] That year he also hoped to travel north, but feeling pinched by his slender budget, he disconsolately wrote to Emma, "I fear I shall have to give up going to Glasgow."[39]

Touring Germany and Austria in July 1909, he visited the city of Darmstadt, telling Emma that "The most interesting place to me is the artists' colony."[40] At the Secession Building in Vienna, a student employed there told him she knew *The Craftsman* magazine and gave him a tour of the premises before he was introduced to the architect and designer Josef Hoffmann.[41] Warner found Hoffmann forthright and voluble, but he was distressed that their conversation had been inconclusive and, further, that Hoffmann had seemed overly concerned about money. "I was left almost alone to meet a man who could not understand a word of English. But at last he came and we had a 5 minute talk. He wanted first to know how much pay our professors received...and we both talked much. He did not understand me and I understood little of what he said but the man himself in interesting."[42]

In 1909, Warner moved his family into a house he had designed and built in the town of Bronxville, just north of New York City. That September, Louise Shrimpton wrote an article about this house for *Good Housekeeping* magazine. Shrimpton recorded that all the living room and dining room furniture, "with the exception of a few antique pieces, was designed by Mr. Warner."

Shrimpton's article suggests the depth of his embrace of Arts and Crafts tradition. Beside the Craftsman furniture in this house, there were imported curtains with "an English conventional design," and a Voysey-designed silk and wool double cloth that was hung as a portiere in the reception room doorway. LaMont and Emma Warner crafted their own lamps and lampshades from abalone shells and cockleshells.

HENRY WILKINSON (1869–1931)

Wilkinson practiced architecture in Syracuse between 1892 and 1902, designing a commercial building in downtown Syracuse as well as several substantial fieldstone and shingle houses.[43] At some point before the summer of 1900 he met Gustave Stickley, who hired him to design "New Furniture" for the Grand Rapids market that July. At the end of the year, Stickley advanced him $700, which Wilkinson earned by freelancing at a very generous rate of $100 a week; Stickley obviously valued Wilkinson's abilities.[44]

Henry Wilkinson was born in Syracuse. In 1890 he graduated from Cornell University in nearby Ithaca with a degree in architecture. He studied under Charles Babcock (1829–1913), an architect and teacher devoted to the Gothic Revival and a vocal admirer of Ruskin. Through Babcock, Wilkinson had an early exposure to ideas relevant to the Arts and Crafts movement, which had, in large measure, grown out of the Gothic Revival.

In 1891, the twenty-two-year-old Wilkinson traveled east to Boston to set up in practice for himself, opening an office in a handsome new office tower, the Ames Building.[45] Whatever his professional hopes may have been, this venture

14

15

was evidently not a financial success, and it folded a year later. But this young man's foray turned out to be important in other ways. He found work as a freelance draftsman for Ralph Adams Cram (1863–1942), who became a life-long friend.[46] Cram was a "medievalist" and an admirer of the guild system. He thought of himself as an American disciple of William Morris and the English Arts and Crafts, and later in the decade, he and his architectural partner Bertram Goodhue (1869–1924) would be among the founders of the Society of Arts and Crafts, Boston. Cram was also susceptible to "the spell of Japan," an influence that has been discerned in some of his residential commissions of the time.[47]

Henry Wilkinson thus came into contact, early in his career, with two gifted young architects conversant with the Arts and Crafts movement and the Gothic Revival, and who were sympathetic toward Japanese art and architecture. Wilkinson later told his family that, like Cram, he counted himself a follower of Morris.[48]

By late January 1901, Wilkinson had begun dividing his time between Syracuse and New York City, where he hoped to move his architectural practice.[49] That year he formed a partnership with another architect, H. Van Buren Magonigle

12/13 Renderings of house interior and exterior by Henry Wilkinson, from *The Craftsman,* February 1902.

14 Fireplace designed by Wilkinson for the Uptegrove Building in 1902.

15 Fireplace in the Craftsman Building, resembling the Uptegrove fireplace; it is likely Wilkinson's design.

(1867–1935), and the new firm opened an office on lower Fifth Avenue.[50] Wilkinson kept his Syracuse connections, however. In February 1902, *The Craftsman* published "The Planning of a Home," an unsigned article accompanied by plans and drawings of a house he had designed. The interior of this proposed house offered the Craftsman architectural virtues of "space, simplicity, and solidity," and it anticipated what would come to be known as the Craftsman house:

open planning, with the downstairs dominated by one vast room; a liberal use of expressed wooden structure, for instance in wainscoting, ceiling beams and built-ins; and a fireplace faced with Grueby tiles. Although the drawings had shortcomings, *The Craftsman* article was good publicity. As Claude Bragdon wrote to his mother, "I guess I told you Wilkinson and Magonigle got two jobs from a little house of theirs published in The Craftsman."[51]

One commission that must have come to Wilkinson & Magonigle through Stickley was their design for the Uptegrove Building in New York City. Completed in the summer of 1902 and erected next to the Uptegrove's Manhattan lumberyard, the new office building was a handsome, Classical structure faced with brick.[52]

Inside the building, Wilkinson's Arts and Crafts tastes were more in evidence: exposed ceiling beams, massive wooden posts, and Craftsman furniture. A photograph published in *Architectural Record* shows that the fireplace in the office was nearly identical to the fireplace Stickley had installed in the Craftsman Building lecture hall during its remodeling of 1901–02. Stickley never credited any architect with this renovation. But these Grueby-tiled fireplaces are the evidence that it was the work of Henry Wilkinson, who was thus the author of one of the first Craftsman interiors ever built.

The furniture made by the Stickley firm during the periods of Wilkinson's employment often had a medieval appearance: for instance, the spaces between the curving back slats of the "Bungalow" chair suggest a pointed Gothic arch. This curve reappeared on a Stickley settle, bookcase, and other pieces, first made in early 1901. Because he was steeped in the Gothic through his training with Babcock and his early experience with Cram, these designs are attributable to Henry Wilkinson.

APPENDIX TWO: THE STICKLEY FALL-FRONT DESK 1900–1905

DIMENSIONS:
H 46" W 23 5/8" D 6 7/8"
INITIAL PUBLICATION:
"New Furniture from the
Workshops of Gustave
Stickley, Cabinet Maker,"
fall 1900
DESIGNER:
Attributed to Henry Wilkinson

In the relatively short span of sixteen years, Stickley's Arts and Crafts enterprise developed and built about a thousand different furniture designs—a daunting breadth of changing taste and detail. This appendix attempts to distill that process in a manageable way by a visual analysis of one form—the fall-front desk—as it evolved from 1900 to 1905. Its purpose is to present the essential facts of design change at the Craftsman Workshops with a minimum of words, letting images of the desks themselves demonstrate the process. The chronological sequence in this appendix begins with the exuberance of "New Furniture" in 1900 and proceeds to the rationalized "Standard Stickley" of the firm's mature production years. All the examples shown here are from contemporary collections, and each is a significant expression of the art of Gustav Stickley and his Craftsman designers.

THE #505 CHALET DESK OF 1900

A good example of the "New Furniture" Stickley introduced in 1900 is his "Chalet" desk. The desk's fall-front is framed with four boards fastened to one another with tongue-in-groove joints and enclosing a slightly raised central panel. When it is closed, the fall-front is held in place by a hand-cut wooden knob that fits into the subtle protrusion of the desk's upper shelf. When the fall-front is open, the horizontal line of its cantilever echoes the line of the long, projecting (and inexplicably curvaceous) feet. Three shallow arches are cut into the lower edge of the fall-front. They are faint though symmetrical hints, perhaps, of the Art Nouveau whiplash or the "lift" motif seen on some of Stickley's other 1900 furniture.

Near the base of the desk a shelf holds a rectangular wastebasket of hand-woven rush. The integral basket is clever, even functional. Its truer purpose, however, is visual, with the lighter color and varied texture of the rush contrasting pleasingly with the smooth, dark-stained wood. Moreover, the basket is an essential compositional element that gives definition to the space between the lower edge of the fall-front and the open shelf below. The back of the desk appears to be a flat panel, but it is actually a group of vertical planks joined with internal splines, a characteristic Stickley construction technique of the following three years. Two wide boards form the flanks of the desk, and they are locked to its horizontal shelves with four keyed tenons on either side.[1]

The Chalet desk has an awkward charm, and it is irresistible both for what it is and for the promise it makes to the future. It is a daring design that, despite its geometric shapes, seems more biomorphic than mechanical, and looks at first glance perhaps less like a desk than some fantastic bird with talons and spurs on its over-long feet. Yet this small, seemingly frail piece of furniture is clearly a built object: it bristles with tenon-and-key joints and other symbols of structure. In the end it is not quite a functional piece of furniture; it is instead a highly original arrangement of planks and articulated joints. The Chalet desk tells a story about the idea of joining wood, but at this stage in the development of Craftsman design that is still a story with more style and structure than substance.[2]

DIMENSIONS:
H 41" W 27" D 14"

INITIAL PUBLICATION:
"Things Wrought by the
United Crafts," summer 1901

DESIGNER:
Attributed to Henry Wilkinson
or LaMont Warner

DIMENSIONS:
H 47 1/2" W 32 3/4" D 13 3/4"

INITIAL PUBLICATION:
"Retail Plates," 1902

DESIGNER:
Attributed to LaMont Warner

THE #521 FALL-FRONT DESK OF 1901

This small desk, first made in the summer of 1901, typifies the Stickley firm's work of that year. Like the 1900 Chalet desk, it has a fall-front over an open shelf and three tiers of tenon-and-key joints on its sides. But it is otherwise quite unlike the earlier desk. The fall-front is made of four horizontal planks; below it are three drawers supported by a Tudor arch that braces the heavy case. Abrupt, angular setbacks are cut into the flat plank sides of the desk to mark the location of the shelf and to serve—visually—as stabilizing feet. The desk is overtly structural, and retains the exaggerated verticality and pronounced joints of the Chalet desk. It is, however, both a more substantial object than the earlier desk and a more functional one, and is not so overwhelmed by structure. Although it is not perfect—the pyramidal wooden knobs, for example, are uncomfortably at odds with the hammered iron key escutcheon—it is

one of Stickley's most accomplished fall-front desks and a true advance beyond his work of the year before.[3]

This fall-front desk is rigorously upright and structural, yet it apparently owes its basic shape to a fall-front "secretaire" designed in 1901 by Baillie Scott and built on a similar small scale (see figure at left). Compared to the Stickley model, the Baillie Scott desk is a more subtle, decorous performance, its sleek rectilinearity softened by tinted inlays and a segmental arch above its open shelf.

THE #552 FALL-FRONT DESK OF 1902

This fall-front desk—an evolution of the 1901 fall-front desk discussed above—exhibits the crisp rectilinearity of Stickley's 1902 furniture. It is a more functional cabinet in comparison to the two fall-front desks that precede it in this appendix. It is more chaste, more rational, its profile more trim, though in gaining these attributes—and despite its emphatic vertical thrust—it has lost a measure of that kinetic energy that vivified the earlier Chalet desk. Structure has been played down, but it is still important to the composition. Instead of ranks of tenon-and-key joints lining the sides, there are now three rectangular tenon ends sawed flush with the surface of the wood. Because end grain readily absorbs stain, these tenons are slightly darker than the surrounding boards, and they punctuate the sides of the desk with their geometric shapes. The overall appearance of this desk is that of a taut slab enlivened by the flake of its quarter-sawn oak and by the light-catching strap hinges held to the wood with pyramidal-headed screws. The facade, however, is slightly marred by the uneasy juxtaposition of the smooth, cast brass drawer pulls and the hammered strapwork.

These strap hinges are worth noticing for what they are not. In Craftsman publications Stickley asserted that "applied ornament" was inconsistent with the honesty of the structural style. He was perennially critical of the common industry practice of adorning furniture with elaborate, machine-carved, glued-on ornament. Yet these straps are, in fact, applied ornament: they are not actually part of the hinge assembly. They are employed here largely for their associative value, and are meant to conjure the strapwork hinges drawn across the planks of a medieval door. An article in *Furniture Trade Review* observed this evocative quality, saying, "The hardware…lends an attractive air. The hinges often extend clear across the door…carrying one back to medieval times."[4] These long straps do have a structural purpose—they help hold together the planks they are mounted on. But like the structurally unnecessary exposed tenon ends on the sides of this desk, they reveal Stickley's "romanticized rationalism." As hinges they are only decorative symbols.

DIMENSIONS:
H 44" W 30" D 12 7/8"
INITIAL PUBLICATION:
"Structure and Ornament in
the Craftsman Workshops,"
The Craftsman, January 1904
DESIGNER:
Attributed to Harvey Ellis

THE INLAID FALL-FRONT DESK OF 1903

Designed in late 1903, this diminutive desk has a wide, beveled cornice, a simple key escutcheon, and a beveled molding applied to its frame-and-panel fall-front. The front of the desk is inlaid with a conventionalized plant motif, a thin vertical line rising to a disk. There is an open shelf near the base, and the entire front of the desk is canted slightly forward. Because this desk so clearly bespeaks Harvey Ellis's hand it has traditionally been ascribed to him, and rightly so. Its story, however, is more complicated than that attribution suggests.

ALUMINUM CLOCK AND
STATIONERY CASE
Designed by C. F. A. Voysey
Made by W. H. Tingey and A. W. Simpson

The roots of this inlaid Craftsman fall-front desk are largely to be found in two Voysey writing cabinets that Stickley had attentively looked over in London. He had seen one of them at the January 1903 Arts and Crafts Exhibition Society exhibition (it is visible on the left side of the photograph of Voysey's exhibit space in chapter three), and he had acquired the other one, apparently from J.S. Henry. Stickley exhibited the one he bought at the Craftsman Building in March and April 1903 and then published it in his magazine that August (also illustrated in chapter three). Both Voysey writing cabinets had a beveled cornice above a trapezoidal profile, with an inlaid fall-front on the upper part of the case and an open bookshelf below. Ellis must have seen the first cabinet—the one Stickley did not buy—when it was published in the April 1903 issue of *House and Garden*. And he had the second cabinet literally before his eyes when it was on public view in the Craftsman Building. He then designed this Craftsman desk using the Voysey cabinets as a point of departure. But he did not design this desk by himself.

In May 1903 Claude Bragdon was designing a house for the Reverend W.S. Rainsford in Murray Bay, Quebec, and the commission included furniture.[5]

Bragdon's furniture designs for Rainsford seem generally sturdy and comfortable, a cottage-like blend of elements borrowed from Voysey, Baillie Scott, and Stickley. His Rainsford fall-front desk is essentially a taller version of the Voysey writing cabinets; like Ellis, Bragdon probably saw the first Voysey cabinet in *House and Garden*, and the second cabinet when it was shown at Stickley's Arts and Crafts exhibition.

The desk Bragdon designed for Reverend Rainsford surely anticipated the later Stickley desk, although there were several significant differences. Bragdon's fall-front, for instance, was not inlaid. It had an awkward hammered-metal plate and pull instead of the simpler and more suitable key escutcheon found on the Stickley desk. The Rainsford desk lacked that subtle but critical unifying visual refinement, the thin strip of beveled, Voyseyesque molding applied to the Stickley fall-front. It also had no back, and would consequently lack structural strength.[6] The floor level cutouts on its sides were sawn into an ogival shape, a nod to the Gothic somewhat out of harmony with the rest of the design; the Stickley version would have a more appropriate plain, flattened arch. What

these desks had in common were a wide, beveled cornice, a fall-front above an open shelf, and, in their side elevations, a canted profile. Thus the profile of this familiar Ellis-designed Stickley desk was in fact first worked out by Claude Bragdon. According to Jean France, the two architects were routinely looking over one another's designs by this time, and Bragdon certainly discussed his Rainsford furniture designs with his friend Harvey Ellis.[7]

When Ellis was working in the Craftsman Building he must have also looked at the other inlaid furniture, designed by G.M. Ellwood and made by J.S. Henry, that Stickley bought in London. The inlay on these pieces was a simple disk surmounting an enamel line; it had the same attenuated shape that would surface on the inlaid Stickley fall-front the following January, and it was clearly

DIMENSIONS:
H 43" W 36" D 14"

INITIAL PUBLICATION:
"The Craftsman Workshops—
Supplement to Catalogue D,"
1905

DESIGNER: Attributed to
LaMont Warner

Ellis's source. LaMont Warner, then completing his third year as a Craftsman designer, must have examined the J.S. Henry furniture as well, if only because Ellwood was apparently his favorite English designer.[8] When Louise Shrimpton later wrote her *Good Housekeeping* article about Warner's house, she credited the design of all the Craftsman furniture in his living room to him; an example of this inlaid Stickley fall-front desk was visible in the photograph of that room. Thanks to his voluminous files, Warner was more familiar with contemporary British furniture than Ellis was, and he apparently contributed to the design of this desk. Though long attributed solely to Ellis, it is more accurate to say that the desk is a synthesis of his own ideas and ideas drawn from several others: Voysey, Stickley, Ellwood, Warner, and, most directly, Claude Bragdon.

THE #729 FALL-FRONT DESK OF 1905

This fall-front desk epitomizes Standard Stickley. Its profile is an evolution of the #525 bookcase of 1901: a rectangular form, with a straight rail running across the gallery top, and flat, slab-like flanks rising in the side elevation to a simple curve. By 1905, Stickley's firm had added to its line a china cabinet, serving table, sideboard, and other pieces, that were variations on this theme. Here these recurrent Craftsman motifs appear on a fall-front desk.

This desk is quite different from the other fall-front desks in this appendix. It has none of the idiosyncratic energy of the 1900 Chalet desk. The overtly structural nature of the 1901 desk and the conspicuous strapwork of the 1902 desk have been abandoned, as has the spare elegance and smaller scale of the inlaid desk of 1903. The construction of this new model is expressed only in the flush dowels that pin the sides to the horizontal rails, and in the modest, barely noticeable chamfered tenon ends that ease their way through the sides at top and bottom. The most prominent decorative feature is the uniform hammered copper hardware that adds attractive parallel lines to the drawer fronts, like rows of buttons on a double-breasted blazer. With its finely tuned proportions, this desk presents a more harmonious and more fully resolved composition than any of the earlier examples. It is a substantial piece of furniture and it efficiently provides a far greater amount of usable space within its handsome and compact form. The standardization of its parts and the simplification of its construction—it has no tenon-and-key joints, no inlay—facilitated quantity production, and it is a viable, convincing, and wholly unified design. In his mature work, Stickley became a more pragmatic furniture maker, and less of a romanticizing experimenter.

1895

1900

1901

1902

1858
Gustave Stickley is born in Osceola, Wisconsin, 9 March.

1875 (ca.)
Stickley's mother moves with her children to Brandt, Pennsylvania, and Gustave begins work in his uncles' chair factory.

1883
Gustave, Albert, and Charles Stickley found the Stickley Brothers Company in Susquehanna, Pennsylvania, and start manufacturing furniture.

Gustave marries Eda Simmons, September 12. They are to have six children: Barbara (1887); Mildred (1888); Hazel (1890); Marion (1893); Gustav, Jr. (1894 ca.); Ruth (1897).

1884
The Stickley Brothers Company begins furniture retailing and manufacturing in Binghamton, New York.

1888
Gustave leaves the Stickley Brothers Company and opens the Stickley & Simonds Company with furniture salesman Elgin A. Simonds, December.

1889
Stickley forms a partnership with G. Tracy Rogers to operate street railways in Binghamton.

1890
Stickley & Simonds opens an office in Auburn, New York, 28 August.

1891
Stickley becomes foreman of the furniture workshop at Auburn State Prison.

1893
Stickley & Simonds erects a new factory near Syracuse in Eastwood, New York.

1895
Stickley travels to Europe, April.

1896
Stickley again travels to Europe, April.

He moves his family to Syracuse, occupying a house at 1001 Walnut Avenue.

1897
Furniture workshop at Auburn State Prison closes.

1898
Stickley forces Simonds out and establishes the Gustave Stickley Company, 5 May.

The Gustave Stickley Company is established as a legal entity, 20 October.

1900
Stickley family moves into a new house at 416 Columbus Avenue, June.

Henry Wilkinson designs furniture for Stickley's firm.

The Gustave Stickley Company introduces its "New Furniture" at the Grand Rapids Furniture Exposition, July.

The Tobey Furniture Company, Chicago, managed by George Clingman, briefly becomes Stickley's distributor.

LaMont Warner joins Stickley's firm as designer and delineator.

Stickley leases office and display space in the Crouse Stables, Syracuse; after remodeling it will become the first Craftsman Building.

1901
The Gustave Stickley Company begins doing business as the United Crafts.

Stickley adopts the joiner's compass shopmark and "Als ik kan" motto.

Written and edited by Irene Sargent, the first issue of *The Craftsman* magazine is published, October.

With the Grueby Faience Company, Stickley exhibits his furniture at the Pan-American Exposition in Buffalo, New York.

Stickley's house is badly damaged by fire, 24 December.

1902
The Craftsman metal shop opens next to the Craftsman Building.

Louise Shrimpton joins the firm as a designer and illustrator.

Jerome Connor leaves the Roycroft Shops to become an artist and metalworker for Stickley's firm.

Advertising first appears in *The Craftsman* magazine, October issue.

The firm exhibits current furniture at the Boston Mechanics Fair.

The interior of Stickley's house is remodeled as a Craftsman interior.

Stickley departs for Europe, December.

1903
Stickley attends the seventh exhibition of the Arts and Crafts Exhibition Society in London, January.

With Theodore Hanford Pond, Stickley holds an Arts and Crafts exhibition at the Craftsman Building, Syracuse, and at the Mechanics Institute, Rochester, March and April.

In *The Craftsman* magazine, E.G.W. Dietrich designs the first house to be called a "Craftsman House," May issue.

Stickley inaugurates the Craftsman textile and needlework department, under the direction of Blanche Baxter.

Harvey Ellis joins Stickley's firm, late May.

Stickley streamlines his first name, changing "Gustave" to "Gustav," ca. May/June.

Stickley retains "Jones the Marqueterie Man" of New York City to execute Craftsman inlay.

Claude Bragdon works in the Craftsman office, July and August.

The Gustave Stickley Company begins to phase out the United Crafts name in favor of a new trade name, The Craftsman Workshops.

The firm displays furniture in a decorative arts exhibition at the Art Institute of Chicago, December.

1904
Harvey Ellis dies, 2 January.

The Craftsman Home-Builders Club is advertised in *The Craftsman* magazine, January.

The firm aggressively markets its goods and services to furniture manufacturers and retailers.

With George Wharton James, Stickley makes a seven-week trip to the West Coast, March and April.

Stickley travels to St. Louis to see the Louisiana Purchase Exposition, June.

Valentine M. Kluge is foreman of the Craftsman metal shop.

Architects Harry L. Gardner, George Nichols, Karl Sailor, Oliver J. Story, and Alfred T. Taylor design Craftsman houses.

Charles Wagner, author of *The Simple Life*, lectures at the Craftsman Building, Syracuse, October.

1903

1904

1910

1915

1916

1905

With publication of "Cabinet Work from the Craftsman Workshops Catalogue D," the firm standardizes its furniture production.

Stickley patents spindle chair designs, August.

The joiner's compass shopmark becomes the firm's registered trademark.

Mary Fanton Roberts joins the editorial staff of *The Craftsman* magazine.

Stickley opens his Branch Exposition Office at 29 West Thirty-fourth Street in New York City, December.

1906

Peter Hansen designs furniture for Gustav Stickley.

Stickley begins dividing his time between his Eastwood factory and his New York City office.

1907

Victor Toothaker is in charge of the Craftsman metal shop.

Stickley begins to contemplate settling his family on a farm near New York City.

1908

Stickley travels to Europe, April.

Stickley starts buying New Jersey real estate and advances his plans for what he now refers to as "Craftsman Farms."

Stickley moves his architectural and editorial departments to 41 West Thirty-fourth Street, October.

The firm opens a Craftsman retail store in Boston, October.

Stickley announces his plan—never realized—to publish *The Yeoman*, a monthly magazine for farmers, October.

The Craftsman Home Building Company is formed to construct Craftsman houses, December.

1909

The Craftsman Publishing Company issues its first book, *Craftsman Homes*, a compilation of Craftsman house plans, April.

1910

Circulation of *The Craftsman* magazine peaks at 22,500.

After undergoing further simplification and rationalization, Stickley's Arts and Crafts furniture enters its final phase.

1911

Stickley and his family move to Craftsman Farms, May and June.

Construction of the log house at Craftsman Farms is completed.

The architect George E. Fowler is hired as a designer of Craftsman houses, most likely in this year.

1912

The firm opens a Craftsman retail store, in Washington, D.C., September.

Stickley's enterprises are consolidated under a new corporate entity, Gustav Stickley The Craftsman Incorporated, October.

Stickley appoints Raymond Riordon to administer the Craftsman Farms School for Citizenship, October.

The second book from the Craftsman Publishing Company, *More Craftsman Homes*, is released, July.

Stickley files a trademark infringement complaint against the Seattle bungalow promoter Jud Yoho; a U.S. Patent Office hearing is held, 1913; Stickley succeeds in retaining exclusive rights to the "Craftsman" trademark.

1913

Stickley leases a new building at 6 East Thirty-ninth Street in New York City, and opens it as the Craftsman Building, October and November.

In the course of this year, Gustav Stickley The Craftsman Incorporated begins to operate at a loss.

1914

Stickley retains Joseph H. Dodson to manage the first and only public offering of the corporation's stock, July.

Helen Speer joins Stickley's firm to design children's furniture.

The firm begins manufacturing reproduction period furniture.

1915

The firm announces bankruptcy, 23 March.

By October, G. Tracy Rogers assumes control of the enterprise.

1916

Stickley launches the historically based Chromewald furniture line, with a new emphasis on vivid colors, which the firm aggressively promotes in the magazine and at the Grand Rapids market, May, June, and September.

Stickley shuttles back and forth between New York and Syracuse.

Publication of *The Craftsman* ceases, December.

Stickley Associated Cabinetmakers is formed, Leopold Stickley, president, and absorbs Gustav Stickley The Craftsman Incorporated, December.

1917

The Craftsman merges with the magazine *Art World*, which takes over its subscription list, January.

Gustav and Eda Stickley move into the Wolcott, a Syracuse boarding house.

Stickley patents an improved couch-bed, March, that he will later plan to manufacture and market with Leopold.

Eda Stickley is paralyzed by a stroke.

To stave off foreclosure, Stickley sells Craftsman Farms to George and Sylvia Farny, August.

1918

Stickley rents half of a duplex house at 832 Sumner Avenue, Syracuse.

1919

Eda Stickley dies, 13 March.

Stickley moves back to 416 Columbus Avenue, now the home of his daughter Barbara and her husband Ben Wiles.

With Ben Wiles, Stickley founds the Lustre Wood Products Company to make toys and children's furniture, June.

1920 (ca.)

Stickley begins two decades of furniture-finish experiments.

1940 (ca.)

Stickley makes his last furniture, several Shaker-like chairs that he gives to family members.

1942

Gustav Stickley dies in Syracuse, New York, 20 April; his ashes are buried in Morningside Cemetery.

ABBREVIATIONS

ACMU   American Cabinet Maker and Upholsterer

CF   Craftsman Farms Archives

FJ   Furniture Journal

FTR   Furniture Trade Review

FW   Furniture World

HFM   Henry Ford Museum and Greenfield Village, Research Center

IS   International Studio

OHA   Onondaga Historical Association

U   The Upholsterer

WL   The Winterthur Library, Joseph Downs Collection of Manuscripts and Printed Ephemera, Stickley Business Papers, Collection 60

INTRODUCTION

1 Several of Stickley's letters to Henry Turner Bailey were written by Emily A. Pickard. They are in the Henry T. Bailey Papers in the Division of Special Collections and University Archives at the University of Oregon Library. Some of Stickley's letters to the ceramist C.F. Binns were written by Josephine K. Brown and others were written by Muriel Irwin MacDonald. The Binns letters are in the Charles Fergus Binns Papers, College Archives, New York State College of Ceramics at Alfred University. Other than the fact that Pickard was an employee of Stickley's firm for about a decade and Brown was for many years his private secretary, little is known about either woman. McDonald, however, was an important contributor to the *Craftsman* magazine.

2 Gustav Stickley, "Cabinet Work from the Craftsman Workshops—Catalogue D" (1905): 1–2.

3 Mildred Stickley Cruess, interview by Robert Judson Clark, Rochester, NY, handwritten notes and typed transcript, 6 January 1973.

CHAPTER 1

1 *The National Cyclopedia of American Biography* 14 (New York: James T. White & Co., 1918): 290–291. The information in his entry, including date of birth, was provided by Stickley and the date he specified is accepted for this book. However, the date of birth on his death certificate and his headstone, for which his daughter Barbara was the source, is 9 March 1857. To cloud this point further, his birth date given in the 1900 United States Census is 9 March 1860.

2 Marilyn Fish, *Gustav Stickley Heritage & Early Years* (North Caldwell, NJ: Little Pond Press, 1997), and Marilyn Fish, Gustav Stickley 1884–1900: The Stickley Brothers, Stickley & Simonds, and the Gustave Stickley Co. (North Caldwell, NJ: Little Pond Press, 1999). These works are essential guides to Stickley's early life.

3 Stickley discarded the "e" in "Gustave" between May and June 1903 and adopted the more American and up-to-date "Gustav." This was initially a cosmetic rather than a formal name change, and legal documents executed in his behalf as late as 1909 retain the earlier spelling. For a brief period, in New York City directories of 1907–08 he referred to himself as "Gustav Stickley, publisher," and in another, separate (and mystifying) listing, "Augustus Stickley, furniture maker." To the extent possible, the following chapters will reflect Stickley's preferences: he will be "Gustave" until mid-1903, and "Gustav" thereafter.

4 Charles Stickley (1860–1928), Albert Stickley (1862–1928), Leopold Stickley (1869–1957), John George Stickley (1871–1921). Fish has established the following dates for the daughters: Louisa (1848–1929), Mary, b. 1851; Emma, b. 1864; and Christina, b. 1866.

5 John Dewey, *The School and Society 1899*; reprint, (Carbondale: Southern Illinois University Press): 18.

6 "Chips from the Craftsman Workshops" (1906): n. p.

7 Clues to Stickley's early reading habits are found in the 1906 "Chips" and his entry in *The National Cyclopedia of American Biography*, both cited above; and in Gustav Stickley, "Thoughts Occasioned by an Anniversary: A Plea for a Democratic Art," *The Craftsman 7* (October 1904): 43–64. It must be said, however, that these clues appear in Craftsman promotional literature and it is not possible to gauge their reliability; it seems more plausible that Stickley discovered the writings of Carlyle, Ruskin, and Morris later in life.

8 The Winterthur Library, Joseph Downs Collection of Manuscripts and Printed Ephemera, Stickley Business Papers, Collection 60 (hereafter WL), Box 51; this transaction occurred on 30 May 1888.

9 This information on Rogers is found in William Foote Seward, Editor-in-Chief, *Binghamton and Broome County New York A History* (New York and Chicago: Lewis Historical Publishing Company, Inc., 1924): 26–27.

10 *American Cabinet Maker and Upholsterer* (hereafter ACMU) 37 (7 July 1888): 15.

11 The address of Simonds's New York City office, at 18 E. 18th Street, appears in ACMU 38 (19 March 1889): 18.

12 Eventually, non-family members joined. Other board members by 1898 were Frederick A. Arwine, Fred H. Mills, J.M. Stevenson, W.J. Robinson, and William D. Brewster, president of the Jones Furniture Company of Syracuse. WL Boxes 19 and 20.

13 WL Box 19; for Stickley's move to Auburn and early years in Syracuse, see Fish, Gustav Stickley 1884–1900.

14 Marion Stickley Flaccus, Elaine Naramore interview, 12 April 1982, transcript in the collection of the Joint Free Public Library of Morristown and Morris Township (New Jersey).

15 There is an old canard claiming that Stickley made the first electric chair while he was working at the Auburn prison. This story does not withstand scrutiny. In a letter to Bruce Johnson, dated 21 November, 1994, Robert Mitchell, Correction Counselor, Auburn Correctional Facility, confirmed the following: Dr. Alfred P. Southwick, a dentist, was the first proponent of electrocution as a humane form of capital punishment; the electrical apparatus for the chair was developed by two other men, Dr. Carlos McDonnell and Alfonse Rockwell; and a third, Dr. George Fell, designed the first electric chair in 1887. As reported in the *New York Times* of 1 January 1890, an electric chair was tested at the prison on 31 December 1889. The first execution by electric chair, that of a convicted murderer named William Kemmler, took place in Auburn on 6 August 1890. Stickley was still in Binghamton when these events occurred and the firm was not in Auburn until after Kemmler's execution.

16 ACMU 47 (6 May 1893): 23.

17 "Walter Plumb, designer ... has accepted an engagement with the Stickley & Simonds Co., Syracuse, N.Y." *Furniture World* (hereafter FW) 4 (12 November 1896): 16. Plumb is also identified as an employee in WL 76 x 101.8; he later worked for Elgin Simonds at the Boston-based firm of Barnard & Simonds; see FW 5 (21 December 1899): 34.

18 "Furniture buyers who visit Syracuse are generally entertained at the Century Club by the local manufacturers. This is the swell club of the city." FW 5 (6 May 1897): 6. Stickley was a member of this club.

19 Stickley returned to the United States on 4 April 1895; he sailed on a German liner, the Teutonic, and departed from Liverpool; information from www.ellisislandrecords.org.

20 FW 4 (19 November 1896): 11.

21 FW 3 (9 July 1896):57. The trade journal research underlying this section was conducted, separately, by David Cathers and Marilyn Fish, who have shared their discoveries with one another for several years.

22 There is one possible exception, uncovered by Michael Clark and Jill Thomas-Clark: according to an 1895 *Furniture World* news item, Stickley & Simonds was said to be upholstering some of its chairs with "Morris velvets." See FW 2, (3 October 1895): 28.

23 Some of the information in this paragraph is from the Yates file, Onondaga Historical Association (Hereafter OHA).

24 WL Box 51. The agreement that Stickley and Rogers made with Averill and Gregory to receive ten percent of the hotel's profits is dated 8 March 1893; the only record of payment that survives is for 1896.

25 According to Michael Clark and Jill Thomas-Clark, Stickley applied for a patent on a "sandpapering-wheel" on 12 September 1895.

26 WL Box 51. Stickley's wood bending machine was patented in the United States on 2 July 1895.

27 For America's fascination with Japan in the late nineteenth century, see William Hosley. *The Japan Idea: Art and Life in Victorian America* (Hartford, CT: Wadsworth Atheneum, 1990).

28 *The Upholsterer* (hereafter U) 17–18 (December 1897): 38.

29 FW 6 (11 November 1897): 7, 8.

30 Gustav Stickley, "Thoughts Occasioned by an Anniversary: A Plea for Democratic Art," *The Craftsman 7* (October 1904): 42.

31 FW 7 (12 May 1898): 8.

32 On 2 May 1898, Simonds advertised in the *Syracuse Herald* offering three fine horses and two carriages for quick sale: "All of the above are first-class and bought for private use, and only used for a short time. Will sell very reasonable." OHA clipping.

33 "E.A. Simonds, lately of the Stickley & Simonds Co., has joined C.J. Brown, of Boston, and the Brown & Simonds Co. [has] been formed .... The new company will place on the market a line of cabinet novelties. Mr. Simonds also has an interest in the Hayden & Crouch Mfg. Co., Rochester, New York, who will put on the market a line of high-class chairs like that made by the Stickley & Simonds Co." U 19 (June 1898): 59. Simonds established the Elgin A. Simonds Company in Syracuse in 1901 and this firm, managed by a

former salesman, T. Ashley Dent, and later by Dent's son, survived into the 1930s; Simonds died in January 1903, at the age of forty-nine, and a large obituary appeared in ACMU 67 (7 February 1903): 8–9.

CHAPTER 2

1 "The Gustave Stickley Co., who succeeded the Stickley & Simonds Co., Syracuse, announce that they will continue their line of dining chairs in the patterns which in the past have been particularly successful…being of the Colonial, Chippendale, Old Dutch and Sheraton." U 20 (20 September 1898): 60.

2 FW 7 (17 November 1898): 5.

3 This claim about Stickley's early career is supported by a passage incorporated into his entry in *The National Cyclopedia of American Biography*: "With the demands of a large business upon his hands, Mr. Stickley for a time was compelled to go with the tide and keep in line with other manufacturers, but in 1900 he began to make all kinds of furniture after his own designs." *The National Cyclopedia of American Biography* 14 (New York: James T. White & Co., 1918): 290–291.

4 Information from Karolee Harris, Grand Rapids Public Library, via e-mail, 29 July 2002.

5 FW 10 (9 November 1899): 8.

6 Gustav Stickley, "Thoughts Occasioned by an Anniversary: A Plea for a Democratic Art," *The Craftsman* 7 (October 1904): 43–64.

7 For example: *House Beautiful*, 1896; *International Studio*, 1897 (this was the American edition of *Studio* [1893], with an added American section at the back; each issue of *International Studio* followed by one month the corresponding issue of *Studio*); *Deutsche Kunst und Dekoration*, 1897; *Dekorative Kunst*, 1897; *Kunst und Kundsthandwerk*, 1898; *Keramic Studio*, 1899. Barbara Stickley Wiles said that her father subscribed to English and French art periodicals and also to *Deutsche Kunst und Dekoration*; interview with Clark, 7 October 1972. Arts and Crafts societies were started in Boston, Chicago, and Rochester, New York, in 1897 and many similar groups were formed in other cities by the turn of the twentieth century.

8 Gustav Stickley, "Chips from the Craftsman Workshops" (1906): n. p.

9 "Yeddo" was a popular variant of "Edo," which was the name of Tokyo before the 1868 Meiji Restoration.

10 "There are suggestions all through the Stickley line of the things made by Rohlfs. It is stated that Mr. Stickley got his first idea from the Rohlfs furniture." FJ 13 (25 August 1900): 4; for a fuller discussion of Rohlfs's influence on Stickley, see David Cathers. *Furniture of the American Arts and Crafts Movement* (Philmont: Turn of the Century Editions, 1996): p. 33–34.

11 For Stickley's description of quarter-sawing, see "Home Training in Cabinet Work: The Texture and Qualities of Natural Woods, Their Individuality and Friendliness," *The Craftsman* 8 (July 1905): 524–534.

12 *Chicago Tribune* (7 October 1900).

13 When cabinet wood is "'filled' with a prepared wood filler made from a finely ground silex" and then varnished, the finishing process "destroys the texture by covering it with an enamel that completely alters its character…. [T]he woodiness of texture that is so interesting has given place to an artificial smoothness of finish that passes for fineness of finish." Unsigned, "Home Training in Cabinet Work: Practical Talks on Structural Wood Working," *The Craftsman* 9 (October 1905): 123–125.

14 "Chips from the Craftsman Workshops," n.p.

15 Claude Bragdon to Katherine Bragdon (his mother) and May Bragdon (his sister), Syracuse, NY, December 27, 1900. Family Correspondence (1st) 1900–1923, Bragdon Family Papers, Rush Rhees Library, University of Rochester.

16 *Furniture Journal* (hereafter FJ) 13 (10 July 1900): 14.

17 "Novelty" was a commonly used trade term: "Mr. Stickley has…succeeded in turning out some handsome designs that cannot fail to impress the buyers of fine goods favorably. The line will contain a variety of novelties." ACMU 62 (30 June 1900): 37–38.

18 *Furniture Trade Review* (hereafter FTR) 20 (10 August 1900): 14.

19 FJ 13 (25 August 1900): 4.

20 Ibid.

21 Research by Marjorie Searl of the Memorial Art Gallery of the University of Rochester, Robert Rust, and David Cathers has unearthed this particular Stickley-Hubbard connection. A Stickley Bungalow chair is visible in a 1902 Roycroft book catalog; a Stickley Chalet table stamped with a Roycroft campus inventory mark is in a private New York State collection; a Stickley flower-shaped Adder table, descended from the Hubbard family, is in the collection of the Metropolitan Museum of Art. The import of these facts remained a puzzle until Searl discovered letters written by a Roycroft employee in July 1900 saying that Hubbard had "attended a furniture exhibition" while traveling and spent "all he made on the lecture on furniture and is going to have it shipped here." Lyman Chandler to Florence Irvine Chandler, East Aurora, NY, 24 July 1900, University of Rochester Department of Rare Books and Special Collections.

22 Ibid.

23 FW 4–5 (25 April 1897): 7.

24 Anna Tobin D'Ambrosio, "The Distinction of Being Different": *Joseph P. McHugh and the American Arts and Crafts Movement* (Utica, NY: Munson-William-Proctor Institute, 1993): 18.

25 The use of trademarks was not then a common practice in the industry. An unsigned article in the October 1900 *American Cabinet Maker and Upholsterer* reported: "Heretofore the public's ideas of furniture have been formed mainly by the dealer. [But some] manufacturers propose to have their particular productions better known and appreciated by the buyer at retail, and with this object in view, will create and make known identifying marks." "Trade-Mark Habit Contagious," ACMU 63 (20 October 1900): 112.

26 Not every piece of furniture in this advertisement came from Stickley. The "weathered oak buffet" on the top right, for instance, had been made by another Tobey supplier, the Michigan Chair Company. See the *Grand Rapids Furniture Record* 6 (January 1903): 147.

27 Margaret Edgewood, "Some Sensible Furniture," *House Beautiful* 8 (October 1900): 653–655.

28 Syracuse city directory, 1901.

29 Stickley bought this house from Moses Lewis, a clerk employed by Simon Rosenbloom, a Syracuse dry goods merchant who carried Stickley furniture in his store.

30 ACMU 63 (22 December 1900): 31. Stickley's first expenses for this building were recorded on 3 March 1901, in WL 76 x 101.11; the 1903 Syracuse city directory shows that he shared the building with the Orleans Sandstone Company, Syracuse Improvements Company, and the Warner-Quinlan Asphalt Company; I thank Coy L. Ludwig for providing information on the building's other tenants.

31 "What is Wrought in the Craftsman Workshops" (1904): 7–13.

32 This brief discussion of the Syracuse Craftsman Building was informed by: Coy L. Ludwig, *The Arts and Crafts Movement in Central New York State 1890s–1920s,* (Hamilton, NY: The Gallery Association of New York State, 1983): 63; Cleota Reed, "Near the Yates," in Bert Denker, ed., The Substance of Style, (Winterthur, DE: The Henry Francis DuPont Winterthur Museum, 1996): 359–374; and Mary Ann Smith, *Gustav Stickley The Craftsman* (Syracuse: Syracuse University Press, 1983): 24–26.

33 Ernest J. Bowden, "Versatility of Talent Lights Entire Career," *Syracuse Post-Standard*, 15 September 1932, obituary clipping in the Onondaga County Public Library.

34 Barbara Stickley Wiles, interview by author, 27 March 1978.

35 Ibid.

36 Sargent ends her essay, for instance, with stirring words: "…we are putting forth our personal efforts to realize the meaning of an art developed by the people, for the people, as a reciprocal joy for the maker and user." The closing words of William Morris's 1879 lecture "The Art of the People" similarly invoked "glorious art, made by the people and for the people, as a happiness to the maker and user." "Chips" begins by proclaiming that "Our object is to substitute the luxury of taste for the luxury of costliness." In her Morris monograph in the October 1901 *Craftsman*, Sargent quotes these similar words from the 1861 Morris & Company prospectus: "and it is believed that good decoration involving rather the luxury of taste than the luxury of costliness will be found much less expensive than is generally supposed."

37 Cleota Reed discovered the handwritten manuscript of this essay among Sargent's papers at Syracuse University. As Reed has written in "Gustav Stickley and Irene Sargent: United Crafts and The Craftsman," the 4,000-word text has few corrections and seems to have flowed effortlessly from Sargent's pen. It is dated 13 January 1901.

38 Stickley applied for a patent for his new logo on 9 September 1901, describing it in his application as "A pair of compasses and the words 'Als ik kan.' Used since January 1, 1901."

39 *The Craftsman* 1 (October 1901): fourth cover.

40 "In 1902, [Stickley's firm] was run on a profit-sharing basis; $2,000 was set aside to be divided among the workmen. This sum was divided with shares of $5 to $100, the amount awarded to each craftsman being based upon the character of work and length of employment." See Mabel Tuke Priestman, "History of the Arts and Crafts Movement in America," *House Beautiful* 20 (November 1906): 14.

41 A factory inventory taken on 1 January 1901, listed a seat machine, tenon machine, inlaying machine, dowel machine, embossing machine, molding machine, as well as sanders, lathes, circular saws, and surface planers, all driven by a powerful Edison dynamo; Leopold Stickley, foreman from 1899 through 1901 and a company director in 1901–02, oversaw the use of this machinery.

42 For instance, as to financial matters, WL Box 19 records a meeting of the firm's board of directors on 19 February 1901, at which it was decided to borrow $10,000 from Merchants National Bank of Syracuse, for use as operating capital; the loan was secured by the firm's tools, machinery, and real estate. As to legal matters, Stickley's patent attorney, Howard P. Denison, filed design patents for three Stickley designs in September 1901: a library table desk, patent #35,044; a table, patent #35,045; and a chair body, patent #35,082. These patent documents are in a private collection.

43 Unsigned, "Famous Crouse Stable Becomes A Furniture Display House Leased by the Stickley Company," *Syracuse Post-Standard,* 10 March 1901; OHA clipping.

44 WL 76 x 101.11

45 Irene Sargent's text for the 1901 "Chips" catalog discusses the color of Stickley's furniture, but describes it as being achieved with wood stains and makes no mention of fuming. The earliest reference to Stickley's use of fuming appears in the first issue of the *The Craftsman,* in October 1901, suggesting that the process had been adopted in the intervening months.

46 I thank Stickley Furniture Company corporate historian Michael Danial and furniture conservator David Parsons for their insights into the promotional value of fuming. Stickley probably got the idea for fuming from English furniture makers, where the practice eventually became so widespread that Hermann Muthesius was able to write in 1904 that "Furniture in…fumed oak is very popular in the wider market." See Hermann Muthesius. *The English House* (1904–05; reprint New York: Rizzoli International Publications Inc., 1979): 197.

47 Stickley explained his fuming process, certainly omitting some key details, in "Home Training in Cabinet Work: Practical Talks on Structural Woodworking: Seventh of the Series," *The Craftsman* 9 (October 1905): 123–125.

48 Gustav Stickley, "Thoughts Occasioned by an Anniversary: A Plea for Democratic Art," *The Craftsman* 7 (October 1904): 43–64

49 Gustav Stickley, "The Structural Style in Cabinet-Making," *House Beautiful* 15 (December 1903): 19–23. This was Stickley's most definitive discussion of the "structural style," and was almost certainly written in 1901 or 1902, probably by Irene Sargent. By the time it appeared in print it was less relevant to the Harvey Ellis-designed furniture Stickley was then making.

50 "Chips from the Craftsman Workshops—Number II" (1907): 38.

51 Stickley, "Thoughts Occasioned."

52 Quoted in Clive Wainwright, "A.W.N. Pugin and the Progress of Design as Applied to Manufacture," in Paul Atterbury, ed., *A.W.N. Pugin—Master of the Gothic Revival* (New Haven, CT: Yale University Press, 1995): 164.

53 Quoted in Chris Brooks, *The Gothic Revival* (London: Phaidon Press, 1999): 238.

54 Clive Wainwright, "Furniture," in Paul Atterbury and Clive Wainwright, ed., *Pugin—A Gothic Passion,* (New Haven, CT and London: Yale University Press, 1994): 127–142.

55 Wainwright, "A.W.N. Pugin and the Progress of Design," p.171.

56 See Frances Collard, "Furniture," 164–165, and Clive Wainwright, "Morris in Context," in Linda Parry, ed., *William Morris* (New York: Harry N. Abrams, 1996): 164–165 and 355.

57 Irene Sargent, "The Gothic Revival," *The Craftsman* 1 (March 1902): 1–32.

58 See, for example, the section on Baillie Scott in Charles Holme, ed., "Modern British Domestic Architecture and Decoration," Special Summer Number of *The Studio* (1901): 157–63; see also ACMU 61 (20 January 1900): cover.

59 "Furniture Made at the Pyghtle Works, by John P. White, Designed by M.H. Baillie Scott," (1901).

60 Baillie Scott wrote, "It has always been a great pleasure for me to receive the Craftsman, and I have before written you expressing my sympathy and interest in your work." See "What is Wrought in the Craftsman Workshops" (1904): 73.

61 WL 76 x 101. 11 records the firm's exposition expenses as $811.60.

62 Clara Ruge, "Das Kunstgewerbe Amerikas," *Kunst und Kunsthandwerk* 5 (March 1902): 126–148.

63 Unsigned, "Furniture from the Eastwood Craftsmen," *Art Interchange* 47 (November 1901): 109.

64 *House Beautiful* 10 (November 1901): 326.

65 A photograph taken of Charles Greene, taken at the Pan-American Exposition, is in the possession of Robert Judson Clark.

66 "Associate Craftsmen," U 26 (December 1901): 26.

67 Gustav Stickley to Henry Turner Bailey, Syracuse, NY, 18 May 1901; Henry Turner Bailey Papers, Division of Special Collections and University Archives, University of Oregon Libraries.

68 "Things Wrought," (1901): n. p.

69 Unsigned, "Ernest I. White, Prominent Lawyer, Marks 81st Birthday," *Syracuse Post-Standard,* 4 October 1950; clipping in the Ernest I. White file, OHA.

70 FJ 17 (10 October 1902): 4.

71 Barbara Stickley Wiles, interview by Robert Judson Clark, Syracuse, NY, 4 August 1971.

72 Mildred Stickley Cruess interview.

CHAPTER 3

1 "Things Wrought by the United Crafts" (1902): 12.

2 Ibid., p. 7.

3 Stickley made his last recorded payment to Wilkinson, for $200, on 18 September 1901; WL 76 x 101. 11.

4 "Chips II," (1907): 40–41.

5 See, for example, *International Studio* (hereafter IS) 17 (August 1902): 91–104; for the Mackintoshes' exhibit in Turin, see Alan Crawford, *Charles Rennie Mackintosh* (London: Thames and Hudson, 1995): 95–99.

6 In August 1903, for instance, *The Craftsman* published several designs for Craftsman portieres, one of which was directly inspired by the rose motif stenciled onto some of the chairs the Mackintoshes took to Turin. See Unsigned, "Some Craftsman Designs for Door Draperies," *The Craftsman* 4 (August 1903): 387–389.

7 Unsigned, "The International Exhibition of Modern Decorative Art at Turin—The Scottish Section," IS 17 (August 1902): 91–104.

8 In 1902 the firm issued a set of line drawings of Craftsman furniture arranged in room settings. These drawings were unsigned, but their hand-lettered captions reveal them to have been Shrimpton's work. Her lettering style was identified by her nephew, Sturtevant Pratt, in an interview by the author in Manlius, NY, 8 July 1996.

9 "Museum of Fine Arts Fifteenth Annual Report of the School of Drawing and Painting" (1891): 4.

10 "William Morris: His Thoughts, Theories and Opinions Upon Work in a Factory," *The Craftsman* 5 (December 1903): 245–253.

11 *Handicraft* 2 (November 1902): 190.

12 Oliver Coleman. "'Ready-Made' Furniture," *House Beautiful* 12 (November 1902): 383–388.

13 Gustave Stickley, "Critical Correspondence," *The Craftsman* 4 (April 1903): 58-59; and (May 1903): 138–140.

14 John Ruskin, "The Nature of Gothic," *The Stones of Venice, vol. 2* (New York: John Wiley & Son, 1889): xxv.

15 U 28 (December 1902): 56d, 56e.

16 Robert Judson Clark is the source of this key insight.

17 George Jack (1855–1932) was born in the United States, immigrated to Britain before he was twenty, and became the head furniture designer for Morris & Company in 1890. The andirons designed by him are visible on page 161 of "A Visit"; they were earlier published in *Studio 2* (1893): 16; it is not known if Stickley actually owned such andirons or if they were only a delineator's fancy.

18 *The Craftsman* 3 (January 1903): 260.

19 Coleman, "'Ready-Made' Furniture."

20 "Gift of Match Case by United Craftsmen," *Syracuse Post-Standard,* 14 December 1902: 6

21 In *The Forgotten Rebel,* John Crosby Freeman claimed that Stickley traveled to Europe in 1898, a date subsequently repeated in other books. There is however, no corroborating evidence of an 1898 trip, and it is unlikely that Stickley, busy shutting down Stickley & Simonds and starting up the Gustave Stickley Company, would have had time to leave the country that year.

22 The price is reported in "Crafts Show Now Open," *Syracuse Evening Herald,* (24 March 1903): back page; this Limoges dinner service stayed in Stickley's family for eighty-five years, and most of it was sold at Christie's New York, 10 December 1988, lots 24–27; see also Gabriel P. Weisberg, "Bing Porcelain in America," *Connoisseur* 158 (November 1971):200–203; The dollar equivalency is derived from Scott Derks. *The Value of the Dollar—Prices and Income in the United States 1860–1999* (Lakeville, CT: Gray House Publishing, 1999): 2; and from the American Institute for Economic Research Cost-of-Living Calculator, www.aeir.org/colcalc.htm.

23 Stickley exhibited these objects in Arts and Crafts exhibitions in Syracuse and Rochester in March and April 1903.

24 In a brief review of the exhibition, a writer for *The Upholsterer*, a journal generally sympathetic toward the Arts and Crafts, did not quite know what to make of some of these exhibits. "Mr. Voysey," fussed the reviewer, "is a designer for whom we have the greatest respect, but what earthly excuse can he give for presenting such a chair and such a desk…and what is the idea of making a lounge [the Baillie Scott settle] with sides so low? It certainly doesn't give one comfort. What's the object of it?" Unsigned. "London Arts and Crafts," U 20 (March 1903): 38–40.

25 For Ellwood, see Jeremy Cooper, *Victorian and Edwardian Décor from the Gothic Revival to Art Nouveau* (New York: Abbeville Press, 1987): 216.

26 Duncan Simpson, "Furniture," in John Brandon Jones and others, *C.F.A. Voysey: Architect and Designer 1857–1941* (London: Lund Humphries, 1978): 72.

27 Dietrich's three contributions to *The Craftsman* were "The Cottage Quality" (February 1903): 280–282; "An Interior" (April 1903):57–58; "The Craftsman House" (May 1903):84–92.

28 A.W.N. Pugin, *The Glossary of Ecclesiastical Ornament*, 1844, quoted in Chris Brooks, *The Gothic Revival* (London: Phaidon Press, 1999):240.

29 See Dianne H. Pilgrim, "Decorative Art: The Domestic Environment," in *The American Renaissance, 1876–1917* (New York: The Brooklyn Museum, 1979):110–151.

30 Clarence Cook, *The House Beautiful* (1881; reprint, New York: Dover Publications, 1995):131.

31 Architectural unity may have been a cherished ideal among Arts and Crafts architects, but it was not universally embraced. In an article about bungalows, for instance, the architect Katharine Budd expressed the contrary view: "Furniture which has perfect harmony in style is not only unnecessary, but undesirable as well, in a true bungalow. Irregularity to a certain extent lends additional charm." Katharine C. Budd, "The Bungalow in America," *Architectural Review* 11 (August 1904):221–224.

32 Much of this section is based on the research of Coy L. Ludwig, who generously gave me photocopies of the Syracuse and Rochester newspaper reports on these two major Arts and Crafts exhibitions. He was assisted in his research by Rebecca Lawton and the R.I.T. archivist in 1982, Gladys Taylor. See also Cleota Reed, "Near the Yates: Craft, Machine, and Ideology in Arts and Crafts Syracuse, 1900–1910," in Bert Denker, ed., *The Substance of Style* (Winterthur, DE: Henry Francis duPont Winterthur Museum, 1996):359–374.

33 *Rochester Times*, 20 April 1903.

34 Irene Sargent, "A Recent Arts and Crafts Exhibition," *The Craftsman* 4 (May 1903):69–83.

35 "Exhibition of Arts and Crafts," *Rochester Post,* 9 April 1903.

36 "Arts and Crafts Exhibition Opened Today," *Rochester Post,* 15 April 1903.

37 "Arts and Crafts," Rochester Union, 18 April 1903; "Handiwork Odd and Beautiful," *Rochester Democrat*, 16 April 1903.

CHAPTER 4

1 Anyone writing about Harvey Ellis is indebted to the pioneering exhibition catalog by Jean R. France, Roger G. Kennedy, Blake McKelvey, and Howard S. Merritt, *A Rediscovery—Harvey Ellis: Artist, Architect* (Rochester, NY: Memorial Art Gallery of the University of Rochester, 1972).

2 Ellis's trip to Syracuse was reported in "A Display That All Should See," *Rochester Democrat*, 3 April 1903: n. p.

3 "Removed to This City," *Syracuse Herald*, 30 May 1903, OHA clipping.

4 The 1903 Syracuse city directory lists Ellis as a designer boarding at 524 Montgomery Street, the home of Daniel Gere, a salesman.

5 "New Art Society: The Rochester Society of Arts and Crafts a New Comer in Art Circles," *Rochester Union and Advertiser*, 13 March 1897:9. Typescripts of this article and the article in note 6 were kindly supplied to me by Coy L. Ludwig.

6 "Japanese Prints and French New Poster Exhibition by the New Society," *Rochester Union and Advertiser*, 22 May 1897:10.

7 James D. Kornwolf, *M.H. Baillie Scott and the Arts and Crafts Movement* (Baltimore, MD, and London: The Johns Hopkins Press, 1972): 385.

8 *The Seven Lamps of Architecture, The Stones of Venice,* vol. 1, and *The Poetry of Architecture* (New York: John Wiley & Son, 1880). If Ellis owned the second volume of *The Stones of Venice*, the book in which the seminal essay "The Nature of Gothic" first appeared, it has been lost. University of Rochester, Ellis papers.

9 My thanks to Alan Crawford for confirming the identity of this house and for providing information about it.

10 Some examples of Jarvis's furniture designs are shown in Aymer Vallance, "British Decorative Art in 1899 and the Arts and Crafts Exhibition, Part III," *International Studio* 9 (January 1900): 180–185.

11 Hugh Garden, *Prairie School Review*, reprint, p. 38.

12 Claude Bragdon, *Prairie School Review*, reprint, p. 24.

13 The professional journal *Architecture* featured a similar typographic gesture, and this was no doubt Ellis's source. The May 1903 issue was in his possession when he joined Stickley's firm and is still among his papers.

14 Flaming hearts can have various meanings, but they typically symbolize generalized religious fervor, an interpretation appropriate to Ellis's art. Marie Via, e-mail to the author, 20 September 2000.

15 Claude Bragdon to Katherine Bragdon, Syracuse, NY, 21 July 1903; Bragdon Papers, University of Rochester Library.

16 Bragdon, to Katherine Bragdon, Syracuse, NY, 26(?)July 1903; Bragdon Papers. This is a familiar-sounding complaint; in his 1897 profile of Ellis, Bragdon had criticized his friend's work for being "too fanciful, too exuberant."

17 Bragdon to Henry Wilkinson, Syracuse, NY, 20 July 1903.

18 Bragdon to Katherine Bragdon, Syracuse, NY, 26 July 1903.

19 Bragdon to Katherine Bragdon, Syracuse, NY, 11 August 1903.

20 "[T]he use of different tones of wash for different lights in a window instead of natural shading for the whole, seem origi-nal [to Shaw]." Andrew Saint, *Richard Norman Shaw* (New Haven, CT, and London: Yale University Press, 1977): 188.

21 These interiors were originally published in black and white; they did not appear in color until Stickley published the book *Craftsman Homes* in 1909, six years after Ellis drew them; the colors printed in 1909 vary from the colors described in Ellis's 1903 text.

22 Harvey Ellis, "How to Build a Bungalow," *The Craftsman* 5 (December 1903): 253–260.

23 Unsigned, "Housekeeping in Miniature," *The Craftsman* 4 (June 1903): 192–196.

24 Inlay and marquetry are related crafts. Both involve cutting decorative shapes out of thin pieces of wood or other materials, but with inlay the shapes are laid in to recesses cut into the body of a piece of furniture; with marquetry, the shapes are assembled in a sawn-out wooden ground and then veneered to the surface of the furniture. See Pierre Ramond, *Marquetry* (Paris: Editions H. Vial, 1979). Both techniques were used on Stickley furniture, but all such furniture is today referred to as "inlaid," and for convenience I have used that term throughout this book.

25 FTR 17 (10 November 1896): 24.

26 ACMU 66 (13 September 1902): 6.

27 WL 76x101.11; the date of this initial shipment is the evidence that Stickley's workers had begun making inlaid furniture by this time.

28 According to his death certificate, Ellis died of "chronic endocarditis due to chronic nephritis." Photocopy, Ellis Papers, University of Rochester.

29 Coy L. Ludwig, letter to the author, 10 March 1997.

30 These expenses are recorded in a Stickley ledger now in private hands.

31 "Harvey Ellis. An artist and architect of reputation, was buried in this city [Syracuse] at the expense of acquaintances…. Mr. Ellis had three pictures called Silhouettes at the Paris Exposition, and also at the Pan American. His paintings in the exhibits of the American Watercolor Society of the National Academy of Design are well known among artists…. He had a wife, from whom he was separated, and a brother…. He was also an architect." *New York Times*, 12 January 1904: 1.

32 *The Craftsman* 5 (February 1904): 520.

33 "Catalogue of Original Designs for Decorations and Examples of Art Crafts having Distinctive Artistic Merits," Art Institute of Chicago, 3 December 1903–20 December 1903; Ryerson Library, 708.17311 A784 1902–03.

34 *Chicago Journal*, 5 December 1903, quoted in *The Craftsman* 5 (January 1904): 422.

CHAPTER 5

1 In December 1903, Stickley advertised in such diverse publications as *Handicraft* and *McClure's* announcing a contest to come up with a name for "The Art of the Craftsman Workshops," and he published a booklet, titled "Name This Child," that he mailed to entrants; the contest was unsuccessful and Stickley continued to use the Craftsman name.

2 FJ 21 (December 25, 1904): 4.

3 According to Mary Ann Smith, this house "seems to have been designed by Harvey Ellis, although it was not signed with his initials." See Mary Ann Smith, *Gustav Stickley, The Craftsman*, (Syracuse, NY: Syracuse University Press, 1983): 66; yet this house is so unlike Ellis's work that an attribution to LaMont Warner, Oliver Story, or another of Stickley's staff architects is much more plausible.

4 An item in that month's *Furniture Trade Review* commented on this recent development at Stickley's firm, reporting that "The management includes in its work the designing of houses [and] all sorts of interior decoration." FTR 24 (10 January 1904): 87.

5 FTR 24, (10 October 1904): 35.

6 A full discussion of Gustav Stickley's brothers is beyond the scope of this book, but information on them is available in Michael Clark and Jill Thomas Clark, *The Stickley Brothers* (Salt Lake City: Gibbs Smith Publisher, 2002).

7 Roger Joseph Bourdon, "George Wharton James, Interpreter of the Southwest" (doctoral dissertation, University of California, 1965).

8 Except, perhaps, for the eccentric beginning of the first article, which describes Stickley's visit to an Indian school in Yuma, Arizona; James's notes for this trip are in Notebook #212 Continued and Notebook #216, George Wharton James Papers, Braun Research Library, Southwest Museum, Los Angeles.

9 Bourdon "George Wharton James," 95.

10 George Wharton James, *Traveler's Handbook to California* (Pasadena: self-published, 1904): 291–294.

11 Ben Wiles, Jr., telephone interview by author, 20 March 2000.

12 There are few firm dates for this trip. George Wharton James's Notebook #216 records the 2 April visit to Burton; an item in the *San Francisco Call* for 4 April states that Stickley arrived in that city the day before; an item in *Furniture World* states, "Gustav Stickley returned April 22 from a sojourn in Southern California covering a period of seven weeks." See FW 19 (12 May 1904): 6. Much of Stickley's California itinerary has been reconstructed from [George Wharton James], "Gustav Stickley May Start an Ideal Town Here," *Pasadena Evening Star*, 19 April 1904: 3.

13 "The Tattler," FJ 20 (June 1904): 24; "Gustave Stickley to Found a Community," FW 19 (30 June 1904): 15–16; "Some Plans of Gustave Stickley," FTR 24 (10 July 1904): 89.

14 FJ 20 (10 May 1904): 18.

15 FTR 24 (10 January 1904): 87.

16 Richard Guy Wilson, "'Divine Excellence': The Arts and Crafts Life in California," in Kenneth R. Trapp and others, *The Arts and Crafts Movement in California—Living the Good Life* (Oakland, CA: The Oakland Museum, 1993): 25.

17 George Wharton James Papers, Notebook #216.

18 *San Francisco Sunday Call*, 12 June 1904: 12–3. The text has been reprinted as *Gustav Stickley, The Arts and Crafts Movement in America*, with commentary by David Cathers (Pasadena, CA: Clinker Press, 2001).

19 Karen Weitze, "Utopian Place Making: The Built Environment in Arts and Crafts California," in *The Arts and Crafts Movement in California: Living the Good Life*, p. 81.

20 Mildred Stickley Cruess, interview with Robert Judson Clark, Rochester, NY, 5 August 1971.

21 I thank Edward R. Bosley for providing information on domestic architecture in Pasadena at the time of Stickley's visit.

22 Cheryl Robertson, "Resort to the Rustic—Simple Living and the California Bungalow," in *The Arts and Crafts Movement in California: Living the Good Life*, p. 101.

23 Cruess interview, 5 August 1971.

24 Una Nixson Hopkins, "A Study for Home-Builders," *Good Housekeeping* 45 (March 1906): 259–264.

25 Unsigned, "Wooden Dwellings in California on the Lines of the Old Spanish Adobe," *The Craftsman* 13 (February 1908): 568–572.

26 "[One] type of Pacific coast architecture...shows markedly the influence of the Craftsman movement. These houses for the most part are of excellent proportions, with sloping rooflines, broad verandahs and overhanging eaves." Una Nixson Hopkins, "The Development of Domestic Architecture on the Pacific Coast," *The Craftsman* 13 (January 1908): 455.

27 Edward R. Bosley, *Greene & Greene* (London: Phaidon Press, 2000): 39.

28 Ibid., pp. 56–57.

29 My thanks to Roycroft scholar Robert Rust for first suggesting the likelihood that Stickley and Toothaker met at this time.

30 Gustav Stickley. "The German Exhibit at the Louisiana Purchase Exposition," *The Craftsman* 6 (August 1904): 489–506; Gustav Stickley, "Thoughts Occasioned by an Anniversary: A Plea For Democratic Art," *The Craftsman* 7 (October 1904): 42–61.

31 The Craftsman reprinted the Hoffmann interior from the August 1904 issue of *Art et Decoration*.

32 FTR 24 (10 June 1904): 92.

33 Unsigned, "A False Effort to be Fine," *The Craftsman* 5 (March 1904): 621-625; Gustav Stickley, "From Ugliness to Beauty," *The Craftsman* 7 (December 1904): 310-320.

34 FW 18 (7 January 1904): 9.

35 U 31 (September 1904): 61.

36 David Shi, *The Simple Life* (New York: Oxford University Press, 1985): 183.

37 Ibid., pp. 183–184.

38 Wagner's lecture date appears in *The Craftsman* 7 (October 1904): 97; his lecture fee is recorded in WL 76 x 101.13.

39 Charles Wagner *My Impressions of America*, (New York: McClure, Phillips & Co., 1906): 259.

40 Unsigned "The Work of the United Crafts in Syracuse," FTR 24 (10 April 1904): 77–78.

CHAPTER 6

1 Gustav Stickley, "Chips from the Craftsman Workshops" (1906): 19.

2 Peter Wiles, interview by author, Skaneateles, NY, 26 February 1983.

3 See Stickley factory inventories for 1901 through 1904, WL 76 x 101.1, and "Appraisal of Workshop of Gustav Stickley," 1 June 1914, #4, Box 4, Research Center, Henry Ford Museum and Greenfield Village.

4 Michael Danial, e-mail to author, 1 November 1999.

5 This phrase was coined by Robert Judson Clark.

6 "Chips from the Craftsman Workshops—Number II" (1907): 46.

7 Gustav Stickley, "Craftsman Furnishings" (1906): 5. Few of Stickley's customers bought his maple and mahogany furniture and by 1907 his catalog furniture was offered only in oak.

8 Other representative Standard Stickley prices include: the #210 knock-down settle, $96.50, with leather cushions; the #336 bow-arm Morris chair with leather cushions, $31.50; the #625 hexagonal library table with leather-covered top, $58.50; the #804 sideboard, $85.00.

9 In contrast, the Sears, Roebuck catalog of 1902 offered oak china cabinets for $10.95 to $16.95. Although lacking the design and structural integrity of Stickley furniture, and made of cheaper materials, they were certainly serviceable.

10 Stickley was granted design patents #37,507 and #37,508 for two spindle chairs, on 8 August 1905.

11 Gustav Stickley, "Catalogue of Craftsman Furniture" (1910): 116.

12 Von Erich Haenel, "Das Kunstgewerbe Auf Der Düsseldorfer Kunstausstellung," *Dekorative Kunst* 11 (October 1902): 25–40; and A.S. Levetus, "Modern Austrian Wicker Furniture," IS 21 (February 1904): 323–328. Stickley was shipping Craftsman willow furniture by February 1904, WL 76 x 101.13.

13 *Summary of Inventory*, January 1, 1901, and *Summary of Inventory*, January 1, 1904, WL 76 x 101.1.

14 My thanks to William E. Uptegrove III, Pieter W. Uptegrove, Liese Uptegrove-Ade, and John B. Horton for generously providing information on the Uptegrove lumber business. Thanks also to Germaine Burke for helping to locate Uptegrove family members.

15 The significance of this hardware is that it places Hansen at the L. & J.G. Stickley company in 1907; had he still been working for Gustav Stickley he would have brought home Craftsman hardware to use on this dated linen press.

16 Olive E. Hansen, interview by author, Ann Arbor, MI, 19 June 2001.

17 For the *Craftsman* magazine, in addition to the essays by Cleota Reed cited in chapter 2, see Marilyn Fish, "In the Company of The Craftsman: An Introduction to the New Craftsman Index"; and David Cathers, "The Craftsmanship of Life Itself: Gustav Stickley and The Craftsman Magazine," in *The Craftsman on CD-ROM* (New York: Interactive Bureau, 1998).

18 WL 76 x 101.4580.

19 Unsigned, "The Home of Mr. and Mrs. R.M. Bond in Florida," *The Craftsman* 21 (October 1911): 78–84.

20 FJ 23 (25 September 1905): 39.

21 FJ 24 (25 January 1906): 43.

22 Stickley submitted his trademark for registration on 10 April 1905; see FW 21 (10 September 1906): 80.

23 FTR 24 (10 December 1903): 64.

24 *Directory of Wholesale Furniture Manufacturers of the United States* (1908).

CHAPTER 7

1 Unsigned, "Craftsman Furnishings for the Ordinary Room" *The Craftsman* 21 (October 1911): 105–109.

2 *The Craftsman* 2 (May 1902): 103.

3 Amalie Busck exhibited metalwork at Stickley's 1903 Arts and Crafts exhibition, and both she and Mary Norton later exhibited at the shows held in New York City by the National Society of Craftsmen; see, for example, Eva Lovett, "The Exhibition of the National Society of Craftsmen," *International Studio* 30 (January 1907); LXX–LXXV and Eva Lovett, "The Second Exhibition of the National Society of Craftsmen," *International Studio* 33 (January 1908): XC–CL.

4 Stickley's metal sources included Rome Brass and Copper in Rome, New York, and two New York City metal dealers, U.T. Hungerford Brass and Copper and John Gleason. WL 76 x 101.13 and WL 76 x 101.66.

5 The borax was most likely used as a flux, a substance that protects metal from oxidizing under the high heat of annealing. Muriatic acid (a diluted hydrochloric acid), benzine, and gasoline were used primarily as solvents to clean the metal during the fabrication process; muriatic acid could also have been used as a "pickle" to quench iron after annealing, and gasoline could be used to thin the wax applied to finished pieces. My thanks to Michael Adams of Aurora Studios for his patient explanations of metal working.

6 A Stickley ledger, WL 76 x 101.13, records the firm's purchases of metal castings made by an upstate New York firm, the Oriskany Malleable Metal Works, among others.

7 Janet Ashbee's visit to the Roycroft is recorded in *Ashbee Journal* 1/7 October–December 1900, King's College Library, Cambridge.

8 The Faulkner Bronze Company is discussed in Glennys Wild and Alan Crawford, "Metalwork," in Alan Crawford, ed., *By Hammer and Hand: The Arts and Crafts Movement in Birmingham* (Birmingham: Birmingham Museums and Art Gallery, 1984): 97–118.

9 An apparently identical lantern is visible in a photograph of a Faulkner Bronze Company exhibition stand, reproduced in Glennys Wild, *A. Edward Jones, Metalcraftsman* (Birmingham: Birmingham Museum and Art Gallery, 1980): 14. The two lanterns that appear in photographs on the right side of the *Craftsman* page appear also in a catalog issued by Jesson, Birkitt & Co. Ltd., the successor firm to the Faulkner Bronze Company. The two Faulkner lanterns displayed at the 1903 exhibition of the Arts and Crafts Exhibition Society were designed by the metalworker/designer Anne Stubbs, and the four lanterns pictured in the April 1903 issue of *The Craftsman* are almost certainly her work.

10 The likelihood that Art Fittings Limited was a distributor was suggested to me by Judy Rudoe of the British Museum and Charlotte Tucker of the Birmingham Central Library; my thanks to them both for their help. Stylistic evidence in *The Craftsman* shows that Stickley knew the Birmingham firm of Ernest and Norman Spittle, but it has not been possi-

ble to determine if the metalwork Stickley bought from Art Fittings Limited was made by the Spittles.

11 Don Marek, *Grand Rapids Art Metalwork, 1902–1918* (Grand Rapids: Heartwood, 1999): 57. I thank Don Marek and David A. Taylor of the Library of Congress for generously sharing their research on Art Fittings Limited.

12 These objects can be identified as English not only because of their appearance but because their prices are noted on the backs of the photographs in pounds, shillings, and pence; how and when Warner obtained these photographs, and where they came from, remain a mystery; the most likely explanation is that these are photographs of Birmingham metalwork that Stickley brought back from his 1903 visit to England.

13 Unsigned, "Skilled Workmen of Syracuse No. 6—Valentine M. Kluge," *Syracuse Journal*, 3 December 1904, p. 5.

14 According to an undated brochure of Toothaker's wrought iron lamp designs issued by the Charles V. Daiger Company of Boston, "At forge, at anvil, at bench, at desk—he is equally at ease.... He believes in modern methods of doing business."

15 A business letter on Craftsman letterhead, dated 19 January 1911 and dictated by Toothaker, is in a private collection; his obituary in the 25 March 1932 *East Aurora Advertiser* says that he joined Roycroft in 1911.

16 For a revealing discussion of the materials and methods used in the patination process, as well as several formulas for coloring solutions, see the chapter "Coloring and Finishing Art Metalwork," in Arthur F. Payne, *Art Metalwork With Inexpensive Equipment* (Peoria, IL: The Manual Arts Press) 1914.

17 During the years that the Craftsman metal shop was active, Benedict Studios, the Onondaga Metal Shop, the L. & J.G. Stickley Company, Knaus & Arwine, and the Valentine M. Kluge Company, all of them upstate New York firms, made Arts and Crafts metalwork similar to Stickley's, sometimes producing nearly identical designs; there is not enough of a historical record to sort out the activities of these firms, although the principals all knew one another and several worked for Gustav Stickley before establishing businesses of their own, and metalworkers must have moved among them, carrying knowledge of designs and finishing processes.

18 Completed iron pieces were first blackened; this was done, apparently, by coating them with lampblack or, according to one *Craftsman* article, by smearing on beeswax and holding the piece over a smoky fire. The uneven surface was then rubbed with a fine emery cloth to create highlights, "like tarnished silver," that contrasted with the matte black remaining in the hand-hammered depressions. See Unsigned, "Work Ennobles," *The Craftsman* 4 (May 1903): 133–137; a Craftsman writer described the process of patinating copper in "Craftsman Metal Work: Designed and Made According to the Same Principles That Rule the Furniture," in *Gustav Stickley, Craftsman Homes* (New York: Craftsman Publishing Company) 1909: 162–164; this article makes no references to the immersion method.

19 Claude Bragdon to Katherine Bragdon, Syracuse, NY, 21 July 1903; Bragdon Papers.

20 According to Syracuse city directories, Baxter was a teacher at the Dakin Brothers Business College in Syracuse from 1901 to 1903.

21 "What is Wrought in the Craftsman Workshops," p. 17.

22 The names of Stickley's in-house and freelance textile workers listed here have been assembled by combining information from several sources: the firm's ledgers, WL 76 x 101.13 and WL 76 x 101. 26; Syracuse city directories and census data of the era; and a birthday poem written for LaMont Warner's daughter Victorine signed by nineteen Stickley employees. It has not been possible to construct a definitive list of these artisans.

23 Stickley's ledgers record textile purchases from Donald Brothers and G.P. & J. Baker; my thanks to Linda Parry for sharing invaluable background information on these firms.

24 WL 76 x 101.13.

25 "Craftsman Furnishings for the Home," (1912): 27.

26 "Needle-Work from The Craftsman Workshops," (1905): 2.

27 Shrimpton's designs for a gingko pillow, table cover, and curtain were published in an unsigned article, "A Study of the Gingko-Tree," *The Craftsman* 6 (July 1904): 406–408.

28 I am very grateful to Rita Curry-Pittman and Dianne Ayres for sharing this important discovery with me.

29 Stickley's factory inventory for 1914 records that there were three "stitching machines...in sewing room." HFM.

30 "Craftsman Furnishings for the Home," p. 13.

31 The quotation on metalwork is from "Chips from the Craftsman Workshops–Number II" (1907): 44; the textile quotation is from "Craftsman Furniture" (1910): 4–5.

CHAPTER 8

1 Ben Wiles, Jr., interview by author, Syracuse, NY, 6 September 1996.

2 FJ 25, (25 December 1906): 132–133.

3 James A. McCreery (1825?–1903) and Ashley Abraham Van Tine (1821–1890) were both leading Manhattan-based retailers about whom little is known today. McCreery had large stores on Twenty-third Street and Thirty-fourth Street in New York City and another in Pittsburgh, and his obituary called him "the first merchant prince of New York." See the *New York Times*, 28 February 1903: 9, 5. Van Tine, generally referred to as Vantine, imported and sold Oriental wares in New York from about 1866, and partners continued the firm after his death. See Henry Hall, ed., *America's Successful Men of Affairs, Vol. 1* (New York: The New York Herald Tribune, 1895): 689–691.

4 The saga of Stickley's unhappy Vantine experience appears in three issues of FTR 24: 10 April 1904, p. 36; 10 May 1904, p. 38; and 10 June 10, 1904, p. 80.

5 Unsigned. "Als ik kan," *The Craftsman* 9 (December 1905): 434–440.

6 FTR 26 (10 December 1905): 100.

7 Unsigned, "The Homes of the Craftsman," *The Craftsman* 23 (October 1912): 128.

8 ACMU 73, (6 January 1906): 7.

9 In his 21 November 1907 letter to Edward Schirmer in Syracuse, Stickley wrote, "I can look at them [furniture sketches] when I come up for Thanksgiving."

10 Edith Wiles Bradford, telephone interview by author, 5

January 1997; it must, however, be noted that some surviving family members do not believe that Gustav was ever anything other than a faithful husband to Eda.

11 Alvan F. Sanborn, "Leaders in American Arts and Crafts," *Good Housekeeping* 47 (February 1907): 146–152.

12 For Mary Fanton Roberts and *The Craftsman*, see Marilyn Fish, *The New Craftsman Index* (Lambertville, NY: The Arts and Crafts Quarterly Press, 1997): 9–25.

13 Ibid., p. 20.

14 Alice M. Rathbone, "Concerning Cottages and Content," *The Craftsman* 5 (March 1904): 593–598.

15 All circulation figures are taken from N.W. Ayer & Son's *American Newspaper Annual and Directory*, for the years cited.

16 My thanks to Ray Stubblebine for identifying this first client. For the house, see Unsigned, "A Craftsman House at Beechhurst Long Island: By the Craftsman Home Building Company," *The Craftsman* 15 (December 1908): xviii–xxix; expenses for this new venture first appear in WL 76 x 101.65.

17 For the early plans for *The Yeoman*, see Unsigned, "To the Readers of the Craftsman: By the Editor," *The Craftsman* 15 (October 1908): ix–xiv; and Unsigned, "To the Readers of the Craftsman: By the Editor," *The Craftsman* 15 (November 1908): xviii–xxvii.

18 WL Box 60; Stickley, his bookkeeper Charles C. White (who was also head of the Craftsman Home Building Company), and his daughter Barbara were the members of its board. This entity issued one-hundred shares of stock, ninety-eight held by Stickley and one each by White and Barbara Stickley.

19 I thank Robert Judson Clark for identifying this firm.

20 Gladys LaCombe Stickley, interview by the author, Rochester, NY, 12 December 1996.

21 Unsigned, "An Invitation to the Opening of the New Craftsman Building," *The Craftsman* 25 (October 1913): 110–116.

22 WL Box 19.

23 WL Box 17B.

24 Gustav Stickley, "Homes," *The Craftsman* 24 (July 1913): 421–427.

25 Gustav Stickley, "The Craftsman Movement: Its Origin and Growth," *The Craftsman* 25 (October 1913): 17–26.

26 Stickley's firm marketed the Craftsman fireplace as a complete heating and ventilation system suitable for any home. In 1912, hopeful of deriving income from his new invention, Stickley patented it in the United States, Canada, and several European countries; patent documents are in a private collection.

27 Unsigned, "A New Way to Shop in America," *The Craftsman* 27 (January 1915): 435.

28 Unsigned, "Home-Making in America," *The Craftsman* 27 (November 1914): 193, 225–229.

29 Helen Speer, "The Mode of the Nursery," *Country Life in America* 41 (November 1921): 57–59.

30 "A New Way to Shop."

31 The first expenses for the restaurant—$140 for furniture and $763.84 for fabric—were recorded in a Stickley ledger on 14 October 1913; WL 76 x 101.45. For the firm's depiction of the restaurant see Unsigned, "The Craftsman Restaurant: By A Visitor," *The Craftsman* 25 (January 1914): 362–368, 397–398.

32 "Your old men shall dream dreams, your young men shall see visions." Joel, 2:28.

33 Gustav Stickley III, Naramore interview, n.d., Joint Free Public Library of Morristown and Morris Plains.

34 Stickley, "Homes," p. 427.

35 WL Box 16; the firm issued five hundred shares of common stock, 498 of which were controlled by Gustav, Eda, and Barbara Stickley.

36 WL Box 20; Stickley maintained a line of credit with the Merchants National Bank of Syracuse, which he drew on for operating expenses, but had otherwise not sought outside capital.

37 "Wages Due Employees of Gustav Stickley, The Craftsman, Incorporated (N.Y. Branch) Up to and Including March 23, 1915." WL Box 18.

38 WL Box 18 Joseph H. Dodson. Dodson (1860–1949) was a prosperous and well-connected stockbroker. He lived in Kankakee, Illinois in a house he named "Bird Lodge." This was in fact the B. Harley Bradley house designed by Frank Lloyd Wright in 1900.

39 "The outbreak of war in 1914 caught the [stock] market by surprise. A sudden wave of international liquidation [i.e., selling] converged on the New York markets, and the Stock Exchange closed from July 31 to December 12." Sidney Homer and Richard Sylla, *A History of Interest Rates, 3rd Revised Edition* (New Brunswick, NJ: Rutgers University Press, 1996): 344.

40 *New York Times*, 1 August 1914–14 August 1914.

41 WL Box 18 Joseph H. Dodson (A) contains a typescript of the text of the prospectus in draft form; a copy of the printed prospectus is in a private collection.

42 Bruce Barnes, telephone interview by author, 7 August 2001.

43 Ibid.

CHAPTER 9

1 John Ruskin to Dora Lees, Abbeville, 25 September 1868, My Dearest Dora, n.d., 57–58; Quoted in Tim Hilton, *John Ruskin: The Later Years* (New Haven and London: Yale University Press, 2000): 142.

2 For a discussion of this impulse, see T.J. Jackson Lears, *No Place of Grace, Antimodernism and the Transformation of American Culture, 1880–1920* (Chicago & London: University of Chicago Press, 1994).

3 Gustav Stickley to Henry Bailey, 22 March 1907; Henry Turner Bailey Papers, Division of Special Collections and University Archives, University of Oregon Libraries.

4 This chapter is not meant to explore every facet of Craftsman Farms. For more on this subject see David Cathers, ed., *Gustav Stickley's Craftsman Farms—A Pictorial History* (Morris Plains, NJ: Turn of the Century Editions in Association with The Craftsman Farms Press, 1999); Marilyn B. Fish, "Craftsman Farms: Landscape and Building Program," *Arts & Crafts Quarterly 4* (15 January 1991): 34–9; and "Craftsman Farms School: Theory, location and curriculum," *Arts and Crafts Quarterly* 4, (April 15, 1991): 4–7; and Mark Alan Hewitt, *Gustav Stickley's Craftsman Farms: The Quest for an Arts and Crafts Utopia* (Syracuse, NY: Syracuse University Press, 2001).

5 Barbara Stickley Wiles interview by Robert Judson Clark.

6 WL 76 x 101.65 and real estate documents in Morris County Recorder's Office.

7 WL 76 x 101.4579; this was $2,000 less than he had paid for the house in 1900. He sold the house to Isaac Fleischman, the president of the Fleischman Furniture Company, a well-known Syracuse manufacturer; Michael Danial, e-mail to author, 27 August 2002.

8 Mrs. John A. Riker, interview with Robert Judson Clark, Basking Ridge, NJ, 8 January 1972.

9 Gustav Stickley, "The Purpose of Craftsman Farms" (1911), from the Mary Fanton Roberts Papers, 1900–1956, Archives of American Art, p. 1.

10 Unsigned, "A Visit to Craftsman Farms: The Study of an Educational Ideal," *The Craftsman* 18 (September 1910): 638–646.

11 G. Edward White, *The Eastern Establishment and the Western Experience: The West of Frederic Remington, Theodore Roosevelt, and Owen Wister* (Austin, TX: University of Texas Press, 1989): 172–179.

12 David Shi, *The Simple Life: Plain Living and High Thinking in American Culture* (New York and Oxford: Oxford University Press, 1985): 202–204.

13 *Jerseyman* (1 April 1910), clipping at the Joint Free Public Library of Morristown and Morris Plains.

14 *The Craftsman* 18 (September 1910): 638.

15 Unsigned, "Another Talk With the Host of Craftsman Farms: The Country and Long Life," *The Craftsman* 19 (February 1911): 485–488.

16 Unsigned, "The First Craftsman Village and a School Where Boys Learn to Work," *The Craftsman* 14 (June 1908): x–xx.

17 Unsigned, "The Value of a Country Education to Every Boy: A Talk With the Host of Craftsman Farms," *The Craftsman* 19 (January 1911): 389–394.

18 John Dewey, *The School and Society* (Carbondale and Edwardsville, IL: Southern Illinois University Press, 1980). Some of Dewey's words obviously resonated with Stickley, for instance: "No number of object lessons, got up as object lessons for the sake of giving information, can afford even the shadow of a substitute for acquaintance with the plants and animals of the farm and garden acquired through actual living among them and caring for them" (p. 8). "We must conceive of work in wood or metal, of weaving, sewing, and cooking, as methods of living and learning, not as distinct studies" (p. 10). "In critical moments we all realize that the only discipline that stands by us, the only training that becomes intuition, is that got through life itself…we learn from experience" (p. 12). On Dewey, see Louis Menand, *The Metaphysical Club* (New York: Farrar, Straus and Giroux, 2001); for Dewey's influence on Stickley, see Hewitt, *Gustav Stickley's Craftsman Farms*, pp. 71–78; for early twentieth-century attitudes toward "book learning," see White, *The Eastern Establishment*, p. 18.

19 *The Craftsman* 18 (September 1910): 644.

20 White, *The Eastern Establishment*, p. 7.

21 Their dates were: Theodore Roosevelt (1858–1919); Owen Wister (1860–1939); Frederic Remington (1861–1909); Sources: *Who Was Who in America 1898–1968* (Chicago: Marquis Who's Who Inc., 1968); and *The New York Times Obituary Index 1858–1968* (New York: The New York Times, 1970.)

22 Mary Fanton Roberts (writing as Giles Edgerton), "Frederic Remington: Painter and Sculptor," *The Craftsman* 15 (March 1909): 658–670.

23 Quoted in White, *The Eastern Establishment*, p. 91.

24 Unsigned, "Als ik kan: A School for Citizenship," *The Craftsman* 23 (October 1912): 119–121.

25 Raymond Riordon, "A Visit to Craftsman Farms: The Impression it Made and the Result: The Gustav Stickley School for Citizenship," *The Craftsman* 23 (November 1912): 151–164.

26 White, "The Eastern Establishment," p. 23. One earlier English example was the New School, Abbotsholme, a school where formal classroom education was punctuated with potato digging, fence mending, woodcutting, and other farm chores; it was founded in Derbyshire in 1889 by Dr. Cecil Reddie and its mention in *The Craftsman* magazine is evidence that it was known to Stickley.

27 Raymond Riordon, "Interlaken, An Outdoor School Where Boys Through Their Own Efforts Learn How to Think and How to Work," *The Craftsman* 22 (May 1912): 177–186.

28 *The Craftsman* 23 (November 1912): 151.

29 Muriel Jennings Case, interview with the author, East Aurora, NY, 8 November 1996; Mrs. Case, who was born in 1904, was a daughter of the Roycrofter Walter Jennings and remembered seeing the Roycroft school boys when she was eight or nine years old.

30 *Jerseyman* (7 November 1913), and Morristown YMCA Yearbooks at the Joint Free Public Library of Morristown and Morris Plains.

31 Raymond Riordon files, Highland, New York, Historical Society; none of Riordon's school buildings survive and the site is now owned by the State of New York.

32 Shi, "The Simple Life," p. 194.

33 For instance, the similar advocacy of Edward Bok, editor of *Ladies' Home Journal*, predated Stickley's and reached a wider audience; see Ibid., esp. pp. 183–189.

34 Unsigned, "A Country Home for the Business Man: A Second Visit to Craftsman Farms," *The Craftsman* 19 (October 1910): 55–62.

35 For a detailed discussion of the construction of the log house see Hewitt, *Gustav Stickley's Craftsman Farms*, esp. pp. 117–135.

36 Natalie Curtis, "The New Log House at Craftsman Farms: An Architectural Development of the Log Cabin," *The Craftsman* 21 (November 1911): 196–203.

37 Sally J. Kinsey, "Gustav Stickley and the Early Years of The Craftsman, 1901–1906" (master's thesis, Graduate School of Syracuse University, 1972): 16.

38 The colors of the log house interior are discussed in Beth Ann McPherson, "The Furnishings of Craftsman Farms," in Cathers, ed. *Gustav Stickley's Craftsman Farms: A Pictorial History*, pp. 35–39.

39 Stickley, "The Purpose of Craftsman Farms," p. 1.

40 "Als ik kan—Farm Life as the Basis of Practical Education," *The Craftsman* 16 (May 1909): 243-245 refers to Stickley as a farmer. In another instance, as he was being sworn in to give evidence in his 1913 trademark infringement suit against the bungalow builder Jud Yoho, Stickley gave his occupation as "Farmer." The wealthy man who became a "farmer" was such a stock figure that *Good Housekeeping* magazine parodied this trend with a verse titled "Back to the Soil":
Every farmer boy wants to be a schoolteacher,
Every schoolteacher hopes to be an editor,
Every editor would like to be a banker,
Every banker would like to be a trust magnate,
And every trust magnate hopes someday to own a farm and have chickens and cows.
We end where we begin.
Good Housekeeping 45 (October 1905): 435.

41 Marion Stickley Flaccus, interview by Naramore, 12 April 1982, Joint Free Public Library of Morristown and Morris Plains.

42 The log house is described as a "Craftsman manor house" in Stickley's 1914 stock prospectus.

43 Gustav Stickley, "Chips from the Craftsman Workshops," *The Craftsman* 5 (March 1904): 629.

44 Marion Stickley Flaccus, interview by Naramore.

45 Barbara Stickley Wiles, interview by Clark.

46 Marion Stickley Flaccus, interview by Naramore.

47 Ibid.

48 Ruth Cruess Glesmann, telephone interview by author, 18 December 1996.

49 Ibid.

50 Gustav Stickley III, interview by Naramore, no date, transcript in the collection of the Joint Free Public Library of Morristown and Morris Plains. In other interviews Stickley's daughters Barbara and Marion both recalled the troubled relationship between their father and their brother.

51 Gladys LaCombe Stickley, interview by author, Rochester, NY, 12 December 1996.

52 Quoted in "The Strenuous Life," *The Craftsman* 4 (January 1904): 412.

53 *The Craftsman* 18 (September 1910): 641.

54 Gladys LaCombe Stickley, interview by author.

CHAPTER 10

1 *The Craftsman* 29 (December 1915): 307.

2 Unsigned, "More Color in the Home: Painted Furniture Inspired by Peasant Art," *The Craftsman* 28 (June 1915): 245–254.

3 Stickley may have gotten the idea for rubbing paint in this manner from the "More Color in the Home" article in the June 1915 *Craftsman*. According to that article, the "peasant" furniture was "first given a coat of paint—usually blue—which is wiped off before it dries. The paint sinks into the pores of the wood, emphasizing the grain and giving a wonderful satin sheen to the surface." Stickley's Chromewald was essentially a refinement of that process.

4 *The Craftsman* 30 (September 1916): 625.

5 Mary Fanton Roberts, "One Man's Story," *The Craftsman* 30 (May 1916): 195.

6 See Gardner Teall, "The Modern Colonial House," *The Craftsman* 24 (April 1913): 61–68; Mary Fanton Roberts, "Science in Art, As Shown in the International Exhibition of Paintings and Sculpture," *The Craftsman* 24 (May 1913): 216–218; and Mary Fanton Roberts, "The New Russian Stage, A Blaze of Color," *The Craftsman* 29 (December 1915): 257–269, 322.

7 Barbara Stickley Wiles, interview by Clark.

8 The book value of the entire Craftsman enterprise at the time of the bankruptcy was optimistically computed by Stickley's financial staff at $408,000. The outside appraiser's valuation, however, came to not quite $131,000. While conflicting figures in Stickley's business papers make it difficult to gauge his firm's liabilities exactly, the reported amount at the time of the bankruptcy was $175,000; two months later the figure was said to be $230,000. Whatever the actual amount may have been, it was considerably greater than the firm's assets. For details of the bankruptcy see these sources: "Court Appraisal of Assets of Gustav Stickley The Craftsman Incorporated as of March 23, 1915" and "Financial Statement of Gustav Stickley, The Craftsman, Inc. March 23, 1915," WL Boxes 17B and 18; see also "Creditors Force Gustav Stickley Into Bankruptcy," *Syracuse Post-Standard*, 23 March 1915, and "Stickley Makes Offer," *Syracuse Post-Standard*, 15 June 1915. OHA clippings.

9 For instance, in addition to the building's $60,000 yearly rent and its large payroll, Stickley spent $69,000 on interior improvements and fixtures, and that money was essentially thrown away. Immediately after the bankruptcy the court-appointed appraiser valued these improvements at a mere $6,000, less than a tenth of what Stickley had spent on them. WL Box 18.

10 For a discussion of interest rates in the United States in the first two decades of the twentieth century, see Sidney Homer and Richard Sylla, *A History of Interest Rates, 3rd Revised Edition* (New Brunswick, NJ: Rutgers University Press, 1996): 330–365.

11 *New York Sun*, undated clipping in a private collection.

12 *New York Times*, 24 March 1915, clipping in a private collection.

13 "The Company's ability to meet [its] payments seemed to us entirely speculative because of the uncertainty of business conditions at present and for some time in the future…the Company's lack of working capital under this plan and also because of the entire dependence for success upon the continued good health of Mr. Stickley, the President, who is now 57 years of age." Creditors' statement, 3 April 1915, WL Box 19.

14 WL Box 18, "Craftsman Statement of Liabilities."

15 This announcement was made in a circular letter mailed to customers in May 1916. CF archives.

16 WL Box 18, "To the stockholders of the company," 30 June 1916.

17 WL Box 16, Howard E. Brown to L.W. Emerick, New York City, 4 October 1915.

18 HFM Box 5, #4 and #5.

19 WL Box 16, Howard E. Brown to L.W. Emerick, New York City, 30 December 1915.

20 HFM Box 5, #5 contains a letter dated 19 January 1917, from Gustav Stickley to Mrs. Harriet P. Early of East Providence, Rhode Island, along with a $10.50 dividend check for her three shares of preferred stock. Stickley, with more optimism than was warranted, told Mrs. Early that "we are getting our wholesale business in order and we are hoping that the coming year may be a prosperous one for us."

21 Board meeting minutes remain in the possession of the Stickley Furniture Company.

22 HFM Box 5, #5 contains a copy of a telegram: "Mrs. G. Stickley, The Wolcott, Syracuse, New York, Will be home about eleven tonight. Gustav Stickley."

23 The patent papers are available from the United States Patent Office. After filing an amended patent application in 1919, Stickley was granted patent number 1,521,975 in January 1925, and assigned the rights to the Stickley Extension Bed Company.

24 Donald A. Davidoff and Stephen Gray, *Innovation and Derivation: The Contribution of L. & J.G. Stickley to the Arts and Crafts Movement* (Morris Plains, NJ: The Craftsman Farms Foundation, 1995): 44.

25 "Gustav Stickley — My Grandfather," some notes by Ben Wiles, Jr., November 1992.

26 Barbara Stickley Wiles, interview by author.

27 WL Box 51.

28 WL Box 16, Howard E. Brown to L.W. Emerick, 13 August 1917.

29 Edith Wiles Bradford, telephone interview by author, 5 January 1997; and Ruth Cruess Glesmann, telephone interview by author, 18 December 1996. Eda Simmons Stickley died on 13 March 1919.

30 Ruth Cruess Glesmann, telephone interview by author; also, Ben Wiles, Jr., interview by author.

31 LustreWood Products Company, Inc., Certificate of Incorporation, June 22, 1919. Photocopy provided by Coy L. Ludwig.

32 Coy L. Ludwig has painstakingly reconstructed the Stickley family's addresses in Syracuse and Rochester in the 1920s and 1930s.

33 Gladys LaCombe Stickley, interview by author.

34 Ben Wiles, Jr, "Gustav Stickley — My Grandfather."

35 Edith Wiles Bradford, telephone interview by author.

36 I am very grateful to Ruth Cruess Glesmann and her family for making photocopies of these invaluable letters available.

37 Marshall Larrabee, of Skaneateles Handicrafters, Inc., telephone interview by author, 5 December 1996.

38 The funeral took place at the Fairchild & Meech funeral home and was conducted by Rev. Dr. Ray Freeman Jenney of the Park Central Presbyterian Church, the church the Stickleys had attended throughout their Syracuse years.

39 Ruth Cruess Glesmann, telephone interview by author, 10 August 2001; Ben Wiles, Jr., telephone interview by author, 27 August 2001; Edith Wiles Bradford, telephone interview by author, 31 August 2001; these three Stickley grandchildren, all in their twenties in 1942, attended the funeral.

40 The brief obituary in the *Syracuse Post-Standard* of 21 April 1942, said that Stickley had been a "furniture manufacturer, publisher, and operator of the first electric streetcar line in America." Obituaries also appeared on 22 April in the *New York Times* and the *Morristown (NJ) Daily Record*. No obituaries appeared in the furniture trade press in the months following Stickley's death.

EPILOGUE

1 Unsigned. "Three Rivers Farm," *Architectural Review* 11 [Boston], (January 1904): 56–9.

2 H. W. Hillman. "An Electric Day," *Good Housekeeping* 43, (June 1906): 615–20.

3 Unsigned. "Furniture from the Eastwood Craftsmen," *Art Interchange* 47, (November 1901): 109.

APPENDIX ONE

1 The standard work on Ellis is by Jean R. France and others; Marilyn Fish is the best source on Roberts and Cleota Reed has written extensively about Sargent.

2 See, for instance, WL 76 x 101.13.

3 LaMont Warner to Emma Warner, Paris, 8 July 1907.

4 Much of the biographical information in this section comes from Bragdon's two memoirs, *Merely Players,* 1929, and *More Lives Than One,* 1938.

5 I gratefully acknowledge Jean R. France for sharing her great fund of Bragdon lore with me.

6 *More Lives Than One,* p. 40.

7 Claude Bragdon, *Merely Players* (New York: Alfred A. Knopf, 1929): 72.

8 Claude Bragdon, "Harvey Ellis," *Brochure Series of Architectural Illustration* 3 (September 1897): 139–146; Harvey Ellis, "Claude Fayette Bragdon," *Brochure Series of Architectural Illustration* 3 (October 1897): 153–157.

9 A photograph of the Baillie Scott cabinet had been published shortly before Bragdon adapted it for Stein. See M.H. Baillie Scott, "Decoration and Furniture for the New Palace, Darmstadt," *International Studio* 7 (March 1899): 108.

10 Mark Girouard, *Sweetness and Light: The "Queen Anne" Movement,* 1860–1900 (New Haven and London: Yale University Press, 1977): 44, 107.

11 Thomas W. Cutler, *A Grammar of Japanese Ornament and Design* (London: B.T. Batsford, 1880).

12 Much of this section is based on the research of others: see Marie Via and Marjorie Searl, *Head, Heart and Hand: Elbert Hubbard and the Roycrofters* (Rochester, NY: University of Rochester Press, 1994): 116 and 134; Connor's work as a designer for Stickley's firm is documented in Giollamuire O´ Murchú, *Jerome Connor: Irish-American Sculptor, 1874–1943* (Dublin: The National Gallery of Ireland, 1993): 74. Connor's move to Syracuse happened too late for him to appear in the 1902 Syracuse city directory, but the directories for 1903 through 1906 list him as a sculptor working at 108 Wellington Place and living at 302 James Street; Anne Connor was listed as a

hand bookbinder. Sales of Connor's work at the Craftsman Building are recorded in WL 76 x 101.13.

13 Olive E. Hansen has in her possession a postcard dated 12 March 1907, mailed to Peter Hansen at his Fayetteville address. I thank Olive Hansen for providing much of the information given here about her late father-in-law, Peter Hansen.

14 Olive E. Hansen, letter to the author, 4 November 1995.

15 This information is in a letter from Hans and Otto Reimers to William and Olive E. Hansen, July 23, 1970; Olive Hansen also has in her possession a postcard addressed to Peter Hansen at a Potsdam address and dated 1902. Hansen later told Louise Shrimpton's nephew, Sturtevant Pratt, that he had left Germany by swimming through the North Sea. Sturtevant Pratt, interview by author, Manlius, NY, 8 July 1996.

16 This information on Howe has been gathered from several sources, including his listing in the 1918–1919 *Who's Who in America*; the *Reader's Guide to Periodical Literature*; the *Avery Index to Architectural Periodicals*; James Ward, *Architects in Practice in New York, 1900–1940* (Union, NJ: J & D Associates, 1989): 37; and several exhibition annuals published by the Architectural League of New York between 1888 and 1927. Howe is identified as a Tiffany employee in Robert Koch, *Louis C. Tiffany, Rebel in Glass* (New York: Crown Publishers, 1966): 80, 136, 142.

17 For more on Jones, see David Cathers, "Gustav Stickley, George H. Jones, and the Making of Inlaid Craftsman Furniture," *Style 1900* 13 (February 2000): 54–60.

18 Unsigned, "Skilled Workmen of Syracuse No. 6 — Valentine M. Kluge," *Syracuse Journal*, 3 December 1904: 5.

19 Syracuse City Directory, 1907, p. 1174.

20 The Arts and Crafts dealer David Rudd has seen a few examples of metal trays and other flatwork stamped "VMKCO." David Rudd, telephone interview by author 4 September 2002.

21 In 1902 the firm issued a set of "retail plates," drawings of Craftsman furniture for use by its customers. These drawings were unsigned, but the style of their hand-lettered captions was distinctly Shrimpton's. Her lettering style was identified by her nephew, Sturtevant Pratt, in an interview by the author, 8 July 1996.

22 Shrimpton's occupation is listed as "designer" in the 1903 and 1905 Syracuse city directories and in the 1905 New York State census.

23 "Museum of Fine Arts Fifteenth Annual Report of the School of Drawing and Painting," (1891) n.p.

24 Louise Shrimpton, "Decorating the Children's Rooms," in Richardson Wright, ed., *Inside the House of Good Taste* (New York: McBride, Nast & Company, 1915): 145–155.

25 My thanks to Bruce Smith for bringing the *Palette and Bench* articles to my attention.

26 Louise Shrimpton, "Handicraft: Wood-Working for the Home," *Good Housekeeping* 48 (October 1908): 412–415.

27 Shrimpton returned to the Syracuse area in 1910 and stayed there the rest of her life. She became chief designer of the Syracuse Ornamental Company and retired in the mid-1940s; Sturtevant Pratt interview by author, 8 July 1996.

28 See, for instance, Helen Speer, "Furniture for Children," *House Beautiful 34* (April 1914): 145; Helen Speer, "The Mode of the Nursery," *Country Life in America* 41

(November 1921): 57–59; and Unsigned, "The Make-Believe World of Toys," *The Craftsman* 27 (December 1914): 286–293. Information about Speer is taken from New York City directories for the years cited.

29 My thanks to Warren Moffet, former East Aurora town historian, and Donald Dayer, the present town historian, for much of this information.

30 Warner was first listed as a Stickley employee in September 1900, WL 76 x 101.7. His name appeared in the Syracuse city directory from 1900 through 1906.

31 Some of the student exercises he completed at Pratt show him working in a Japanesque manner, and in April of Warner's senior year, Dow organized an exhibition of Hiroshige color prints at the school's art gallery. See *Pratt Institute Monthly* 6 (May 1898): 247.

32 Warner's Teachers College job application is now archived in Special Collections, Millbank Memorial Library, Office Records, vol. 15 Vi-Z. On the application Warner wrote that he "worked six years as designer and head draftsman at the Craftsman office with Gustav Stickley—furniture and decorations," and that he pro-duced "drawings for 'The Craftsman' magazine monthly for the first five years.

33 Designs of furniture and interiors by Frank Brangwyn, C.J.H. Cooper, G.M. Ellwood, Ambrose Heal, Wickham Jarvis, A.H. Mackmurdo, Edgar Wood, and others are to be found in Warner's "Modern English" file; there are also photographs of four Morris & Co. armchairs.

34 Charles Holme, ed., *Modern British Domestic Architecture and Decoration* (London: The Studio, 1901).

35 LaMont Warner to Emma Warner, Antwerp, 28 May 1907.

36 LaMont Warner to Emma Warner, Brussels, 8 June 1907.

37 He brought away a Guild business card, which is still among his papers; there is no indication, however, that he and Ashbee met.

38 LaMont Warner to Emma Warner, London, 20 June 1909.

39 LaMont Warner to Emma Warner, London, 24 June 1909.

40 LaMont Warner to Emma Warner, Darmstadt, 4 August 1909.

41 Bound volumes of the 1901–1904 *Craftsman* from the library of the Weiner Werkstätte, with specially designed covers and the firm's bookplate, are known today. They were sold at Christie's New York December 13, 1986, lot 473.

42 LaMont Warner to Emma Warner, Vienna, 24 July 1909; perhaps this awkward exchange can be explained not just by language difficulties but by Hoffmann's nature: according to Eduard F. Sekler, Hoffmann was "not easily approachable…. He found it embarrassing to be visited by foreign admirers." See Eduard F. Sekler. *Josef Hoffman: Monograph and Catalogue of Works* (Princeton, NJ: Princeton University Press, 1985): 231.

43 For instance, the W.K. Pierce house, ca. 1902; see also Wilkinson's Champlin house in *The Book of One Hundred Houses* (Chicago, IL: Herbert Stone & Company, 1902): 52–57.

44 In comparison, Stickley was then paying his three high-est-level executives, Frederick A. Arwine, W.D. Brewster and Leopold Stickley, salaries of $166 a month. See WL 76 x 101.11.

45 The Ames Building, at 1 Court Street, completed in 1889, was designed by the successors to H.H. Richardson, the firm of Shepley, Rutan and Coolidge, which had an office there. See Donlyn Lyndon, *The City Observed: Boston* (New York: Random House, 1982): 13–14.

46 J. Burke Wilkinson, telephone interview by author, 10 January 1999.

47 Douglass Shand-Tucci. *Boston Bohemia 1881–1900*: *Ralph Adams Cram, Life and Architecture* (Amherst, MA: University of Massachusetts Press, 1995): 96–97.

48 J. Burke Wilkinson, telephone interview by author, 9 February 1997.

49 Claude Bragdon to Katherine Bragdon, Syracuse, NY, 1 January 1901.

50 Magonigle would later become a prominent architect, much better known during the 1910s and 1920s than his former partner Wilkinson, and active in the American Institute of Architects and the Architectural League of New York.

51 Claude Bragdon to Katherine Bragdon, Syracuse, NY, 26 (?) July 1903.

52 ACMU 6 (10 May 1902): 9.

APPENDIX TWO

1 My thanks to William Porter for his expert comments on the construction of this desk.

2 Stickley produced a less flamboyant version of this desk, without the sawn-out decoration of the top rail and with straight-lined feet, in 1901 and 1902.

3 I thank Stephen Gray for his detailed comments on the construction of this desk.

4 Unsigned, "Beauty Along Utilitarian Lines," FTR 24, (10 January 1904): 87.

5 Bragdon Papers, Tube 81, Rainsford House, May 1903, University of Rochester Library.

6 I thank David Parsons for his insightful comments on the construction of this desk.

7 Jean R. France, conversation with the author, September 7, 2000.

8 There are more clippings of Ellwood's work in Warner's files than of any other English designer.

A. STICKLEY CATALOGS AND BOOKLETS

1900 "New Furniture from the Workshop of Gustave Stickley, Cabinet Maker."

1901 "Chips from the Workshops of Gustave Stickley." Unsigned text by Irene Sargent.
"Chips from the Workshops of the United Crafts."
"Retail Plates."
"Things Wrought by the United Crafts."

1902 "Retail Plates."
"Things Wrought by the United Crafts." Unsigned text attributed to Irene Sargent.

1903 "The Simple Structural Style of Household Furniture."
"Name This Child."

1904 "Safecraft—Catalogue C."
"What is Wrought in the Craftsman Workshops."

1905 "Cabinet Work from the Craftsman Workshops—Catalogue D."
"Craftsman Furnishings."
"The Craftsman's Story."
"The Craftsman Workshops—Supplement to Catalogue D."
"Hand-Wrought Metal Work."
"Needle-Work from the Craftsman Workshops."

1906 "Chips from the Craftsman Workshops."
"Craftsman Furnishings."
"Christ Among His Fellow Men." Text by Harriet Joor, with a foreword by Gustav Stickley.

1907 "Chips from the Craftsman Workshops—Number II."
"Descriptive Price List of Craftsman Furniture, with Retail Plates."

1908 "Craftsman Fabrics and Needlework."

1909 "Catalogue of Craftsman Furniture."
"Some Chips from the Craftsman Workshops."

1910 "Catalogue of Craftsman Furniture."
"The Craftsman House."
"Craftsman Premium Catalogue."

1912 "Craftsman Furnishings for the Home."
"24 Craftsman Houses."
"What They Say About The Craftsman."
"Craftsman Furniture."

1913 "Craftsman Furniture."
"Craftsman Houses—A Book for Home-Makers."
"Craftsman Service for Home-Builders."

1914 "$150,000 7% Cumulative Preferred Stock Offering of Gustav Stickley The Craftsman Incorporated and The Craftsman Magazine Inc."
"Craftsman Restaurant."
"A Summary of Craftsman Enterprises."
"Woodwork and How to Finish It."

1915 "Craftsman Department of Interior Furnishings."

B. PERIODICALS

American Cabinet Maker and Upholsterer (1886–1916)

The Craftsman (1901–1916)

Furniture Journal (1896–1931)

Furniture Trade Review (1894–1916)

Furniture World (1895–1942)

Good Housekeeping (1901–1914)

Handicraft (1902–1904)

The House Beautiful (1896–1910)

House and Garden (1901–1915)

International Studio (1897–1916)

The Upholstery Dealer and Decorative Furnisher (1901–1906)

The Upholsterer (1896–1921)

C. UNPUBLISHED SOURCES

Bourdon, Roger. "George Wharton James, Interpreter of the Southwest." Doctoral dissertation, University of California, Los Angeles, 1965

Early, Marcia. "*The Craftsman* (1901–1916) as the Principal Spokesman of the Craftsman Movement in America with a Short Study of the Craftsman House Projects." Master's thesis, New York University, 1963.

Kinsey, Sally J. "Gustav Stickley and the Early Years of *The Craftsman*, 1901–1916." Master's thesis, Syracuse University, 1972.

Gustav Stickley Business Papers. Collection 60. The Winterthur Library. Joseph Downs Collection of Manuscripts and Printed Ephemera.

LaMont Warner Papers. Collection 647. The Winterthur Library. Joseph Downs Collection of Manuscripts and Printed Ephemera.

D. PUBLISHED SOURCES

Anderson, Timothy J., Eudorah M. Moore and Robert W. Winter. *California Design 1910*. Salt Lake City: Peregrine Smith Books, 1980.

Atterbury, Paul, ed. A.W.N. *Pugin: Master of Gothic Revival*. New Haven, CT, and London: Yale University Press, 1995.

Audsley, George Ashdown. *The Ornamental Arts of Japan*. New York: Charles Scribner's Sons, 1883.

Ayres, Dianne, Timothy Hansen, Beth Ann McPherson, and Tommy Arthur McPherson II. *American Arts and Crafts Textiles*. New York: Harry N. Abrams, Inc., 2002.

Baillie Scott, M.H. "Decoration and Furniture for the New Palace, Darmstadt." *International Studio 7* (March 1899): 107–113.

_____ . "Furniture Made at the Pyghtle Works Bedford by John P. White Designed by M. H. Baillie Scott," 1901.

_____ . "Some Furniture for the New Palace, Darmstadt." *International Studio 5* (August 1898): 91–97.

Bartinique, Patricia A., ed. *Gustav Stickley: His Craft*. Parsippany, NJ: The Craftsman Farms Foundation, 1992.

Billcliffe, Roger. *Charles Rennie Mackintosh: The Complete Furniture, Furniture Drawings & Interior Designs*. New York: Taplinger, 1979.

Bosley, Edward R. *Greene & Greene*. London: Phaidon Press, 2000.

Bragdon, Claude. *Merely Players*. New York: Alfred A. Knopf, 1929.

_____ . *More Lives Than One*. New York: Alfred A. Knopf, 1938.

Brooks, Chris. *The Gothic Revival*. London: Phaidon Press, 1999.

Carruthers, Annette, and Mary Greensted. *Good Citizen's Furniture: The Arts and Crafts Collection at Cheltenham*. London: Cheltenham Art Gallery and Museums in association with Lund Humphries, 1994.

Cathers, David. *Furniture of the American Arts and Crafts Movement*. Rev. ed. Philmont, NY: Turn of the Century Editions, 1996.

_____ , ed. *Gustav Stickley's Craftsman Farms—A Pictorial History*. Morris Plains, NJ: Turn of the Century Editions in association with The Craftsman Farms Press, 1999.

Chaves, Ann. *Basic Embroidery Stitches*. Pasadena, CA: The Clinker Press, 2001.

Clark, Michael, and Jill Thomas Clark. *The Stickley Brothers*, Salt Lake City, UT: Gibbs Smith Publisher, 2002.

Clark, Robert Judson, ed. *The Arts and Crafts Movement in America 1876–1916*. Princeton, NJ: Princeton University Press, 1972.

Cook, Clarence. *The House Beautiful*. 1881. Reprint, New York: Dover Publications, 1995.

Cooper, Jeremy. *Victorian and Edwardian Décor: From the Gothic Revival to Art Nouveau*. New York: Abbeville Press, 1987.

The Craftsman on CD-ROM. New York: Interactive Bureau, 1998.

Crawford, Alan, ed. *By Hammer and Hand: The Arts and Crafts Movement in Birmingham*. Birmingham, UK: Birmingham Museums and Art Gallery, 1984.

_____ . *C.R. Ashbee: Architect, Designer, and Romantic Socialist*. New Haven, CT, and London: Yale University Press, 1985.

_____ . *Charles Rennie Mackintosh*. London: Thames and Hudson, 1995.

Darling, Sharon. *Chicago Furniture: Art, Craft, & Industry, 1833–1933*. New York: W.W. Norton and Company, 1984.

Davidoff, Donald A., and Stephen Gray. *Innovation and Derivation: The Contribution of L. & J.G. Stickley to the Arts and Crafts Movement*. Parsippany, NJ: The Craftsman Farms Foundation, 1995.

de Wolfe, Elsie. *The House in Good Taste*. New York: Century and Co., 1913.

Finegold, Rupert, and William Seitz. *Silversmithing*. Radnor, PA: Chilton Book Company, 1983.

Fish, Marilyn. *Gustav Stickley 1884–1900: The Stickley Brothers, Stickley & Simonds, and the Gustave Stickley Company*. North Caldwell, NJ: Little Pond Press, 1999.

_____ . *Gustav Stickley: Heritage and Early Years*. North Caldwell, NJ: Little Pond Press, 1997.

_____ . *The New Craftsman Index*. Lambertville, NJ: The Arts and Crafts Quarterly Press, 1997.

Fisher, Alexander, et al. "The Arts and Crafts Exhibition at the New Gallery." *Art Workers' Quarterly 1–2* (April 1903): 53–80.

France, Jean R., Roger G. Kennedy, Blake McKelvey, and Howard S. Merritt. *A Rediscovery—Harvey Ellis: Artist, Architect*. Rochester, NY: Memorial Art Gallery of the University of Rochester, 1972.

Freeman, John Crosby. *The Forgotten Rebel: Gustav Stickley and His Craftsman Mission Furniture*. Watkins Glen, NY: Century House, 1966.

Girouard, Mark. *Sweetness and Light: The "Queen Anne" Movement 1860–1900*. New Haven, CT, and London: Yale University Press, 1977.

Gray, Stephen. *The Collected Works of Gustav Stickley*. Rev. ed. New York: Turn of the Century Editions, 1989.

_____ . *The Early Work of Gustav Stickley*. Philmont, NY: Turn of the Century Editions, 1996.

Greensted, Mary. *Gimson and the Barnsleys: "Wonderful*

Furniture of a Commonplace Kind." Gloucestershire, UK: Alan Sutton Publishing Ltd., 1991.

Harvey, Charles, and Jon Press. *William Morris: Design and Enterprise in Victorian Britain*. Manchester, UK: Manchester University Press, 1991.

Hewitt, Mark Alan. *Gustav Stickley's Craftsman Farms: The Quest for an Arts and Crafts Utopia,* Syracuse, NY: Syracuse University Press, 2001.

Hilton, Tim. *John Ruskin: The Early Years*. New Haven, CT and London: Yale University Press, 1985.

_____ . *John Ruskin: The Later Years*. New Haven, CT and London: Yale University Press, 2000.

Hitchmough, Wendy. *C.F.A. Voysey*. London: Phaidon Press, 1995.

Holme, Charles, ed. *Modern British Domestic Architecture and Decoration*. London: The Studio, 1901.

James, George Wharton. *California Scrapbook: A Collection of Articles by George Wharton James*. Los Angeles: N. A. Kovack, 1945.

_____ . *Traveler's Handbook to Southern California*. Pasadena: self-published, 1904.

Kaplan, Wendy. *Leading "The Simple Life": The Arts and Crafts Movement in Britain, 1880–1910*, Miami Beach, FL: The Wolfsonian–Florida International University, 1999.

_____ , ed. *"The Art that is Life": The Arts and Crafts Movement in America, 1875–1920*, Boston: Museum of Fine Arts, 1987.

Konody, P.G. "Die Arts und Crafts Austellung in London." *Kunst und Kunsthandwerk* 6 (1903): 70–92.

Kornwolf, James D. M.H. *Baillie Scott and the Arts and Crafts Movement*. Baltimore, MD: John Hopkins University Press, 1972.

Lancaster, Clay. *The Japanese Influence in America*. New York: Abbeville Press, 1983.

Larson, Roger Keith. *Controversial James: An Essay on the Life and Work of George Wharton James*. San Francisco: The Book Club of California, 1991.

Lears, T.J. Jackson. *No Place of Grace: Antimodernism and the Transformation of American Culture, 1876–1914*. New York: Pantheon, 1981.

Ludwig, Coy L. *The Arts and Crafts Movement in New York State, 1890s–1920s*. Hamilton, NY: Gallery Association of New York State, 1983.

Marek, Don. *Grand Rapids Art Metalwork, 1902–1918,* Grand Rapids, MI: Heartwood, 1999.

Murchú, Giollamure O. *Jerome Connor: Irish-American Sculptor, 1874–1943*. Dublin: The National Gallery of Ireland, 1993.

Muthesius, Hermann. "Die Glasgower Kunstbewegung: Charles R. Mackintosh und Margaret MacDonald-Mackintosh." *Dekorative Kunst 9* (March 1902): 193–214.

_____ . *The English House. 1904–1905*. Reprint New York: Rizzoli, 1979.

Parry, Linda. *From East to West: Textiles from G.P. & J. Baker*. London: G.P. & J. Baker, 1984.

_____ . *Textiles of the Arts and Crafts Movement*. London: Thames and Hudson Ltd., 1988.

Payne, Arthur F. *Art Metalwork With Inexpensive Equipment*. Peoria, IL: The Manual Arts Press, 1914.

Prairie School Review 5 (first and second quarters, 1968).

Reed, Cleota. "Irene Sargent: Rediscovering a Lost Legend." *Courier* 16 (Summer 1979): 3–13.

_____ . "Gustav Stickley and Irene Sargent: United Crafts and *The Craftsman.*" *Courier* 30 (1995): 35–50.

_____ . "Near the Yates: Craft, Machine, and Ideology in Arts and Crafts Syracuse, 1900–1910." in Bert Denker, ed. *The Substance of Style*. Winterthur, DE: Henry Francis du Pont Wintherthur Museum, 1996.

Rudd, David. "Wrought in Syracuse: Onondaga Metal Shops & Benedict Art Studio." *Style: 1900* 11 (1998): 58–61.

Ruge, Clara. "Das Kunstgewerbe Amerikas." *Kunst und Kunsthandwerk* 5 (1902): 126–48

Saint, Andrew. *Richard Norman Shaw*. New Haven, CT, and London: Yale University Press, 1976.

Shi, David E. *The Simple Life: Plain Living and High Thinking in American Culture*. New York: Oxford University Press, 1985.

Smith, Mary Ann. *Gustav Stickley The Craftsman*. Syracuse, NY: Syracuse University Press, 1983.

Sparrow, W. Shaw, ed. *The British Home of Today: A Book of Modern Domestic Architecture*. New York: A.C. Armstrong and Son, 1904.

Stansky, Peter. *Redesigning the World: William Morris, the 1880s, and the Arts and Crafts*. Princeton, NJ: Princeton University Press, 1985.

Stickley, Gustav. *Craftsman Homes*. New York: The Craftsman Publishing Company, 1909.

_____ . *More Craftsman Homes*. New York: The Craftsman Publishing Company, 1912.

Thovez, Dr. Enrico, and others. "The International Exhibition of Decorative Art at Turin," *International Studio* 17 and 18 (1902–03): 44–52; 91–104; 251–259; 130–134; 188–197.

Unsigned. "The Arts and Crafts Exhibition at the New Gallery," *International Studio* 19 and 20 (1903): 27–40; 117–127; 179–260; 22–33.

Via, Marie. "Beloved Vagabond: The Paintings and Drawings of Harvey Ellis." *Arts and Crafts Quarterly* 4 (1991): 26–32.

Via, Marie, and Marjorie Searl. *Head, Heart and Hand: Elbert Hubbard and the Roycrofters*. Rochester, NY: University of Rochester Press, 1994.

Wagner, Charles. *My Impressions of America*. New York: McClure, Phillips & Co., 1906.

_____ . *The Simple Life*. New York: McClure, Phillips & Co., 1904.

Ward, James. *Architects in Practice in New York, 1900-1940*. Union, NJ: J&D Associates, 1989.

Weitze, Karen J. *California's Mission Revival*. Los Angeles: Hennessey & Ingalls, 1984.

White, G. Edward. *The Eastern Establishment and the Western Experience: The West of Frederic Remington, Theodore Roosevelt, and Owen Wister*. Austin, TX: University of Texas Press, 1989.

Wilson, Richard Guy, Dianne H. Pilgrim, and Richard N. Murray. *The American Renaissance, 1876–1917*. Brooklyn, NY: The Brooklyn Museum, 1979.

Winter, Robert W., ed. *Toward A Simpler Way of Life: The Arts and Crafts Architects of California*. Los Angeles: University of California Press, 1997.

Wright, Richardson, ed. *Inside the House of Good Taste*. New York: Robert M. McBride & Company, 1915.

E. OTHER SOURCES

Binghamton City Directories (1884–1890)
New York City Directories (1897–1917)
New York State Census (1895, 1905, 1915)
Rochester City Directories (1877–1903; 1925–1930)
Syracuse City Directories (1896–1930)
United States Census (1900, 1910, 1920)

F. INTERVIEWS BY DAVID CATHERS

Edith Wiles Bradford, telephone interview, January 5, 1997; January 11, 1997; August 31, 2001.

Peter W. Bragdon, telephone interview, October 10, 1997.

Muriel Jennings Case, East Aurora, NY, November 8, 1996.

Ruth Cruess Glesmann, telephone interview, December 18, 1996; August 11, 2001.

Olive E. Hansen, Ann Arbor, MI, June 18, 2001.

Sturtevant Pratt, Manlius, NY, July 8, 1996.

Elinora Price, Fayetteville, NY, July 8, 1996.

Gladys LaCombe Stickley, Rochester, NY, December 12, 1996.

Gustav Stickley III, telephone interview, January 13, 1997.

Louise Bowman Stickley, Fayetteville, NY, June 30, 1979.

Ellen Von Arx, telephone interview, November 7, 2000.

Ann Wiles, Skaneateles, NY, October 12, 1996.

Ben Wiles, Jr., Syracuse, NY, February 27, 1983; September 6, 1996; October 13, 1996; telephone interview, August 27, 2001.

Barbara Stickley Wiles, Syracuse, NY, March 27, 1978; September 20, 1978.

Peter Wiles, Skaneateles, NY, February 26, 1983.

J. Burke Wilkinson, telephone interview, February 9, 1997.

BY ROBERT JUDSON CLARK

Mildred Stickley Cruess, Rochester, NY, August 4, 1971; January 6, 1973; March 19, 1973; handwritten notes and typed transcript.

Mrs. John R. Riker, Basking Ridge, NJ, January 8, 1972; typed transcript.

Mrs. Mildred Vogelius and Mr. Warren L. Babcock, Jr., Mendham, NJ, September 15, 1979; typed transcript.

Barbara Stickley Wiles, Syracuse, NY, August 4, 1971; October 7, 1972; handwritten notes and typed transcript.

BY ELAINE NARAMORE

Marion Stickley Flaccus, April 12, 1982; typed transcript of tape recording in the collection of the Joint Free Public Library of Morristown and Morris Plains, NJ.

Gustav Stickley III, n. d.; typed transcript of tape recording in the collection of the Joint Free Public Library of Morristown and Morris Plains, NJ.

ACKNOWLEDGMENTS

A study of the life and work of Gustav Stickley must be a collaborative venture. Although any errors or infelicities in the text are my own, to a very great degree this book exists because of the freely given assistance of many knowledgeable people.

First is Robert Judson Clark, who helped shape this book, offered illuminating insights throughout the writing process, and gave an invaluable close reading to an earlier version of the manuscript. He has never formally been my teacher, but he was the first to make me aware of Gustav Stickley and I am indebted to him above all others.

My thanks as well to Coy L. Ludwig, for his ideas, for the extensive source materials that he generously made available to me, and for the kindness of his hospitality whenever I have visited Syracuse.

I can never adequately acknowledge all those who have been helpful, but every person listed here has enhanced this book in some significant way:

Rebekah Ambrose, Onondaga Historical Association; Michael Adams; Alfred and Aminy Audi, the Stickley Furniture Company; Dianne Ayres and Timothy Hansen; Bruce Barnes and Joseph Cunningham; Patricia Bartinique; David E. Berman; Edward R. Bosley; Allen and Vonda Breed; John H. Bryan, Crab Tree Farm; Beth Cathers; Ann and André Chaves; Michael Clark and Jill Thomas-Clark; Jerry Cohen; David Conradsen, the St. Louis Art Museum; Alan Crawford; Kathleen Cummings; Rita Curry-Pittman; Michael Danial, the Stickley Furniture Company; Sharon Darling; Donald Davidoff and Susan Tarlow; Audel Davis; Elaine and Robert Dillof; Martin Eidelberg; Marilyn Fish; Jean R. France; John Crosby Freeman; Peggy Gilges; Tim Gleason; Stephen Gray; Mary Greensted; Olive E. Hansen; Mark Alan Hewitt; Wendy Hitchmough; Bruce Johnson; Robert Kaplan; Wendy Kaplan; H. Allan Knox; David W. Lowden; Boice Lydell; Don Marek; Michael McCracken; Michele McHugh; Kennon G. Miedema; Warren C. Moffett; David Parsons; Linda Parry; J. B. Porter; William and Patsy Porter; The late Sturtevant Pratt; Elinora Price; David Rago; Cleota Reed; Debbie Goldwein Rudd and David Rudd; Robert Rust; Marjorie Searl; Beverly Sierpina; Suzanne Sliker; Bruce Smith and Yoshiko Yamamoto; Mary Ann Smith; John D. Spencer; Ray Stubblebine; David A. Taylor, the Library of Congress; Jan Toftey; John Toomey; Pieter Uptegrove; William E. Uptegrove III; Alexander Vertikoff; Marie Via; J. Burke Wilkinson; Robert W. Winter.

I have also drawn on the resources of numerous libraries, museums, archives, and local historical societies, and I am grateful for their help.

Alfred University, Scholes Library of Ceramics, Elizabeth Gulacsy, Art Librarian and Archivist
Archives of American Art
The Art Institute of Chicago, Ryerson Library
Auburn (NY) Correctional Facility, Michael Pettigrass, historian
The Bernice Bienenstock Furniture Library, Carl Vuncannon, Director
Birmingham (England) Central Library, Charlotte Tucker, Local Studies Librarian
Birmingham (England) Museum and Art Gallery, Glennys Wild, Senior Curator, Art Department
The British Museum, Judy Rudoe, Keeper, Department of Medieval and Later Antiquities
Broome County (NY) Historical Society, Charles J. Browne and Gerald Smith
Cayuga County (NY) Historian's Office, Malcolm O. Goodelle, Assistant County Historian
Cornell University, Carl A. Kroch Library, Elaine Engst, University Archivist
Crab Tree Farm, Jo Hormuth, Kathleen Kasprzak, Dru Muskovin, Emily Zaiden
The Craftsman Farms Foundation, Beth Ann McPherson, Tommy McPherson, Nancy Willans
East Aurora (NY) Historian's Office, Donald Dayer, Town Historian
Henry Ford Museum and Greenfield Village, Research Center
Highland (NY) Historian's Office, Lindsay Sullivan, Town Historian
King's College Library, Cambridge, Modern Archive, Jacqueline Cox, Archivist
The Landmark Society of Western New York, Cynthia Howk, Architectural Research Coordinator
Minnesota Historical Society, Denise Carlson, Reference Librarian
Missouri Historical Society, Duane Sneddeker, Curator of Prints and Photographs
Moravian Pottery and Tile Works, Vance A. Koehler, Curator of Historic Properties
Joint Free Public Library of Morristown and Morris Plains, Local History Collections, Claire Kissil, Senior Librarian
National Arts Club, Carol Lowry, Curator
New York County, Surrogate's Court Records
The New York Genealogical and Biographical Society
The New-York Historical Society, Eric Robinson, Reference Assistant
The New York Public Library
Office of Vital Records, Syracuse, NY
Office of Vital Statistics, Binghamton, NY
Onondaga County (NY) Clerks' Office
Onondaga County (NY) Public Library, Local History and Genealogy, Gary Jones, Librarian
Rochester Institute of Technology, Kari Horowicz
Royal Institute of British Architects, Eleanor Gawne, Curator of Manuscripts and Archives
School of the Museum of Fine Arts, Boston, Amy Lucker, Laura Sundstrom and Kristin Bierfelt, Museum School Librarians
Society for the Preservation of New England Antiquities, Rebecca Aronson, Archivist
Southwest Museum, Braun Research Library, Kim Walters, Library Director
Syracuse University Archives, Mary O'Brien, Archivist
University of Oregon Library System, Linda J. Long, Manuscripts Librarian
University of Rochester, Rush Rhees Library, Mary Huth
Victoria and Albert Museum, Archive of Art & Design, Blythe House, Eva White, Archivist
Victoria and Albert Museum, Department of Furniture and Woodwork, Sorrel Hershberg, Rebecca Milner
Winterthur Museum, Garden & Library, E. Richard McKinstry and Neville Thompson
www.ellisislandrecords.com

I am especially indebted to Stickley family members who shared family lore; for their candor and kindness I thank them sincerely.

Edith Wiles Bradford; the late Mildred Stickley Cruess (interviewed by Robert Judson Clark in 1971); Barbara and Henry Fuldner; Louis G. Glesmann III; Ruth Cruess Glesmann; Cynthia and Timothy McGinn; Robert and Linda Preim; the late Louise Stickley; the late Gladys LaCombe Stickley; Gustav Stickley III; Doree Rose Stroffolino; Ellen Von Arx; Ann Wiles; Ben and Betty Wiles; the late Peter Wiles; the late Barbara Stickley Wiles (interviewed by Robert Judson Clark in 1971 and by David Cathers in 1978)

My thanks to my exemplary editor, Megan McFarland, to Jesse Donaldson, to the designer Ariel Apte, and to Karen Stein and everyone at Phaidon Press who has helped bring this book into being.

And, as ever, this book is for Susan.

2267/61

Numbers indicate page number. t = top, b = bottom, l = left, c = center, r = right, f = far

Reproduced from *The American Bungalow 1880-1930,* by Clay Lancaster (New York: Dover Publications, 1995): 114

Courtesy Bernice Bienenstock Furniture Library, High Point, North Carolina: 28r, 119r

© Danny Bright: 22t, 26, 43

Broome County Historical Society: 14, 15, 203

Courtesy Amanda Brown, photos © John Farnach: 196, 199

Courtesy Cathers and Dembrosky Gallery, New York City, photos © Beth Phillips: 40, 48, 49, 89-90, 127, 166

Courtesy Cathers and Dembrosky Gallery, New York City, photos © Tony Sahara: 42l, 137tr

© Christies Images: 80, 126, 130r

Courtesy Robert Judson Clark: 94, 115, 175, 219b

Courtesy Crab Tree Farm: 151

Courtesy Crab Tree Farm, photos © Danny Bright: 46, 47, 54, 72l, 95, 98, 124, 132, 133r, 150cl, 152, 158-159, 163, 220t

Craftsman Auctions: 31r, 129, 135, 137b, 150fr, 164r

The Craftsman on CD-ROM: 11, 48-49, 51l, 56l, 60-61, 62, 63, 64, 66, 70r, 72r, 73tl, 73b, 92, 93, 100tl, 100bl, 106, 110l, 112, 116, 117, 119l, 120b, 121, 122, 131c, 131r, 134r, 138, 140, 144, 147, 148, 154, 156, 157, 162, 164l, 165, 168r, 169, 170, 174, 176, 177l, 178, 181, 189, 190r, 191, 198, 200l, 213c, 213r, 216

The Craftsman Farms Foundation, Parsippany, New Jersey: 2, 4-5, 18-19, 21, 172, 184-185, 188, 190l, 192, 194, 205b, 206

Courtesy Sharon Darling: 34

Courtesy Elaine and Robert Dillof, photos © Danny Bright: 30, 31c

East Aurora, New York, Historian's Office: 153

© John Farnach: 65, 128l, 128r, 207c, 207r

Courtesy Barbara and Henry Fuldner: 16r

Courtesy Stephen Gray, photos © Danny Bright: 12, 142, 219tl, 219tr

The Guild of Handicraft Trust: 60

Courtesy Harvey M. Kaplan: 102-103

Courtesy Michael Lehr, photos © Beth Phillips: 6, 218

Minnesota Historical Society, Harvey Ellis Papers: 82l

Museum of the City of New York, Print Archives: 24-25

New York Public Library: 28l, 67, 71, 83r, 96l, 107c, 108b, 168l, 179, 200r, 205t, 208, 209r, 210r, 220bl

Onondaga Historical Association Museum & Research Center, Syracuse, New York: 37, 51r, 68, 76l, 212l

Onondaga County Public Library: 76r

© Beth Phillips: 45, 52, 55, 56, 104, 182

Private Collection: 16l, 17, 22b, 23, 35, 36, 57r, 59, 70l, 82r, 84-85, 97, 99l, 107l, 107r, 108t, 110r, 120, 131l, 133l, 136, 137tl, 149r, 161, 187, 195, 209l, 212r, 213l, 214, 215l, 217l, 220br, 222, 223

Courtesy David Rago: 100r

Courtesy Debbie and David Rudd, photo © John Farnach: 42r

Courtesy Robert Rust / Pamela McCrary Collection: 111, 146

Courtesy Bill and Debbie Schu, photo © John Farnach: 29

Courtesy John Spencer, Riverrow Bookshop: 73tl

Rochester Institute of Technology, Archives and Special Collections, Wallace Library: 78, 79

University of Rochester Library, Department of Rare Books & Special Collections, 33, 86, 87, 210l
© Courtney Frisse

Courtesy Philip and Marguerite Stevens, photo © John Farnach: 221

Courtesy Stickley Furniture Company: 58, 109, 215r

Strong Museum, Rochester, New York: 83l

Courtesy Ray Stubblebine: 50, 96r, 130l

Syracuse University Archives. All rights reserved: 39

Courtesy David Taylor, Library of Congress: 150fl

Courtesy Treadway Gallery: 30l, photo © Ross van Pelt; 44r, photo © Joseph Higgins; 99r, photo © David Kalonick

Courtesy Liese Uptegrove-Ade, curator, Uptegrove Family Archives: 134l

V&A Picture Library: 44l

Courtesy Betty and Ben Wiles, Jr., photo © John Farnach: 1; 207l

The Winterthur Library, Arts Photographic Collection: 160

The Winterthur Library, Joseph Downs Collection of Manuscipts and Printed Ephemera: 32, 149l, 150cr

The Winterthur Library: Printed Book and Periodical Collection: 38l, 38r, 94-75, 145, 155, 217r

Phaidon Press Limited
Regent's Wharf
All Saints Street
London N1 9PA

Phaidon Press, Inc.
180 Varick Street
New York, NY 10014

www.phaidon.com

First published 2003
© 2003 Phaidon Press Limited

ISBN 0 7148 4030 0

A CIP catalogue record for this book is available from the British Library.

Designed by Ariel Apte, of mgmt.
Printed in China

FRONTISPIECE: Gustav Stickley ca. 1907
OVERLEAF: Gustav Stickley ca. 1942

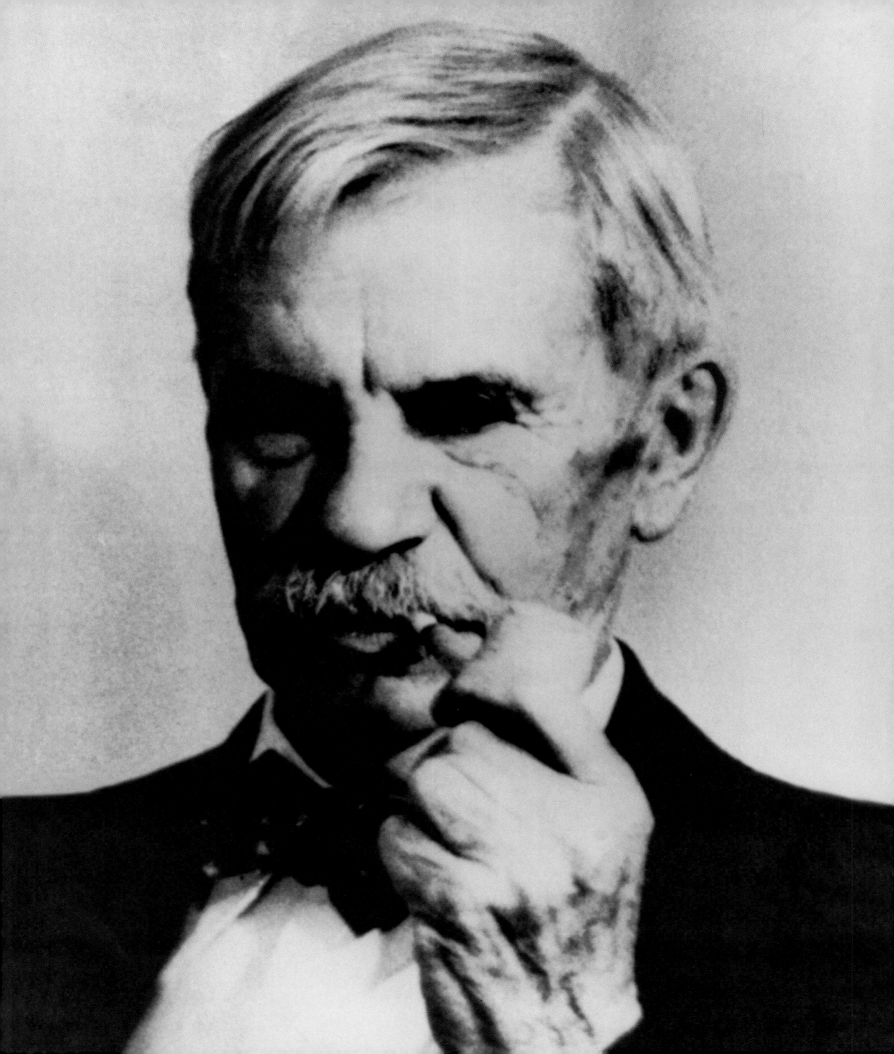